A publication of the

AMERICAN ASSOCIATION FOR HIGHER EDUCATION
National Center for Higher Education
One Dupont Circle, Northeast
Washington, D.C. 20036

DYCKMAN W. VERMILYE, *Executive Director*

The American Association for Higher Education, AAHE,
promotes higher education and provides a national
voice for individual members. AAHE, founded in 1870,
is the only national higher education organization
open to faculty members, administrators, graduate
students, and trustees without regard to rank, discipline,
or type or size of institution. AAHE is dedicated to
the professional development of college and university
educators, to the achievement of their educational
objectives, and to the improvement of conditions
of service.

New Teaching New Learning

G. Kerry Smith, EDITOR

1971

CURRENT ISSUES IN HIGHER EDUCATION

ASSOCIATE EDITORS, *Joseph Axelrod,*
Tom Erhard, Winfred L. Godwin,
Lewis B. Mayhew

NEW TEACHING NEW LEARNING

 Jossey-Bass Inc., Publishers

San Francisco · Washington · London · 1971

NEW TEACHING, NEW LEARNING
G. Kerry Smith, Editor

Copyright © 1971 by American Association for Higher Education
Jossey-Bass, Inc., Publishers

Published in Great Britain by
Jossey-Bass, Inc., Publishers
St. George's House
44 Hatton Garden, London E.C. 1

Library of Congress Catalogue Card Number LC 72–173856

International Standard Book Number ISBN 0–87589–113–6

Manufactured in the United States of America

JACKET DESIGN BY WILLI BAUM, SAN FRANCISCO

FIRST EDITION

Code 7128

THE JOSSEY-BASS SERIES IN HIGHER EDUCATION

JOSEPH AXELROD
San Francisco State College and
University of California, Berkeley

MERVIN B. FREEDMAN
San Francisco State College and
Wright Institute, Berkeley

Preface

In the concluding paragraph of the Preface to *The Troubled Campus,* the preceding volume of *Current Issues in Higher Education,* I commented on the urgency of the authors who were at that time, in effect, issuing a warning and a call to action to the academic community. In this Preface I would like to state my belief that some action *has* taken place. In the perspective of Clark Kerr's masterful historical review (the last chapter of this volume) of over three hundred years of higher education and its relation to society and in view of the multiple revolutions which are shaking and shaping us so profoundly, I would not be so bold as to claim that major changes can take place and be observed in one year's time. As a society we are still traveling on a narrow rope bridge above a deep chasm, but we can see glimpses of green on the other side. Clearly, five significant markers have been reached in the past year: increased interest in the teaching-learning process by academics; evolution of an "out-going" attitude in higher education as evidenced by such developments as external degrees, universities without walls, North American Open University, and the Commission on Nontraditional Study; a sharp change of mood from the high-water mark to protest at the time of the Cambodian invasion to the uneasy calm of 1970–1971—a calm some interpret as a sign of improvement and others as a sign of resignation or despondence;

progress in the fight for the rights of women; and national awareness of the ecological movement.

At the Twenty-Sixth National Conference of the American Association for Higher Education (AAHE), where the essays in this volume were presented, the several sessions dealing with the teaching-learning process were filled with capacity audiences. In previous years this was not typically the case. Admittedly this is only one indicator of academic concern, but it is worth noting, particularly since critics have attributed the alienation of students in part to bad, indifferent, or impersonal teaching. Harold Hodgkinson in his essay in this volume proposes class visits by colleagues to evaluate teaching. When similar suggestions were made in a conference ten years ago, they were largely rejected by indignant faculty members. In the current atmosphere, however, there is acceptance of this practice on the part of many faculty members. And when Lawrence Dennis made what seemed at first blush to be an unrealistic prediction that by 1976 a University of North America would be established, no one could have guessed that an actual try at that, the North American Open University, would be chartered even before the publication of this book. The stern financial problems facing the colleges and universities have complicated experiments with open admissions. Comments on the potentiality and limits of these movements occupied several sessions at recent conferences of AAHE.

As for ecology, rarely has such a far-reaching movement gained so much national support so quickly. To a large extent students and faculty can be credited with having drummed up that support. The evidence is strong that there will be significant follow-through. And with regard to the movement for equal opportunities and rights for women there has been significant action by the federal government affecting equal pay for women faculty in colleges and universities. This action is clearly an outgrowth of activity by the women's lib movement. How much political power will be generated by the various political coalitions spawned by this movement remains to be seen. Congresswoman Edith Green, eminently qualified on this subject as both a remarkable woman and a Representative with considerable clout, continues her persistent and successful pressure for federal support for rights for women.

It is my belief that the past year has witnessed a national shift in mood and direction, and this change is indicated in the 1970 and 1971 titles for this book; they reflect the shift from our preoccupation with *The Troubled Campus* to our concern with *New Teaching, New Learning* and ways to achieve new arrangements and structures.

The AAHE is grateful to the American College Testing Program for cosponsoring the appearance of the following authors at the Twenty-Sixth National Conference: Alexander Astin, Louis Benezet, Amitai Etzioni, Clark Kerr, John Monro, Charles Silberman, and Immanuel Wallerstein. I wish also to thank John F. Warner for his excellent editorial assistance.

Washington, D.C.   G. KERRY SMITH
September 1971

Contents

Contributors

JACK N. ARBOLINO, executive director, Council on College-Level Examinations, College Entrance Examination Board

ALEXANDER W. ASTIN, director of research, American Council on Education

LOUIS T. BENEZET, president, State University of New York at Albany

PAUL L. BRIAND, JR., professor of English, State University of New York at Oswego

DAVID S. BUSHNELL, director of research, Project FOCUS, American Association of Junior Colleges

JOHN J. CORSON, chairman of the board, Fry Consultants

BERTRAM H. DAVIS, general secretary, American Association of University Professors

W. JOSEPH DEHNER, JR., trustee, Princeton University, and student, Harvard Law School

LAWRENCE E. DENNIS, provost and director, Massachusetts State College System

AMITAI ETZIONI, chairman, Department of Sociology, Columbia University

JERRY G. GAFF, assistant research psychologist, Center for Research and Development in Higher Education, University of California, Berkeley

SAMUEL B. GOULD, chancellor, emeritus, State University of New York, and director, McKinsey and Company

FRED F. HARCLEROAD, president, American College Testing Program

HAROLD L. HODGKINSON, project director, Center for Research and Development in Higher Education, University of California, Berkeley

PHYLLIS E. KAYE, campus program coordinator, National Center for Dispute Settlement, American Arbitration Association, Washington, D.C.

CLARK KERR, chairman and executive director, Carnegie Commission on Higher Education

RICHARD L. MILLER, executive director, Michigan Council of State College Presidents

JOHN MONRO, visiting professor in freshman studies, Miles College

GEORGE A. MORGAN, director of institutional research and associate professor of psychology, Hiram College

RUTH M. OLTMAN, staff associate for higher education, American Association of University Women

ROBERT M. O'NEIL, professor of law, School of Law, University of California, Berkeley, and counsel, Assembly on University Goals and Governance

MORTON A. RAUH, vice-president, emeritus, Antioch College

ED RIDDICK, national research director, Operation Breadbasket, Southern Christian Leadership Conference

CHARLES E. SILBERMAN, member, Board of Editors, *Fortune* Magazine, and Field Foundation Fellow

RUSSELL I. THACKREY, writer, consultant, and executive director, emeritus, National Association of State Universities and Land-Grant Colleges

WILLIAM W. VAN ALSTYNE, professor of law, Duke University

IMMANUEL WALLERSTEIN, associate professor of sociology, Columbia University, and fellow, Center for the Study of Behavioral Sciences

ROBERT C. WILSON, research psychologist, Center for Research and Development in Higher Education, University of California, Berkeley

New
Teaching
New
Learning

❧ Prologue: ❧

The New University

Joseph Axelrod

T he twenty-seven essays contained in *New Teaching, New Learning* explore the teaching-learning process and the settings and structures that surround and often support—but also often impede—teaching and learning in American colleges and universities. The essays embrace six major areas of this subject. Parts One and Two concentrate directly on teaching and learning. Part Three is devoted to various aspects of the college population: low-ability students, ethnic-minority students, the poor, and women. Part Four investigates the decision-making structures that will determine the future character of teaching and learning in postsecondary institutions. Part Five deals with professors as employees, not as teachers per se—an increasingly important distinction. And Part Six attempts a reinterpretation of the essence of higher education, both to help educators reconceive it and to help other segments of the American public understand it.

1

The New Teaching

The four essays of Part One focus specifically on teaching. The authors of the first two essays, John Monro and Paul Briand, have been devoting the major portion of their time to classroom teaching and write from that experience. The authors of the other two essays of Part One, Jerry Gaff, Robert Wilson, and Harold Hodgkinson, are former classroom teachers who are now devoting a major portion of their time to research on the nature and improvement of teaching. Several major aspects of college teaching are examined in these essays; they include concrete observations about the act of teaching, descriptions of the value contexts surrounding teaching, and analyses of the assessment systems that are applied to teaching.

Like each of the essays in this volume, John Monro's "Teaching in a Black College" is taken from an address given at the Twenty-Sixth National Conference on Higher Education. Monro, a former Harvard University dean now visiting professor in freshmen studies at Miles College, told his conference audience that he had had serious doubts about giving a talk on this subject: not only was he a white teacher discussing problems of black colleges, he explained, but he had come late to his task. In the end, however, he decided to accept the invitation. "The least I can do, in return for the very real privilege of working four years at a black college," he said, "is to try to report out some things I have observed and felt." The essay shows how well—indeed, how memorably—Monro has achieved his purpose.

It is impossible to do justice to the essay in these introductory notes. The perceptive reader will find, in "Teaching at a Black College," the quality known as "soul." Much of the essay is purely factual, but enormous meaning is wedged between its lines. It is at one and the same time an analysis of the problems of black colleges, a report of recent developments, a personal memoir, and an appeal to other educators to share in this experience, not merely with words and dollars, but with their bodies and minds.

Teaching, of course, is not easy under even excellent conditions. It is especially difficult at a black college. Monro speaks of the "intricate and apparently paradoxical effort" of faculty members at Miles College, who must help their black students prepare for full professional participation in a world dominated by whites and, simultaneously, help the students strengthen their sense of self and their sense of community as black men and women.

A completely different teaching problem is approached by Paul Briand, professor of English at the Oswego campus of the State University of New York, in "Turning Students On Through Multimedia." Briand describes how he organized and taught a "turned-on course in English composition—turned-on because it is plugged in to multimedia." The essay contains implications that go far beyond the teaching of composition, for Briand's new departures and unusual techniques are applicable to most other skill and content fields of learning.

Although it was not Briand's intention, his essay will remind many college teachers and administrators how slow our progress in the uses of educational technology has been. Ten or fifteen years ago, when the exciting possibilities of technology in the classroom became fairly well known, many people believed that the kind of classroom Briand describes would have become, by this time, typical. The essay thus points up the gap between our present state of technological knowledge and the general teaching practice in most of our college courses.

The remaining two essays in Part One move away from concrete contexts for teaching to an analytic level. These essays show why the years ahead will not bring very much change in teaching styles, unless campus climates and reward systems are altered to encourage change and to become supportive of good teaching. Jerry Gaff and Robert Wilson, in "Faculty Values and Improving Teaching," present data from two studies. The first is an extensive multicampus survey of college and university faculty members, carried out by the Center for Research and Development in Higher Education at the University of California, where Wilson and Gaff hold posts as research specialists. The study reveals that most of the charges frequently leveled against college and university professors—alleging lack of interest in teaching— do not hold true for most faculty members. The researchers discovered that while college and university teachers are indeed a very diverse lot, the vast majority of them favor greater emphasis on teaching and greater rewards for excellence in teaching.

In their presentation, Gaff and Wilson draw profiles of two teacher types. One type favors academic change; the other opposes it. The data on which these profiles are drawn also show that these two faculty types differ in other significant ways. The two types hold different views of what a college education should be, and they teach their classes according to quite different teaching models.

In the second study, conducted for the Project to Improve College Teaching—a joint project of the Association of American Colleges and the American Association of University Professors—Gaff and Wilson present data to demonstrate that few colleges and universities maintain climates that their faculties view as sufficiently supportive of teaching. The authors insist, however, that the quality of teaching can be improved if certain changes are made in policies and practices related to the reward system.

In the last essay in Part One, "Assessment and Reward Systems," Harold Hodgkinson, project director at the Center for Research and Development in Higher Education, examines the nature of the reward system for the college professor. Faculty members are not adequately rewarded for excellence in teaching, and part of the problem lies in our present incapability to assess the quality of teaching. Hodgkinson argues that class visits not only are appropriate for this purpose but are, in fact, indispensable. A college teacher cannot be adequately judged unless someone qualified to observe and assess the teaching process watches him teach. But a single semiannual visit, Hodgkinson asserts, does not provide even the most acute observer an adequate basis for assessment. Multiple visits must occur over a period of time, frequently enough to allow the visitor to observe the teacher's growth pattern—for that pattern provides the frame in which the quality of a teacher's performance on any given day assumes significance. Hodgkinson thus stresses the developmental character of a faculty member's career as teacher.

The four essays of Part One emphasize the importance of the teaching process and its central role in higher education. We find cause, in these essays, for both uneasiness and encouragement. Today's typical college teacher carries out his teaching tasks in contexts that do not, on the whole, help him grow as a teacher or encourage improvement in teaching methods and styles. A young person beginning his college teaching career encounters a complex mythology that is hostile to any systematic analysis of the teaching process, and he finds in his older colleagues an almost paranoid fear of change. And yet, in this quite discouraging context, there is—as the essays of Part One show—considerable evidence which suggests that the turning point has already appeared. More than ever before, administrators are now working toward flexible contexts for teaching, and professors are becoming tolerant of teaching styles that differ from their own. Above all, college and university teachers have come to realize that they must go beyond a special knowledge of their subjects and a general interest in their students if they are to fulfill their teaching tasks with distinction.

But it is not very likely that any substantial changes for affecting the teaching function can take place unless there is substantial rebuilding of the structures designed to support the learning process. Some ways in which restructuring may be accomplished provide the subject for the essays of Part Two.

The New Learning

The essays of Part Two make it painfully clear that college and university resources are not organized efficiently enough to meet the needs for education beyond the high school. Perhaps the greatest obstacle in the way of effective use of resources is the degree system. Since it ties educational opportunity to class meetings and binds certification to course enrollment, the degree system is enormously wasteful. It discourages young adults from attempting to master a field of knowledge or a set of skills on their own, and, except under very special circumstances, it does not recognize such an achievement once it is completed.

A second obstacle to an efficient use of our resources is the concept of majors and minors that dominates academic programs. This concept has been responsible for an increasing crisscross of specialized academic programs which, most of us realize, resulted from past pressures now no longer felt and present expediencies soon to disappear. These unwieldly and inflexible curricular structures, which maintain a stranglehold on academic life, cannot adequately serve the future needs of our students and our nation.

A third obstacle is the great gap that exists between the community college and the public it is designed to serve. Everyone agrees that the community college must prepare itself to play an immeasurably significant role in American postsecondary education during the coming decades. But of all institutions, it appears least ready to meet its challenge and its opportunity—to a large extent because the total educational establishment has not allowed the community college to develop its own character and shape.

The essays of Part Two focus on these problems. They suggest some ways to introduce flexibility into the degree system, to design new curricula that are not built on traditional majors, and to plan for change in the community college. In the first two essays of Part Two, Lawrence Dennis and Jack Arbolino present proposals for radically new structures leading to external degrees. In the last two essays, George Morgan describes a new curriculum focused on the interdisciplinary principle and maximum student responsibility, and David S. Bushnell suggests how community colleges might begin to organize for the inevitable changes the world expects to see them make.

Lawrence Dennis, provost and director of the Massachusetts State College System, presents a blueprint for a new educational institution, The University of North America. As the title, "The Other End of Sesame Street," suggests, Dennis takes a multimedia approach. But his new institution is based only partly on the Sesame Street model; its more central concept is based on the open university in Great Britain.

The University of North America would exist, not as another campus, but as a confederation of regional higher education institutions and agencies. Its students would be mainly adults (anyone over the age of fifteen) who would work systematically toward the university degree. The basic teaching medium would be public broadcasting—that is, television and radio—supplemented by tutorials, conferences, and seminars. The blueprint emphasizes a new role in higher education for the Corporation of Public Broadcasting, and it asks us to abandon, once and for all, the myth that face-to-face contact in walled classrooms is necessary for effective learning.

Dennis' plan is staggering in its implications. Many readers will undoubtedly feel that it is unrealistic, but others will surely find it a possible solution to the seemingly insurmountable problems that post-secondary education must face during the coming decades. Perhaps the most persuasive argument in favor of Dennis' proposal is the fact that every facet of it is already technologically feasible. Dennis believes that in one way or another—either because professionals in higher education will be willing to take the initiative or because they will be forced to respond to pressures from outside the profession—the open university will become "a fact of life in this country in the last years of the present decade."

Jack Arbolino, in "A Plan for External Degrees," also envisions a national university, but his concept differs somewhat from Dennis'. Arbolino, executive director of the Council on College-Level Examinations of the College Entrance Examination Board, argues that the present degree structure in American colleges and universities is outmoded and badly in need of reform, and he presents a bold new plan in which a national university, perhaps federally chartered, would award external degrees. Unlike Dennis' institution, however, Arbolino's new university would not engage in instruction. Since Arbolino is concerned with the possible threat that his national university may pose to established colleges and universities, he outlines a compromise plan for external degrees where requirements would be met partly through individual campuses and partly through the national university.

To any observer of the American higher education scene, it is quite clear that basic reform in our total degree structure is long overdue. It is therefore reasonable to anticipate the establishment of external degrees. But if such a development occurs, one wonders whether it will affect only exceptional students, or whether it will involve, as many educators hope, millions of adults at every age in all walks of life. No one can say for certain.

In the meantime, the existing machinery is still in need of repair, and individual colleges and universities need to continue their plans to reform their own degree programs. An illustration of such a plan is given in the next essay of Part Three, "A New Interdisciplinary Curriculum," where George Morgan, director of institutional research at Hiram College, describes a new curriculum established at his campus. The curriculum emphasizes integrated studies and increased student freedom, based on these principles: greater responsibility of the student for his own education; interdisciplinary organization of subject matter; emphasis on effective written communication and effective discussion; new modes of teacher-student interaction in the classroom; and integration through a single, explicit approach—namely, the rational exploration of contemporary society. An evaluation of the new curriculum is in progress, and the preliminary results, reported by Morgan, are encouraging. He identifies a number of practices that have not worked, but he tells us that the principles on which the new curriculum is based have proved to be sound.

David Bushnell's essay, "Community College: Organizing for Change," is a preliminary report on Project Focus—a project of the American Association of Junior Colleges—written by its director of research. Bushnell surveys the accomplishments and weaknesses of the American junior college and emphasizes the need for change. The disparity between goals and current practices, Bushnell says, is revealed in a number of ways: in the general education programs of junior and community colleges, in their counseling and guidance programs, in the extended-day programs, and in their provision of community services.

Results thus far are not entirely positive. The ability of the community college to accommodate a diverse set of student needs is "at best limited," Bushnell says. Instructors and curricula are heavily oriented toward serving the able student; the disadvantaged student, when he is finally recruited, is not served well once he arrives on campus. There is little innovation on the instructional level. But despite these criticisms, Bushnell shows that the community college is a remarkable institution, that it has an immensely important role to play, and that in the years ahead it must—and will—rise to the challenge that our society has given it.

The reader of *New Teaching, New Learning* will find the essays of Part Two generally optimistic. Their authors see an enormous potential for postsecondary education in the United States, and their vision stimulates their enthusiasm. But the essays point up the depressing side of the picture as well; a frightening chasm lies between what we now have and what the nation will need.

Nonetheless, no one can deny that progress has been made. Every thoughtful trustee, administrator, faculty member, and student has come, finally, to recognize that the learning process is central to college and university activity. Surely other campus activities are important, too—housing and feeding students and caring for their health; recruiting and promoting professors; applying for research projects; protecting campus buildings and equipment; planning new facilities; increasing library holdings; recruiting ethnic-minority students; providing adequate working conditions for secretaries; purchasing computers; providing parking space for automobiles; and sponsoring sporting and theatrical events. But these activities take on importance only because, in one way or another, they facilitate the learning process.

The general shift of attitude about the centrality of learning is of great significance. It enables us now to go about creating the settings and structures that will put the learning process at the hub of American higher education—for it is not yet there on many campuses—and keep it there during the crucial decades ahead.

The New Student

The essays of Part Three appear under the general title "Exits and Entrances." The phrase comes from Dylan Thomas, a poet who made no attempt to hide his disrespect for the academic world. His hostility was directed, of course, toward the establishment in general (men in Brooks Brothers suits, as Kenneth Rexroth's elegy was later to tell us), but at least part of it must have arisen from his experience with the university as a low-risk enterprise. It is an institution that characteristically undertakes nothing that is not perfectly safe. The poetic irony of the title "Exits and Entrances" sets the theme for the essays, which ask how the higher education establishment—a low-risk enterprise—is responding to pressures to accommodate the high-risk student.

Students generally considered to be high risk are those who are poor, nonwhite, or low in ability—and, under certain circumstances, those who are women. As we put our academic energy, our public dollars, and our faculty time into their education, they are the students about whom we ask: Will our investment pay off? The low-ability student may drop out and add yet another experience of failure to his list. The woman may marry, become a homemaker, and fail to put her expensive university education to use. Are we not wasting on such students the time and energy and money that other students could use?

During the past few years, another element has complicated the question. As the pressures to devote resources to high-risk students have been increasing, the total resources available to higher education have been decreasing. As a consequence, many educators feel that we must invest most of the available resources in our best students; educators who have always held this belief are now more strongly convinced than ever, and those who temporarily abandoned this belief have returned to it. Only by devoting our resources to our best students, they argue, can we maintain and improve the highly developed society we have at present.

The counterargument also sets the good of society as the final goal. The lowest performing members of our society, this argument states, represent the greatest threat to the general welfare; they drain off our resources and contribute little or nothing in return. Hence, substantial improvement in the competence of such members of society would ultimately yield enormous benefits. To deny these people the opportunity to acquire competence is socially irresponsible; to help the individual is to help the society.

The two essays which open Part Three analyze an important aspect of these arguments as they concentrate on the problem of access to college. Alexander Astin, director of research for the American Council on Education, builds his presentation on an obviously sound principle that is suggested by the title of his essay, "College Admissions: A Systems Perspective." The admissions policy of a college or university can be described or judged only when it is seen in its relationships to the entire institution and to the larger systems of which the institution is a part. Astin's data, emerging from the research program of the

American Council on Education, are interpreted from this broad perspective. Amitai Etzioni, chairman of the Department of Sociology, Columbia University, begins his essay, "The Policy of Open Admissions," with a similar point. Decisions about admissions to college not only are important in themselves, Etzioni says, but they are of "far-reaching importance for all parts of the societal system." Although both Astin and Etzioni are analytic in their approach—and both maintain a remarkable objectivity—it will be clear to the reader where they stand. Etzioni recognizes the dilemma but leans toward a policy of selective admissions. Astin, keenly aware of the evidence to support both sides of the argument, leans toward a policy of open admissions.

These different points of view emerge when the two authors touch upon the most controversial aspects of their subject. Is it true that, in order to maintain high academic standards on a campus, an institution must support a policy of selective admissions? Etzioni answers in the affirmative; Astin presents arguments that suggest a negative answer. Is it true that a bright student develops better academically if he goes to a select college—that is, if he is grouped with students of similar ability? Etzioni assumes that it is so, while Astin presents data that suggest the opposite. Not only is there little intellectual value gained for the bright student by attending a highly selective college, Astin asserts, but according to available evidence such a student does not suffer intellectually when he attends a college of average or even below average selectivity. Is a policy of open admissions—involving, as it must, the development and support of new educational programs geared to low-ability students—too expensive to be feasible? Etzioni fears that such programs may be prohibitively expensive; Astin approaches the problem from a different perspective and offers a possible solution.

Many educators agree with Etzioni that open admissions cannot be implemented without economic assistance. The argument holds that students from disadvantaged backgrounds continue to be disadvantaged until such assistance is provided, no matter what policy colleges adopt. Some experts in the field of financing believe that poor but potentially capable students can be most effectively helped by a system of student vouchers. And if the vouchers can be used by these students at private as well as at public institutions, then the fiscal problems facing large numbers of private colleges in the United States can also be alleviated. Persuaded by these arguments and beliefs, the Governor's Commission on Education in Wisconsin recommended adoption of a student voucher system.

The Wisconsin Commission's recommendation is analyzed by Russell Thackrey, executive director, emeritus, National Association of State Universities and Land-Grant Colleges, in his essay "The Case Against the Wisconsin Voucher Plan." Thackrey at once takes issue with the Commission plan, attacking it on both philosophical and pragmatic grounds. The basic philosophy of the Commission, he points out, holds that higher education is primarily of benefit to the individual student rather than to the general society and, therefore, ought to be paid for by the student. The Commission recommended the elimination of direct public support for undergraduate education in the colleges and universities of Wisconsin in order to acquire funds to finance the voucher program. Thackrey presents a persuasive case against the student voucher system, arguing that it will, in the end, benefit neither the young people who are now disadvantaged nor the colleges that are in financial difficulty.

In all probability, the group most discriminated against in higher education at the present time is women. Ruth Oltman, a staff associate of the American Association of University Women, reports on an AAUW survey concerning women in her essay "Women in Higher Education." The object of the survey, begun a year ago, is to provide a comprehensive picture of women at all levels in the academic world—women as students, as faculty, as administrators, and as trustees. The survey data available thus far leave no doubt that women, in almost every respect, do not have equal status with men in the academic world. At every level, women are underrepresented or given positions with little power. Women constitute over 40 per cent of the total student population in four-year colleges and universities in the United States, but they constitute less than 20 per cent of all faculty, with proportionately fewer women in the higher ranks. There is a conspicuous lack of women serving in administrative positions or on boards of trustees.

Oltman recalls that more than a decade ago Theodore Caplow and Reece McGee stated in *The Academic Marketplace* that women academicians were not taken seriously "not because they have low prestige but because they are outside the prestige system entirely." While the situation has improved since Caplow and McGee's book appeared, Oltman points out that the basic problem remains. In addition to giving an excellent historical overview of the problem, Oltman's essay outlines some means that may contribute to its solution.

Part Three closes with an essay by Fred Harcleroad, "Disadvantaged Students and Survival in College." Harcleroad, president of the American College Testing Program, believes high-risk students can survive in college in far greater numbers than have generally been considered possible. Sufficient experience in a wide variety of institutions provides knowledge of successful approaches and of the specialized personnel and counseling services that are necessary to support those approaches.

Harcleroad presents some examples of effective programs. One of them, started in 1968 at a midwestern state college, was designed for students who under normal circumstances would not have been admitted to college. Faculty members on the campus did not know which students belonged to the specially admitted group and which did not. By March 1971, 60 per cent of the original group were still enrolled and making progress toward their degrees. Perhaps the most startling fact which Harcleroad presents in this description has to do with the cost factor: the additional cost of the special program was less than three hundred dollars per student per year beyond the regular basic budget. As Harcleroad points out, "The gain in human potential and individual human welfare from this modest expenditure is almost incalculable."

The essays in Part Three forcibly demonstrate that a traditional teaching-learning process which has proved barely effective in educating low-risk students is hopelessly inadequate for educating high-risk students. Whether improved methods for serving disadvantaged students will be discovered during the coming decade remains to be seen. Meanwhile, these new students must be accommodated in one way or another, for they are making their way into our colleges and universities in increasing numbers.

The New Decision Makers

The future of the new teaching and the new learning on college and university campuses is intimately tied to decisions being made at this very moment—decisions taken, not only by professors and students, but by everyone who shares in the governance of these institutions. Part Four of *New Teaching, New Learning* is devoted, therefore, to decision-making structures and processes in higher education.

In the opening essay, Morton Rauh stresses the need for change in governing boards; if their work is to become meaningful, he says, both their function and the composition of their membership must be redefined. Joseph Dehner presents a new, democratic pattern of governance that discards both the one-man–one-vote concept and the notion of participatory democracy. Phyllis Kaye demonstrates how mediation may succeed in resolving campus conflicts when other means fail. And to conclude Part Four, Robert O'Neil and John Corson describe current trends in university governance, emphasizing the paradoxical nature of recent developments.

Morton Rauh, vice-president, emeritus, of Antioch College, explains the function of university trustees in "Governing Boards: A Redefinition," and he suggests what they must become. Unless changes are made in the role of boards and the composition of their membership, they will soon no longer have reason for existence. "What is left to the trustees but to play meaningless games according to rules barely understood by anyone?" Rauh asks. He then points to four important functions that most boards are not now adequately fulfilling: selecting the president and evaluating his work, planning and maintaining institutional purpose, preserving assets, and acting as the final court in the resolution of issues.

Rauh redefines each of these functions. In his discussion of the responsibility of a governing board to act as the final court in the resolution of issues, he states that this function is "more commonly abused than used." It is imperative for the board to act as a court when all other processes have failed, but too many boards have asserted their right of ultimate authority when other processes have not yet been tried. A case in point is the action taken by the regents of the University of California regarding Angela Davis.

Rauh's redefinition of governing board functions leads him to make suggestions about the composition of the boards. Trustees are currently too business oriented, too old, and too homogeneous in their training and experience. Typically, they are businessmen or lawyers. They should be recruited from a wider pool of talents, Rauh says, from sources as yet scarcely tapped.

Joseph Dehner is a student at Harvard Law School and a trustee at Princeton University. His essay, "Creative Tension and Home Rule," begins with two major points. First, university tensions can become creative forces for progress. Conflict is healthly and creative, Dehner says, when it contributes ultimately to the common good rather than to mutual destruction of the participants. But members of the university community must realize their common purposes and rise above the special interests of various segments of the academic population. Second, there should be community control over community decisions; the resident community should play a role in decision-making. Most alumni and governing board members are not generally residents in the academic community and should not presume to understand its problems. "A university," Dehner maintains, "should be governed by home rule because only home rule can turn tension to creativity and transform conflict into progress." From these two major points emerges the principle of democratic control—a new principle not based on the concept of one-man–one-vote or on the idea of participatory democracy. "It simply means," Dehner explains, "that those who are directly affected by decisions and who have, by experience or position, positive contributions to make should have the primary responsibilities for making those decisions."

Phyllis Kaye, campus program coordinator of the National Center for Dispute Settlement of the American Arbitration Association, maintains, in "Resolving Conflict Through Mediation," that the process of mediation can often succeed in resolving campus conflict and preventing crises when other means fail. One reason for the success of mediation, Kaye asserts, lies in the relationship of a mediator to the parties in conflict: he is not a contender but a neutral off-campus agent sympathetic to all parties in the conflict. The voluntary nature of the mediation process also gives it an advantage. But the key to successful mediation is trust in the mediator by the individuals or groups in conflict. The bulk of Kaye's essay is devoted to descriptions of four campus situations where the National Center for Dispute Settlement was invited to help. The author presents a persuasive case for resolving and even preventing campus conflict.

In "Paradoxes of Campus Power," Robert O'Neil, professor of law at the University of California, Berkeley, presents an analysis of the crosscurrents in campus governance today. He describes these trends provocatively, but with deep seriousness, in the form of paradoxes: the ubiquitous cry for reform and the tenacious grasp on the old structures; the expansion of the decision-making process and the increasing disenfranchisement on campus; the pride taken in institutional diversity and the search for a single governance model to suit all colleges and universities; the increasing participation in governance and the decreasing accountability for decisions taken; the focus on structure in the building of new models and the lip service given to the dynamics of process; the persistent myth of autonomy and a social order so interdependent that the most important decisions on all campuses are largely predetermined. O'Neil thus depicts the truly paradoxical world of academia. The reader cannot fail to find it fascinating, and he will recognize it immediately as the world in which he lives. The essay ends with a summary of several broad avenues to the study and reform of university governance suggested by the Assembly on University Goals and Governance. O'Neil's acute analysis should be of much practical help to students of governance and to the decision makers currently involved in governance procedures.

The final essay of Part Four, "New Developments in Governance" by John Corson, presently chairman of the board of Fry Consultants, identifies the five most frequently proposed modifications in governance patterns for colleges and universities. In the first modification, new mechanisms are set up to make community-wide participation in governance possible. In the second, an attempt is made, as redistribution of power takes place, to redefine the authority of each participant group. The third modification focuses on university leadership. Corson discusses not only the leadership responsibility of the president but also the leadership functions of officers at other levels. His essay on this point confirms Rauh's conclusions. Corson points out, for example, that exacting standards of leadership, applied to existing governing boards, show how much these boards need to be reconstituted. Corson's fourth modification deals with the relationship between authority and accountability, and his fifth has to do with the relationship between decision-making and the new developments in curriculum and degree structure that are altering the landscape in higher education today.

The five essays of Part Four reflect the mounting concern over the nature and process of academic decision-making. But a large number of faculty members on American campuses—especially those who want to concentrate on teaching their courses and pursuing scholarly activities—find the tempest that rages around the question of university governance somewhat senseless. Many of them even view all this activity as a kind of absurd game playing, introduced to the campus from the worlds of politics and business and taken up and played by colleagues who want the excitement such games bring. But faculty members who are indifferent to the problems of academic governance are doing a disservice to themselves and to the world of scholarship. The conflicts on campus in which these professors refuse to participate are often tied to the world outside the university and indirectly affect the lives of men and women and quite possibly the future of mankind. Campus governance games may appear absurd, but they are deadly serious. No one, inside or outside the academic world, can afford to make light of them.

The New Professor

Recent volumes of *Current Issues in Higher Education* have increasingly reflected the concern of educators over the politicization of the university. Essays on this subject appearing in the last three yearbooks have pointed up the dilemma: whether the American university should turn itself into an agent for social reform, or whether it should continue to protect its status, its power, and its financial interest in the governmental-industrial complex.

Part Five opens with an essay that makes an exceedingly important contribution to the continuing dialogue on politicization. In "Academic Freedom and Collective Expressions of Opinion," Columbia University sociologist Immanuel Wallerstein argues the case for the appropriateness—indeed, the necessity—of collective or corporate expressions of opinion by the university. An obvious example is the resolution by faculty senates calling for the end of the war in Indochina. Wallerstein believes that such expressions of opinion are an essential ingredient in the maintenance of a free society. "It is not the presence but the absence of collective expressions," he states, "which is dangerous."

Following the presentation of his general position, Wallerstein reconstructs three counterarguments and systematically demolishes them. Finally he calls for the transformation of the American liberal university into a critical university, and, in a compelling sequence of statements in the last paragraphs of his essay, he develops a definition of the critical university. *Current Issues* readers who have more than an academic interest in academic freedom will want to share Wallerstein's essay with their friends both in and out of the academic community.

The theme of freedom is also central to the next essay, Bertram Davis' " 'Policing' Academic Responsibility". Some faculty members will bristle, while others may merely shrug, when they encounter the idea that professors ought to be policed to make certain they are fulfilling their responsibilities. Davis uses the term in a special way, however, as he examines both sides of the coin—responsibility and freedom. Although it is commonly argued that one cannot have freedom without responsibility, Davis maintains that in the academic world the argument should be reversed: the professor must have conditions that are most favorable to learning and teaching if he is to do an adequate job—and he cannot, therefore, discharge his responsibilities without a high degree of freedom.

Davis, general secretary of the American Association of University Professors, describes the role that the AAUP has played in the struggle for the professor's freedom to teach. Davis asserts that "the record of academic freedom in the United States is stained with numerous incidents which boards of trustees have concurred in, encouraged, and even compelled so that administrative actions violate academic freedom." In institutions where a repressive atmosphere exists, Davis points out, a faculty member has three possible courses of action open to him: he can resign; he can enter a private world where he performs his teaching and other duties in a purely mechanical way, with no one (except a few of his students and a colleague or two) the wiser; or he can join the fight to improve the conditions under which students and professors on his campus go about learning and teaching. Increasingly in our time, professors on repressive campuses have courageously turned to the last of these choices.

Davis' essay serves as an introduction to the two essays that make up the remainder of Part Five. "Prescribing Faculty Workloads" by Richard Miller and "Tenure and Collective Bargaining" by William Van Alstyne deal with the working conditions of the university employee and with methods for controlling these conditions. The general problem that Miller addresses is the increasing control of public institutions, including the processes of institutional management, by state legislatures. Specifically, Miller focuses on the professor's work week and who controls it. Miller, who is executive director of the Michigan Council of State College Presidents, analyzes the situation in his own state, where the legislature has imposed an increasing number of controls on the colleges and universities in the name of productivity and economy. The latest such control prescribes teaching loads for faculty members.

One of the effects of such legislative intrusion into institutional management, Miller predicts, will be a quickening of the pace of unionization. Bargaining confrontation between faculty members and their legislatures seems to him to be inevitable; but he wonders how faculty members can achieve their goals at the present time, when the general feeling among voters is so hostile toward professors. Readers of the 1970 AAHE yearbook will recall the many examples of this hostility presented by Senator Mark O. Hatfield in his essay in that volume.[1] One does not need to look very far for more recent examples than this: California Governor Ronald Reagan received a standing ovation from an audience of a thousand citizens when he told them that the University of California needs not more money but larger teaching loads for its faculty. The governor accompanied his public utterances by action: he vetoed millions of dollars in the university budget (including a cost-of-living salary increase for faculty members) that had been approved by the legislature. There was little public outcry at the governor's action.[2]

The last essay in Part Five explores tenure practices and their possible modification as college and university employees, including the professoriate, move toward collective bargaining. Van Alstyne, professor of law at Duke University, begins with a definition of tenure and offers several examples to show that tenure by no means guarantees lifetime employment. He then investigates the relationship between tenure and the process of collective bargaining. While no clear pattern has as yet emerged, Van Alstyne believes that there will be no serious problem in the academic world "in accommodating the process of collective bargaining to the concept of tenure." He concludes that tenure, far from being threatened with extinction, may well become widespread as a result of an increase in the collective bargaining process on American campuses.

If collective bargaining in industry continues to supply the models for the academic world—which is more than likely—there are several "danger areas" Van Alstyne believes should cause concern. If, for example, a majority of the faculty members at a given campus are new to the academic world, if they are indifferent to academic tradition, and if they are single-mindedly interested in salary increases and fringe benefits, they may bargain for these advantages at the risk of "trading off the protection of tenure or academic due process—or academic freedom."

---

[1] "Public Pressures on Higher Education," in G. K. Smith (Ed.), *The Troubled Campus: Current Issues in Higher Education 1970*. San Francisco: Jossey-Bass, 1970.

[2] Less than a month later, however, the board of regents voted by a large margin to "urgently request" the legislature to override the governor's veto. The strong wording of the regents' request astonished everyone (including the governor himself, who is a member of the board) and pleased academicians everywhere. See R. Moscowitz, "Longer Hours: Reagan for More Teaching at UC," *San Francisco Chronicle*, June 23, 1971, p. 4; and S. Duscha, "Regents: 'Kill UC Fund Veto,' " *Berkeley Daily Gazette*, July 17, 1971, pp. 1–2.

Taken together, the four essays of Part Five deal with the whole range of academic working conditions, including both their spiritual side (such as the freedom to render collective expressions of opinion on political issues) and their material side (such as the control of teaching loads). The authors of these essays point up the relationship between working conditions and the attitude toward faculty members that dominates those bodies that, in one sense or another, employ professors—that is, university management, boards of trustees, state legislatures, and the tax-paying public.

The New University

If education beyond high school is to meet the future needs of our nation and its individual citizens, the role played by colleges and universities in our society and in the lives of its members must be redefined. The goals of higher education, its very nature, must be reinterpreted both for members of the educational profession and for the general public.

The authors of the essays in Part Six attempt such reinterpretation. Ed Riddick and Charles Silberman both emphasize the direct and active role that education needs to play in the society. Despite similarity of content, however, there are great differences in form: Silberman's rhetoric is in the white European tradition; Riddick's is in the black American tradition. Samuel Gould and Louis Benezet are both concerned with the image the public now has of the American university. Despite similarity of theme, however, there are differences in their content: Gould wants to bridge the interpretation gap between the university and the general public; Benezet wants to correct the undue emphasis he finds, both inside and outside the profession, on the economics of education. He places part of the blame for this wrong emphasis on the Carnegie Commission on Higher Education. The Commission's reports have, indeed, emphasized numbers and costs, and its chairman, Clark Kerr, is, indeed, an economist. But interestingly enough, the essay which closes this last part of *New Teaching, New Learning* is written by Clark Kerr, and it does not emphasize numbers and costs. Kerr's essay is basically historical in subject; the current period of uncertainty for higher education is placed in the context of almost 350 years of the existence of American institutions of higher learning.

Riddick told his audience at the Twenty-Sixth National Conference on Higher Education: "We are not fulfilling the prophetic role required of education, and we have turned ourselves into prostitutes." He condemned academicians who rationalize the evils in American society and who condone bigotry and inhumanity. He criticized educational conferences, where academic people meet only with academic people; and he suggested that we invite welfare mothers, city planners, and politicians to take part in our educational dialogues.

The essay based on that speech, "A Race with Disaster," opens Part Six. As national research director for Operation Breadbasket, Southern Christian Leadership Conference, Riddick has observed and analyzed the relationship between academic institutions and other structures within our society. He very much fears that the university has become isolated from the rest of American life, and he warns educators about the consequences of this isolation: "The university must see itself as part of a larger community: the problems of the community are also the problems of the university. The university must not lose sight of this fact. If the university, seeking to save itself, withdraws from the community, it will lose itself. And once lost, it might never find its life and its role again."

Riddick's basic thesis will not be new to the reader. It tells us that the academic community must rejoin the rest of the world if we are to win the race with disaster. But this message cannot be too often repeated, especially when it is presented as eloquently and as cogently as it is in Riddick's essay.

In "The Remaking of American Education," Charles Silberman, a member of the Board of Editors of *Fortune,* also views the crisis in higher education as part of the larger crisis in American society. But Silberman points out that the word *crisis,* in its Greek etymon, signifies a turning point. All is not hopeless, he says, for the turn must come sooner or later. Silberman's thesis can be easily stated: education is a process that people carry on themselves; it is not possible to educate someone else. College and university teaching is, however, typically organized on the basis of a diametrically opposed presupposition. Pursuing the implications of his thesis, Silberman reaches some conclusions that will please those professors who give high status to their teaching function. Silberman believes, for example, that some kind of teaching experience ought to be a part of every student's education because "teaching is the ultimate liberal art." In short, a man cannot be liberally educated without becoming an educator himself.

Some traditional university professors may find Silberman's ideas disturbing. They can, of course, write him off as simply another educational reformer in the tradition W. H. Cowley has called counterrevolutionist. They can deal with him as they have dealt with others whom Cowley places in that tradition—Alexander Meiklejohn and Robert M. Hutchins, for instance.[3] But the majority of readers will, no doubt, be sympathetic to Silberman's ideas. Perhaps they will not find much that is startling or new in the essay, but they will discover that it excellently formulates what they already know.

Samuel Gould, chancellor, emeritus, State University of New York, in "Bridging the Interpretation Gap," begins by asking what can be done about the public's diminished confidence in colleges and universities. He presents several principles which he believes should guide relationships with the public: We must impart information about our activities quickly, accurately, and—above all—frankly. We must talk to people in a language they can understand, not in educational jargon. We must emphasize the positive achievements of the American college and university. We must persuade the public of the values of scholarship. And we must present a picture of the university as a microcosm which reflects all the problems of the wider world; if the public does not like what it sees, it is because it sees itself. We must make the public understand that fact, although we must not state the matter so bluntly. But the public must be persuaded, Gould insists, that the university cannot be held responsible for problems that pervade the entire society.

"Is Higher Education a Commodity?" poses a question which Louis Benezet, president of the State University of New York at Albany, answers in the negative. Benezet maintains that analyses of the financial crisis in higher education have encouraged many people (including the President of the United States) to think of a college education as a commodity, similar to other goods and services an individual purchases for his own benefit. Benezet believes that the Carnegie Commission on Higher Education has, in certain ways, contributed to this erroneous concept. Like Thackrey and Astin, Benezet argues that the chief beneficiary of higher education is not the student but society itself.

While Benezet does not underestimate the importance of economic factors, he does not believe they should determine how new patterns are to be developed for teaching and learning in postsecondary institutions. He adduces an old but still highly regarded principle in the field of educational development. The criteria by which educational change should be planned and ultimately assessed must derive, first

[3] See M. Harris, *Five Counterrevolutionists in Higher Education.* Corvallis, Ore.: Oregon State University Press, 1970.

and foremost, from considerations that make sense educationally; fiscal conditions and other noneducational factors may limit the possibilities, but they must not be permitted to determine solutions. Indeed, Benezet is pleased to report that a new spirit of humanity has pervaded students and the young faculty during the past decade. "If we can maintain the humane spirit," he says, "and at the same time retain substance and process in higher learning, then our campuses will still lead the way to an era finer than any we have seen."

Clark Kerr's essay, "Destiny—Not So Manifest," which closes Part Six and the volume, is primarily an historical piece that surveys the past several centuries and then looks forward into the uncertain future. Kerr traces the history of American higher education over 330 years, discovers only one relatively brief period of substantial uncertainty (the half century from 1820 to 1870), and concludes that we are now in the beginning years of another such period of uncertainty— a period, Kerr says, "of unknown duration and as yet of uncertain outcome." Kerr has played a central role in some of the most controversial activities that have taken place in higher education during the last decade, and he has a reputation as one of the most perceptive current observers of the higher education scene. Readers of this volume will want to give his essay the special attention that it merits.

The essays of Part Six will almost certainly leave the reader uneasy—especially in view of the emphasis some of the authors place on the vast public relations job that must be done if higher education is to be properly interpreted to the general public.

There is a story told about a modern philosopher who was arguing a point with someone vastly inferior to him intellectually. The philosopher found himself speechless, for he was unable to argue at his own level, and he refused to falsify the issue by arguing at his opponent's level. The philosopher was only able to sputter at last: "Your ignorance leaves me stupid!" A sensitive professor sometimes feels that way today when he encounters the arguments typically used to justify reduction of college and university budgets. Moreover, the professor has reason to suspect that upholders of the status quo, many of whom occupy influential positions in the society, have cooperated with conservative politicians in a punitive campaign against all centers of liberal thought, including the college and university campuses. In a culture where it has become the norm for public images to be built by professional image makers, perhaps the professor, too, should turn to the public relations specialist and enlist his aid. Even with this solution, however (aside from the question of funds), many faculty members would no doubt feel uneasy. No public relations specialist, in all probability, is free enough from commercial taint to satisfy the American professoriate.

In any event, one can be sure a typical public relations campaign, whatever its outcome, is hardly the ultimate answer. The most serious inadequacies of the American university will not be remedied in the slightest by an improved public image unless fundamental changes take place in higher education itself. As Kerr makes clear in his essay, the plight of the university is intimately bound to the course of the cultural revolution our society is now experiencing. As Kerr gauges that revolution, he finds that the gap between the intellectual and the general public will likely widen in the years immediately ahead. If, however, the plans and proposals presented in the twenty-seven essays that follow could begin to be implemented within the next few years, we could make solid progress toward closing that gap.

PART ONE:

New Teaching Contexts

The essays of Part One arouse both uneasiness and encouragement. They show the typical faculty member working in a context that does little to help him grow as a teacher. But the essays present also considerable evidence of change: more administrators looking for better ways to reward teaching, more faculty members exploring new teaching styles. Many professors now realize that, to fulfill their teaching tasks with distinction, they must go beyond a special knowledge of their subjects and a general interest in their students.

1

Teaching in a Black College

John Monro

According to the Carnegie Commission on Higher Education, there are in existence 105 black colleges—both large and small, public and private, and almost all located in the deep South. The Carnegie study found that black colleges enroll some 160,000 black students, or 35 per cent, of the overall total of about 450,000 black students now going to colleges across the country. During the mid-sixties, considerably fewer black students attended college (approximately 250,000), and about half of these went to black colleges. Thus, absolute enrollments in black colleges have grown substantially, even though the proportion of the total number of black students has gone down. What happened, of course, was that white colleges made an effort to enroll black students. In addition, the number of community colleges increased rapidly.

Black student enrollments will continue to grow at increasing rates. William Brassiel, professor at the University of Connecticut and a careful scholar of these matters, predicts that by 1978 one million black students will be enrolled in college. This would double the present enrollment. According to Southern Regional Education Board studies, presently in the South something like 15 per cent of all young black men and women get to college, while 50 per cent of all white students continue their schooling. Maybe that simple comparison alone spells out the problem and responsibilities that face us. I have used these figures in order to indicate that we are in a very important boom period in the size of enrollments at black colleges. The number of students has doubled in five years and may double again in the next ten years, which is one indication that we will need all the college space we have and then some. Making generalizations about a hundred or more colleges, either black or white, is difficult. Among black colleges, there are some weak and marginal institutions, and there are some that clearly rank among the very best colleges in the United States. Many black colleges are in the middle, just as with white colleges. Yet, for black colleges as a whole, the opportunities, responsibilities, emphases, and problems differ from those of white colleges. These are the issues that I will try to sketch out briefly.

First, because of the cruel effects of racial discrimination in our society, black colleges must provide for a great number of students who have no money and whose schooling is inadequate. Miles College is a good example. Eighty per cent of the students at Miles College qualify for federal poverty aid, and after twelve years in the Alabama schools most of our students enter college at the ninth grade level in reading, language, and math skills. This is a perfectly typical situation, and, I must say, one that is not restricted to the South or to the black community. In such situations, the job is to get financial support for the students and to set up a curriculum and teaching style that will move the students ahead on basic skills as rapidly and effectively as possible. Black colleges are doing a sound job on both counts. And we had better. In the years ahead, our problems will become more difficult before they get any easier than they are now.

The second problem that faces the black college is the challenging and intricate job of preparing black students for full professional participation in a predominantly white institutional world, while strengthening their sense of self, their sense of identity, and their pride in and responsibility to the black community. On the one hand, we are working toward desegregation. On the other hand, we must sometimes move in the opposite direction in order to stress the identity and power of the black community. These are intricate and apparently paradoxical efforts that generate sharp disagreement and a good deal of pain within the walls of the black college as well as confusion and anxiety in the surrounding white world. The matter is not a simple one and has no easy solution.

Other problems that plague black colleges are that they must conduct business while desperately in need of money and that they must operate in the face of a surrounding white power structure that persistently wonders whether black colleges are not after all a kind of wrongheaded anachronism in a society trying to move toward desegregation. An examination of the position of the black community is necessary before we can answer the charge of anachronism and before we can discuss the curriculum and methods of teaching at black colleges.

Whether we like it or not, in this country there is a white community and a black community, and the white community has control of the political, economic, and institutional power. Since the power structure is characterized by racism—indeed a sick racism—we have a long history of keeping the black community down and out. No community gets anywhere in this country without strong institutional organizations. Organized labor made no progress in our country until labor quit believing that management was its partner. In the past three or four decades, labor forces learned to organize to shut down steel or auto production or to stop the mail or truck transport. Organizing the community of labor was bloody and hard, but it worked. Now General Motors and even the U.S. Post Office sit down and bargain with the work force on equal terms. And I remember, and so do many of my readers, I am sure, the doomsday cries in the 1930s, when workers sat down in the auto plants to block the use of strike breakers. Those outcries are reminiscent of the cries heard when Martin Luther King, Jr., took over downtown Birmingham to stop the money-making there, or when the black people in Watts or Newark or Detroit took over and stopped the money-making there.

In order to survive in America, a group must have respect, and clearly what the dominant white community respects is not piety and courtesy but organized strength in the opposition, especially the kind of organized strength that can interrupt the flow of profits. Thus, I am led to the conclusion that what the black community needs is organized institutional power, or clout as it is called in some parts of the country.

Indeed, I would predict that order and progress will be seen in the relations between black and white communities when the country senses this fundamental fact of our sociology.

The black college finds a place in this sociological scheme by being one center of institutional strength for the black community. We make it our special business to get in touch with badly prepared, poorly financed black students who want to go to college. Such students become our special concern.

The black college also functions as an ideal place to conduct much needed teaching and research on the wretched experience of the black minority in this country since 1600. As powerful and as racist as we obviously are, immediate, intensive studies of our racial attitudes are needed before we launch on further racial wars in Asia. The black college is an extraordinarily important place of learning for white teachers and students who want to begin to set their own lives and attitudes straight. If we think it is important for black students to go to Harvard or Stanford, surely we can see by now that it is doubly important for Harvard and Stanford students to go to Morehouse or Miles. Finally, we must ask: Why not have black colleges? For 350 years we apparently have not been troubled by having all-white colleges in this country, and it is one simple instance of our racism that while all-white colleges seem natural enough, a black college seems anachronistic. Never in their history have black colleges excluded white people as students or faculty; of how many white colleges can the reverse be said?

Let us turn now directly to the curriculum. Black colleges should be offering strong, general education programs and major curricula that will lead our graduates out into professional schools and lines of work—especially, I would add, professional work that has some bearing on the progress of the black community. For example, there are serious shortages of black doctors, lawyers, sociologists, psychologists, economists, and business executives. We should be concentrating on all these fields and introducing them to our students as real options leading to useful careers. Developing strong majors in these professional and preprofessional fields will mean that our faculties will have to be greatly strengthened or that local exchange arrangements with neighborhood universities and colleges will have to be developed.

Some of the fields of study that black colleges should expand or continue to pursue are black studies, education, and urban studies. As for black studies, I am convinced that black colleges can and should develop strong, major programs in fields other than black studies. Education, of course, is a traditional field in the black colleges, but we should now take a different approach. We should be looking forward to the new elementary and secondary schools that can be created, rather than looking backward to the old constricting certification requirements. Many black colleges should be running their own experimental schools. Urban studies will inevitably become a new major field. I do not necessarily criticize traditional curriculum patterns, but I do believe profoundly that the black college should set its priorities so as to meet the critical needs of the black community, rather than to imitate the offerings of prestigious white colleges.

I would like to touch briefly on freshman studies, which is my responsibility at Miles College. Freshman studies is a crucial area because that is the threshold across which we meet our in-coming students. This is where students first discover what college is like; it is when they decide whether college relates, whether it is demanding and important, or whether it is just more rote learning. In our program at Miles we try to figure out what material is important to a student, what will grab his interest. We then exploit that advantage to motivate the student's reading and discussing, to encourage ideas and writing, and to sharpen the basic skills. For example, in general science, we do not start with molecular theory and the intricacies of the cell, important as those may be. We start with the study of human anatomy, a matter of some interest to and indeed of some consequence for teenagers.

In social science we start out with a one-semester course in black history covering the main events, people, and trends, and in the black experience in the United States since about 1800. We put a heavy emphasis on the strategies and the successes and the failures of heroes in the civil rights efforts since 1954. Our freshmen read and report on Frederick Douglass and Booker Washington, W. E. B. DuBois and Marcus Garvey, King and Stokley Carmichael, and Eldridge Cleaver and Franz Fanon. We meet five days a week in small seminars of fifteen students. The teacher's job is to get to know his people and to help them with the troubles they are having.

In the spring semester in social science we introduce the student to problems in all of the social sciences. For example, in my classes, students completed a unit of economics that dealt with problems of inflation, how to protect oneself against loan sharks, how to make sense when buying a car, and the record of labor unions in keeping black people out of decent jobs. You could call this a course in simple economic survival. Very few of our students come away thinking that economics is an irrelevant subject.

Freshman English is critically important of course.[1] We have a lot to accomplish—developing vocabulary and a grasp on basic grammar; generating, organizing, and presenting ideas; reading and understanding the nature of the ideas of other people; learning the elements of rhetoric and how to be intelligently skeptical and critical; and finding out how creative writers represent experience in poetry, stories, and novels and how to recreate that experience for oneself. In all this, black writers are inevitably important to us. We have had our moments of overstressing black letters and neglecting the rest, but we are hitting a better balance now. One reason for this is that our students have let us know they want a better balance.

During the fall semester, my freshman class of fifteen students met every day for one hour. We read *Black Boy* by Richard Wright and several short pieces. We wrote a piece almost every day, in class and out. In the spring, we read *Huckleberry Finn, The Red Badge of Courage,* and *The Invisible Man.* We worked hard every day on grammar and vocabulary. A proficiency examination was set by the College for the first of May in order to test our whole effort. I saw my students in individual conferences, and a staff of upper classmen was available to tutor those who needed it.

How well does our system work? I have made some running accounts of student grade averages in college, checking students' test scores at the time of admission and after graduation. Any student we admit (and we are an open enrollment college), no matter how discouraging things may look at the start, can make it through our college if he stays with it. We have an overwhelming number of individual cases to illustrate this point. We graduated in June 1971 about half the students admitted in 1967. Some of the graduating seniors were from the bottom of the prediction list at admission; some were from the middle; and some were from the top. We lost people at all levels, failed to reach them, failed to hold their interest, failed to get them going. But we know our efforts are reaching many, and we

[1] Studies by professional linguists are now being made on the grammar of black dialects. These include contrastive analyses between black dialect structures and standard English. Teachers of black students can do best in their work in teaching standard English when they understand thoroughly how these various language systems work. There is, of course, nothing intrinsically better about the structural patterns of the standard language, but most of our students want to have command of standard English for office and professional use.

know that not here or anywhere in education are there any instant miracles. We have to make sense in our curriculum, get the best teachers we can, and get them working hard with students. It's an old story; but it works, and we keep learning.

As a final comment, I hope this brief discussion will interest some white teachers young or old to come join us in the work of black colleges. For some, it will be a valuable sabbatical year. For others I would hope it could become an extended period of teaching. I cannot think of a more rewarding place to work for the man or woman who likes to teach students. In thirty-five years of work in higher education I have never known such reward. Teaching or studying at a black college offers the thoughtful white teacher or student the rare and precious opportunity to live and work in the American black community, to begin to see things as they are, and to begin there and then the long, difficult, critical task of curing our country of its terrible, crippling sickness—white racism.

❧ 2 ❧

Turning Students on
Through Multimedia

Paul L. Briand, Jr.

❧❧❧❧❧❧❧❧❧❧

After seventeen years of teaching composition, I was convinced that the art of writing could not be taught, that the craft of writing may be taught, and that the skill of writing could be taught with only indifferent success. Therefore, when my chairman asked me if I would like to work up a program in a multimedia approach to advanced composition, I readily accepted, especially when he offered me the released time in which to do it. Discouraged at my long failure to turn my students on about theme writing, I was ready to try anything.

Initially, I researched the subject—compiling a bibliography of books and articles (the National Council on the Teaching of English has the best single collection) and making a list of materials available in film, film strips, television kinescopes, 35 millimeter slides, transparencies for overhead projectors, records, audio tapes, programmed instruction for teaching machines, and programs in computer-assisted instruction. I had no idea what I would come up with, which made the adventure into multimedia an exciting one. I did know, however, that help was needed in four main areas: theme grading; theme discussion in class (students are bored when the theme is not theirs); the teaching of theme writing (rhetoric frightens students; grammar turns them off; and spelling and punctuation turn them away); and subjects for theme writing (what to write about). I was heartened by what I found, and since the spring semester of 1969 I have been offering my turned-on course in English composition—turned-on because it is plugged in to multimedia.

Theme grading can be a vexing problem for composition instructors. At first I thought I would grade each student's theme on television; he could see me mark and criticize his paper. Each student would have his own reel of video tape, which he could play back on his own time. The student would have a record of his progress that could be replayed any time he wanted to see and hear it again. This proved too expensive and time-consuming, but audio tapes work almost as well. Each student has two or three of his own cassette tapes, which he buys like textbooks, with one hour on each. He writes his paper, records it on tape, and submits both to the instructor. The instructor marks the paper for such visible errors as comma splices and fused sentences, disagreements between subjects and verbs and between pronouns and antecedents, and misspellings. The instructor uses the tape recorder for his comments on such large abstract matters as style and diction, the introduction of subject and establishment of thesis, organization and development, and the conclusion. The student has a record of his progress that can be replayed at will; hopefully his writing will begin to sound like him since he can now hear it (probably for the first time). Having diagnosed the ills of the student's writing, the instructor can also use the tape recorder to recommend treatment for the cure of poor writing. On the student's time, not the instructor's, so many prescribed doses of teaching machine programs can be given for such maladies as "strep" punctuation, viral grammar, and malodorous spelling. For the ambiguous rhetorical problems, the student would have to view and listen to kinescoped, twenty-minute lectures (prerecorded by the instructor from previous classroom theme discussions or taped under controlled conditions in the television studio) on such matters as purpose, organizational patterns, concrete development, sentence variety, and psychological impact of sentence and paragraph arrangement.

Classroom theme discussion is a second area that can be vitalized by using multimedia. The instructor will want to record on television his analyses of representative student papers, since he will use them again for individual theme therapy. He can analyze one paper for one particular problem, another paper for another problem, until he has a good sampling of the maladies of student writing along with the recommended treatments for cure. These minilectures and the teaching machine programs will serve as a library/clinic for students with writing problems.

Another way to discuss particular writing problems in class is to turn the classroom into a writing workshop or a kind of a newspaper cityroom in which the instructor is the editor; he uses an overhead projector on which he edits copy for the benefit of all the writers in the room. The editor/instructor would need a Thermofax or other type of copier machine close by so that he could readily make transparencies and put them on the overhead projector to be edited with grease pencil. I would ask my student writers to write no more than one paragraph on a page, which would not have to fill the page. Then in my discussion of the paragraph transparency, I could proceed from word, to sentence, to paragraph, and to different kinds of paragraphs for introduction, conclusion, and development. These classroom exercises I would not grade, for the student must have a chance to write without pressure and to experiment with ways of writing that he has dared not try before. Since these exercises are not graded, the student can remain anonymous by turning in his work without his name on it.

A third area that can always stand improvement is the teaching of theme writing. I once had a flight instructor who told me he would "learn me" how to fly a light plane, and he did—not by teaching me but by showing me how to fly. So should it be in learning how to write. If the instructor must lecture on certain writing principles, let him keep those lectures short, no more than twenty minutes, so that the class can spend the rest of the time doing what the principles require. Let the students see the instructor actually writing and rewriting different kinds of sentences and paragraphs on the overhead projector. As for the minilectures themselves, I am planning a three-screen projection with 35 millimeter slide transparencies, where each point is made first on the center screen then moved to one of the two side screens as more points are made. For example, I would first show the thesis sentence for a theme on the center panel, then move it to the right panel and hold it there. Next I would show the topic sentences for the paragraphs in the body of the paper on the center panel, then move them to the left panel and hold them there. Finally, I would show the theme from beginning to end, one paragraph at a time, on the center panel. As this is done, I would ask one of the students to read the paragraphs out loud, so the class could enjoy the double advantage of seeing and hearing at the same time. I am planning eighteen of these minilectures with slides, but I do not expect to use more than twelve.

Finding subjects for theme writing is a fourth problem that plagues students and instructors alike. What subjects will interest students sufficiently to enable them to write competently, adequately, and comprehensibly? My students complain no matter what the source of the subjects for theme writing may be—whether the subjects come from me, from a book of readings, or from the students themselves. Nothing seems to turn them on to writing. I have unsuccessfully tried subjects like student unrest, pot, racism, the population explosion, sex, and pollution. I have tried controlled research papers and open research papers. I have tried assigning one long paper, several short papers, papers of one paragraph, and papers of several paragraphs. Because nothing I have tried has worked, I was willing to try something else. The questions I asked myself were: Since my students have no verbal literacy to speak of, do they (because they were brought up on viewing instead of reading) have visual literacy? Can they translate visual and oral messages into verbal, linear literacy? In other words, can they change lines of photographic and electronic dots of light into lines of movable type? Finding an answer to these questions was worth a try.

To this end, I have planned six programs, saturated with ideas and multichanneled in multimedia, so that the students will be assaulted on as many sense levels as possible. The programs will be based primarily on 35 millimeter slide transparencies, projected on three screens and synchronized to sound; the same programs will also use kinescopes and films. For a particular program on war, for example, the 35 millimeter slides could be moved to the two side panels to be held or changed, while a film clip or kinescope of a battle or engagement was shown on the center panel.

The only drawback to such programs is that a great deal of time is required for preparation. Photographs must be taken, developed, mounted, put in trays, viewed, edited, and viewed again; music or narration must be taped, listened to, edited, listened to again, and synchronized to the slides. Thousand of feet of film and kinescope must be viewed, selected, and edited. Even though it is always cheaper to rent film than to buy it, there is the problem that the rented film may not arrive on time. Finally, the instructor, who has already played the roles of writer/editor, television actor, and tape recording artist, must also become a photographer, director, and producer. (Fortunately for the instructor, synchrotape is commercially available for putting audio and visual elements together from one punched tape. Otherwise, he would need helpers to operate slide projectors, tape recorders or record players, and kinescope or movie projectors.)

A multimedia approach to advanced composition would be initially expensive (about three or four thousand dollars), but after that it should be relatively easy to maintain. At the State University College at Oswego, New York, a Learning Resources Center is fully staffed with media specialists and housed in a brand new building with classrooms fanning out from a central core where projection on two and three screens can be made and where television monitors for student viewing jut out from the walls. Classrooms like these are literally wired for multimedia.

Computers are much more expensive, but they will undoubtedly serve the multimedia composition course of the future. The student will sit at a typewriter before a console equipped with several panels for viewing, microphones for talking, and earphones for listening. Presently available are programs in computer-assisted instruction (CAI) for essay analysis of spelling, reading, grammar, rhetorical patterns, and characteristic features of various literary genres. The composition course of the future will be organized around the computer console.

Today, however, composition courses are still in the classroom, but they work better if plugged into multimedia, turned on to slide projectors, movie projectors, three-screen panels for viewing, kinescope on television monitors, cassette tape recorders, and record players. Despite these advances, however, I am still convinced that the art of writing cannot be taught. The skill of writing, however, can be taught —and with great success—by means of a multimedia approach.

3

Faculty Values and Improving Teaching

Jerry G. Gaff, Robert C. Wilson

Students level many charges against college professors, but the central concern focusses on teaching: faculty neglect teaching in favor of research; they avoid contacts with students; and they resist changing traditional classroom practices. One must ask whether these particular criticisms are justified. To learn more about the teaching attitudes, values, and activities of college teachers, we conducted a multicampus survey of college and university faculty members. Six very different schools were canvassed: a campus of a large state university, a large state college, a medium-sized public junior college, a medium-sized private university, a small selective liberal arts college, and a small Protestant denominational college. We were interested in faculty views on several issues that are both controversial and at the core of the teaching process. We asked questions about orientation toward teaching, faculty-student interaction, the reward structure, and educational change. During the winter of 1968–1969, a questionnaire was distributed to all of the faculty members in the four smaller schools and to random samples of four hundred in the two larger ones. Approximately 1,500 questionnaires were sent out, and 70 per cent were returned. (Readers interested in further details on the methodology of this research are invited to correspond with the authors at the Center for Research and Development in Higher Education, Berkeley, California, 94720.)

Our data have mainly shown that many of the common assertions about college professors are not true of the majority of faculty members. Although it has been charged that faculty regard research as more desirable than teaching, we found that most faculty consider teaching a central activity and a major source of satisfaction. For example, when asked to indicate major sources of satisfaction in their lives, faculty members most frequently checked teaching. Most faculty members thought their students viewed them as effective teachers. In addition, most faculty expressed a desire to be advanced primarily on their teaching effectiveness. Our data therefore show a generally high degree of interest in teaching on the part of college faculty members. Indeed, this interest is more than we expected to find, even allowing for the fact that the data were based on self-judgments.

Another common criticism is that teachers have little meaningful interaction with students, especially undergraduates, and especially outside of class. However, we discovered that most faculty establish and maintain a variety of relationships with students outside of class. A large majority of our respondents said that during the two weeks preceding the date of their response, they had met with students to discuss intellectual issues and to give advice about educational and career plans. In addition, during that two-week period a smaller number of teachers, but still a majority, had talked with students about campus issues or personal problems, or had socialized with students on a friendship basis. Thus, our data showed that the majority of faculty have contact with students in prescribed capacities (that is, as teachers and academic advisors) and also as friends and personal counselors).

Faculty members have been accused of maintaining an advancement procedure that rewards research at the expense of teaching. However, about nine out of ten respondents said that teaching effectiveness should be an important criterion in pay and promotion decisions at their schools. At every school we sampled, most of the faculty were critical of the fact that, in actual practice, teaching effectiveness was not given as much weight in advancement decisions as it should be given. To say that faculty want teaching to count for more than it now does in the advancement procedures does not mean that teachers are disinterested in research and scholarly activity. Indeed, the majority of all faculty (except community college faculty) thought that research should be a fairly important criterion for advancement, although not as important as teaching effectiveness. This belief in the importance of research was corroborated by faculty members' responses to other questions. The respondents indicated that involvement in research is likely to help them keep up to date in their fields and be exciting teachers. Indeed, there are now signs of a shift in emphasis as increasing numbers of colleges and universities institute programs of teaching evaluation in an effort to give teaching effectiveness greater weight than is now given in reward systems.

It has been widely asserted that faculty are liberal regarding change in social and political institutions but conservative regarding change in academic institutions. Our data showed, however, that the majority of our respondents actually favored a broad range of educational changes. A substantial majority thought that the proportion of students coming from minority groups should be increased—as should the amount of informal interaction between faculty and students; the number of interdisciplinary courses; the use of independent study; the proportion of courses directed at contemporary social problems; and the granting of academic credit for work in community action projects. The responses indicated that faculty in general are favorably disposed to reforming the conventional structures of college education. Perhaps years of criticism have persuaded most faculty to favor at least certain kinds of academic reform. On the other hand, perhaps the stereotype has been wrong, and faculty have always favored change more than has been recognized. In all of these matters, there is a range of variation among faculty. Some faculty have little interest in teaching; some do have little contact with students; some do think advancement should depend more on research than on teaching; and some do oppose significant change. But these kinds of attitudes, values, and activities simply do not fit the majority of college professors.

We were particularly interested in discovering how faculty members differed from each other on certain issues. For example, we were curious about the different attitudes of those who favored and those who opposed academic change. Not surprisingly, we found that faculty who favored academic reform taught differently and had a different conception of a college education than did those opposed to change. These differences in attitudes may be summarized briefly. Faculty who favor educational change are likely to see development of the student as the purpose of a college education; to emphasize personalization in the educative process; to have permissive views toward the regulation of students' personal lives; to hold a theory of teaching and learning that emphasizes the self-motivating power of students; and to favor giving students significant roles in academic and social policy making. In their classroom teaching, those who favor educational change are likely to be discursive, analytic, and integrative; to encourage student participation; and to employ loosely structured evaluation procedures. Proponents of change also have considerable contact with students outside of class. Such faculty are likely to be in the junior ranks and to come from the humanities and social sciences. Professors who oppose academic change are likely to stress the mastery of vocational and technical competence; to deemphasize the need for close faculty-student relationships; to hold restrictive views of the personal lives of students; to have a theory of teaching and learning that emphasizes external motivations; and to deny students a significant role in academic or social policy making. Opponents of change are likely to emphasize factual understanding; to center classroom work on the instructor; to employ structured evaluation procedures; and to have little contact with students outside of class. Such faculty are disproportionately drawn from the senior ranks and from the natural and applied sciences. However, as we have indicated, these faculty tend to be in the minority. In summary, faculty members are indeed a diverse lot, but most of them are concerned about teaching, students, and academic reform.

In another study, conducted for the Project to Improve College Teaching (a joint project of the Association of American Colleges and the American Association of University Professors), we have analyzed college environments from the teachers' point of view in order to learn what can be done to capitalize on faculty members' positive feelings about teaching, students, and academic change. We had to consider those aspects of the environment that affect the faculty members' motivations to teach. The policies and practices of institutions and the people with whom faculty work closely (both students and teaching colleagues) are environmental factors that have considerable impact on college teachers. The following paragraphs summarize a few of the conclusions that will be presented in detail in a forthcoming monograph. The main conclusion is that few colleges and universities maintain a climate that faculty view as sufficiently supportive of teaching. There is good reason to believe that the quality of college teaching can be improved if some existing policies and practices were changed.

Perhaps the most important institutional policy affecting the motivations of faculty members is the reward structure. In its broadest sense, the reward structure includes both the distribution of extrinsic rewards and the opportunity for faculty to derive intrinsic satisfactions from their work. Frequently, these alternative kinds of incentives are mutually reinforcing. For example, the extrinsic reward of a promotion or a salary increase may increase intrinsic satisfactions; such extrinsic rewards may contribute to the teacher's self-esteem by implying that his colleagues and students believe he is doing a good job. Since national prestige in an academic discipline is usually gained by research and publications, a faculty member (especially one who devotes himself to undergraduates) must look to his own institution for recognition and rewards for his teaching efforts. If faculty are to devote a considerable portion of their time to students and derive personal satisfactions from teaching, there must be a visible structure of rewards for such efforts. This means that, for most institutions, a merit advancement procedure must be employed to allow faculty members to get ahead by developing excellence in teaching.

Another policy related to the issue of an adequate reward structure is the evaluation of teaching. Teaching evaluation serves two general purposes: it provides teachers with feedback that may help them improve their teaching practices; and it may be used to give added weight to teaching in the advancement procedures. In order for these benefits to be realized, the methods for assessing the quality of teaching must be both reliable and systematic. Yet few colleges have a formal procedure that systematically provides reliable evidence of a professor's teaching effectiveness. Feasible procedures that have been used to obtain systematic evidence of effective teaching include classroom visitation by colleagues, self-assessment, and student ratings. By far the most prevalent approach is student ratings, and a considerable body of research indicates that ratings by students are reliable indicators of effective teaching. In a recent study, Milton Hildebrand and Robert C. Wilson suggested that the implementation of evaluative procedures can enhance teaching by helping faculty members improve their own teaching and by allowing decisions about salary, promotion, and tenure to be based in larger measure on evidence of teaching effectiveness.[1]

In addition to the reward structure, the students and colleagues with whom a faculty member works affect the quality of teaching on a campus. The generally held opinion is that faculty-student relationships have value for students alone. The rewards of interaction, however, are not unidirectional; teachers also may benefit from having contact with students. Indeed, our survey indicated that the more contact faculty had with students, the more satisfied teachers were with the stimulation received from students. Faculty who had more contact with students were also more likely to rank themselves among the very best of teachers and to list teaching as one of the major satisfactions in their lives. In short, close contact with students allows faculty members to take pride in their work and to derive intrinsic enjoyment from teaching. Also, interaction with students increases the faculty member's knowledge of the students' academic strengths and weaknesses, interests, problems, and perspectives. Effective curriculum planning and change, sound learning evaluations, and wise academic counseling are some of the faculty activities that require a knowledge of students' abilities and inadequacies. Thus, close relationships with students are important sources of the information faculty members must have to carry out tasks related to effective teaching. Unfortunately, in recent years, many schools have become so large and so fragmented that faculty have not been able to benefit from close relationships with students. Large classes tend to prevent teachers from knowing their students well enough to gain either intellectual stimulation or a sense of having made a contribution to the students' lives. In addition, in large schools—and in many small ones—a faculty member seldom has a student in more than one class; thus, the teacher cannot witness over time the development of any but a handful of students.

In an attempt to encourage close faculty-student relationships many large and growing schools have created cluster colleges, ethnic studies programs, and residential programs. All of these efforts attempt to create more intimate settings within larger institutions where faculty and students can pursue their education with a greater sense of community. Evidence shows that these subcolleges do in fact create closer faculty-student relationships and that faculty and students are more

[1] Milton Hildebrand and Robert C. Wilson, *Effective University Teaching and Its Evaluation*. Berkeley, Calif.: Center for Research and Development in Higher Education, 1970.

satisfied with these new environments than with traditional settings.

In addition, several curricular innovations are designed to reduce the distance between faculty and students. The use of independent study and tutorials has increased as an antidote for the large lecture class. Several schools, such as Johnston College at the University of Redlands and the Experimental College at the University of Alabama, have personalized graduation requirements by means of curricular contracts: each student and a small faculty committee draw up a plan of study (the contract), and the student graduates whenever he completes the contract. Minicourses (short-term courses initiated by either faculty or students to pursue topics that are not otherwise available) have been adopted at Syracuse University and other schools. Freshman seminars on socially relevant topics and taught by senior professors have been introduced at several universities. The creation of subcolleges and curricular innovations are but two of the ways some institutions have tried to take advantage of faculty interest in teaching and to provide settings in which faculty members can enjoy the intrinsic rewards of teaching.

Colleagues are also an important group that significantly influences the environment of teachers; yet few colleges are so organized as to make use of faculty peer groups to improve teaching. Since the increase of specialization has created an array of intellectual subcultures in the faculty, many faculty members have become increasingly oriented toward their national disciplinary associations, which have put little stress on teaching. Moreover, the young Turks in recent years have been pitted against the old guard in issues raised by campus activism.

All of these factors have detracted from a climate in which faculty members reinforce and stimulate one another's interest in teaching. Where such a supportive climate does exist, however, faculty members can help one another become effective teachers. First, fellow faculty members can provide motivation. They can pique the curiosity or stimulate new interests of their colleagues by intellectual discussions. They can generate enthusiasm by creating a sense of working for a common cause, and they can establish priorities by encouraging certain kinds of behavior and discouraging other kinds. Second, colleagues can provide information and criticism. Discussions with colleagues can help a teacher keep up to date by learning about new publications, materials available for classroom use, and developments in professional associations. Colleagues can help a teacher learn more about his students by relating what interests the students, what the students are doing presently, or what they have studied previously. Since most college faculty members have little formal training in teaching, colleagues often serve as informal teacher trainers. Third, colleagues can reinforce a teacher for his efforts and accomplishments. Since faculty members serve on review committees, they can recommend promotions or tenure and thereby affect both the financial status and self-esteem of their colleagues.

The quality of teaching will be improved by any innovation that will bring faculty members closer together and allow them to gain intellectual stimulation, help in their teaching, and a feeling that good teaching is valued. Several efforts to achieve these purposes have been attempted. For example, interdisciplinary courses that cut across the usual academic disciplines to focus on contemporary social problems, intellectual themes, or human experiences are popular with some teachers and students. Such courses have frequently utilized a team of teachers drawn from a variety of disciplines. Also, as we have mentioned, new academic organizations—cluster colleges, ethnic studies programs, residential programs, and noncredit experimental colleges—have been established on many campuses. These new organizational arrangements have attracted much faculty interest and support. And many schools have adopted new governance procedures that involve more people, decentralize decision making, and encourage all participants to support the decisions that are made. In such schools, the power of an oligarchy of old faculty members is being checked, and the chronic tension between the junior and senior ranks may be reduced.

The studies discussed in this essay show that most faculty members are as concerned as their students about effective teaching, faculty-student relationships, and educational change. We have suggested several innovations that could capitalize on the positive attitudes that a majority of faculty members have toward teaching. These innovations could produce more effective teachers by creating an environment that is supportive to good teaching and that will allow faculty members to enjoy the intrinsic rewards of teaching.

❧ 4 ❧

Assessment and Reward Systems

Harold L. Hodgkinson

The literature on student development during the college years reveals one rather interesting finding—if you ask students to name their most important educational experience while in college they seldom list an event that took place in a classroom. My feeling is that if you ask faculty the same question they would probably respond similarly. Sociologist Willard Waller observed over forty years ago that teachers and students come to school at cross purposes and therefore can never be at peace with each other. We all know of cases in which truly inspired teaching and learning take place, but we must ask two questions. First, how often does this occur? And, second, how often can this occur?

Sociology tells us that every organization has two reward systems, one based on competence and one based on service. The reasons for this are clear. As organizational imperatives change, new individuals with new specific techniques must be brought in and allowed to develop new leadership positions. Thus, status must be reserved for the new leadership made necessary by changing conditions. Every organization also needs a large cadre of individuals who will remain and be loyal to the organization. Because of changing organizational needs, one is bound to reach the point where old members are less valuable than they were at first. The gold watch after twenty-five years of service and getting kicked upstairs are only two of a number of industrial reward systems often used to keep people in positions of lesser demand for long periods of time. In most organizations it is vital that a person who is not too competent can be moved out of the mainstream without damaging his ego. Thus, the man who cannot survive in a major organization in New York City may end up as branch manager in Fargo, North Dakota. He has increased his position (title) and the organization goes on relatively unharmed.[1]

While the reward systems in business organizations are firmly established, the field of education has had great difficulty in developing a flexible reward system by which people may be resituated without violating their rights to some kind of personal status and feeling of importance as a human being. From kindergarten to graduate school, teachers are differentially rewarded according to the probable mobility level of their students. Thus, the teacher who works hard with poor students does not receive many rewards, while the teacher who works with bright students is rewarded with greater status and occasionally a high salary. In my own writing, I have referred to this as "the higher education, the higher the better" syndrome.

Most teachers probably agree with this system, but it should not be this way. In fact, teachers who work with students at the remedial level, be it a third grade or college, probably work harder and use their brains more than those who work with the very best students. Still, developing a reward and evaluation system is particularly difficult in education because competence is so hard to define. While in most businesses competence is conceived according to only one or two criteria (the only criterion for an excellent salesman is sales), in education competence becomes a vague concept since the output of the process is so illusive. Thus any system that attempts to assess and reward competence in teaching must be highly flexible and individualistic—at least until teaching and learning outputs can be measured systematically. The reward structure has two general strategies. The first is simply to

---

[1] For a discussion of this tactic, see W. Goode, "The Protection of the Inept." *American Sociological Review,* February 1967.

increase rewards for those jobs that must be performed at the highest level of competence. The second approach is to decrease the level of threat that accompanies these positions so that people will move into new tasks with a greater feeling of security and well-being.

Tenure decisions quite often deny both of these theoretical presuppositions. Individuals are often made to suffer rather cruel punishments: information is deliberately withheld from them; they are seldom given a chance to confront those who make the final decision about their future; and criteria are clothed in educational rhetoric and seldom specified in any detail. It is quite easy to document a large number of cases of promotion and tenure in which the evaluative criteria are whimsical and have little to do with the teacher's performance. In one case, known by this author, the wife of a faculty member had one drink too many at a cocktail party, and thus tenure was denied although no reason was ever given formally. In another, the president's wife made certain, totally unfounded allegations with regard to an individual's moral conduct, and tenure was again denied.

This is not to say that all tenure decisions are irresponsible. Unquestionably, the tenure system does work effectively in a number of cases. However, if teaching is an important professional criterion for promotion within an institution, such decisions are less than professional unless other professionals are in the room watching the teacher teach. Any legitimate system of faculty assessment must not only measure the faculty member in terms of where he is but also in terms of what his growth patterns are. We somehow have the feeling that development takes place only in students—that faculty and administrators do not continue to grow and change. Clearly, some changes do occur. The young faculty member, for example, characteristically has to deal with many new problems. He must learn how to distribute his time between his family and his teaching commitments. He will find that the demands placed upon him are often contradictory; for instance, he learns that he must devote himself to teaching, while he notices that those who get promoted are those who publish and do research. This means again that stresses are placed upon him: he can never fulfill all of the demands that are made.[2]

Our uniform approach to defining teaching competence is per-

[2] For an account of how the young faculty member can "psych out" the reward and distribution systems, see my "Finding the Levers." In W. Morris (Ed.), *Effective College Teaching*. Washington, D.C.: American Council on Education, 1970.

haps at the heart of the issue. A standardized teaching load is one indicator that is used to measure a teacher's effectiveness. It is the equivalent of using a single IQ or SAT score to measure a student's abilities. The standardized load implies that everybody should do the same thing, give the same number of lectures, advise the same number of students, and give the same number of seminars; yet some people may be very good lecturers and very poor advisors, while others are excellent advisors and poor at lecturing. Despite this fact, few institutions have dared tackle the thought of a flexible teaching load in which evaluation would be based on those things the teacher does and likes to do best.

The area of assessment is fraught with difficulties. Consider, for example, the problem of evaluating the dynamic lecturer who gets very good evaluations from his students but is perhaps a trifle superficial. Then compare this type of teacher to a person who may have a significant impact on only 10 per cent of his students, while 80 per cent think he is nothing. In such a situation, one can easily overlook the fact that 10 per cent of the students in a class may have had their lives changed considerably. Which of the two should get tenure?

We might resolve the problem of assessing teacher competence by using pupil achievement scores. The many pitfalls here include establishing the identity of score potentials before students encounter the instructor. How can the influence of other teachers and the effects of nonclassroom experiences be parcelled out? Learning curves are not the end of the argument. Several recent studies projected learning curves over the period of time a student takes a course and then matched these curves with forgetting curves for a similar duration of time after the course is over. Some very interesting things occur in required courses. For example, the learning curve shows a sharp increase near the end of the course when students are cramming to get through the final. Six months to a year after the course is over, the curve shows a decline that is just as steep as the learning curve was. Other courses may indicate a slow learning curve while the student is taking the course and then a continual increase for a year after the course is over. Clearly two different things are going on in the two cases, but the problem of when to measure learning is clear.

A few comments about reward systems seem relevant. Evaluation should exist for the central purpose of helping a person—whether student or teacher—improve his performance. Most evaluation systems, however, work primarily to reject people rather than to help them attain improved performance. Concise criteria would be helpful, but the criteria used for students and for faculty promotion are usually ambiguous and do not allow much individuality, which is important in both teaching and learning. The assessment must continuously be available for the teacher or student, so he may benefit from it whenever he thinks he needs it. Assessments at the end of the year or term will not be terribly useful for the teacher or student who has been told he has failed. The system must make maximum feedback on performance available constantly. In order that the feedback does not have to be labeled in an evaluative way except on a person's past performance, any reward system should be based on intrinsic motivations rather than extrinsic ones. The individual who is being assessed should try to develop his own criteria for increasing competency and should be helped to understand the feedback in terms of his own goals.

The reward and assessment system might encourage the person to improve on his weaknesses as well as his strengths. Compare student grading systems that drive the student away from unfamiliar areas, in which he might not do well and toward those in which he has already succeeded. Developing in new areas or working on weaknesses will be impossible if the system is designed to punish faculty and/or students rather than encourage the individual as he develops clear-cut assessments of his own strengths and weaknesses. At the faculty level any such system must encourage collaboration between colleagues rather than set colleagues against each other. Such artificial status producing devices as teacher of the year awards do not accomplish this sort of collaboration. Assessment and reward systems must directly reflect the educational objectives of both the individual teacher and the college or university. Certain departmental differences in this regard will occur, since departments vary according to the nature of the material and the students. Nevertheless the essential relationship between the objectives of the institution and the methods of assessing performance is a functional one. One last thing that all assessment and reward systems need is a person skilled in a wide variety of assessment procedures (clinical as well as statistical), who would interpret the various evaluation results for both teachers and students. (In an essay where I describe an educational utopia, this person goes under the title of psycho-social registrar.[3] I am now more firmly convinced than ever that every college needs such a person as much as it needs an ombudsman.

In my opinion, it would be desirable to work for something like

[3] H. L. Hodgkinson, "Walden U—A Working Paper." *Soundings,* Summer 1969. Also in H. L. Hodgkinson and M. B. Bloy, Jr. (Eds.), *Identity Crisis in Higher Education.* San Francisco: Jossey-Bass, 1970.

a contract system of evaluation for both faculty and students. The incoming person is asked to state as clearly as possible the goals he would like to attain during his period of residence. The institutional representative than states the ways in which the institution is prepared to commit itself to helping this individual attain these objectives. This then becomes a contract between the institution and the individual. No two contracts would necessarily be alike, as no two individual patterns of development would be alike. But the contract model assumes a longitudinal dimension to life and makes clear that individuals, both teachers and learners, are expected to grow as they stay with the institution. Such contracts can be changed at any time as long as both parties agree to any alteration in the structure. The important characteristic of the contract model is that the assessment procedures to be used will inevitably be based on the structure of the contract itself.

In addition to a contract system, universities should allow for the direct observation of classroom teaching by one's colleagues. During my six years at Bard College in New York State, we improved upon this system of observation to the point where decisions to promote a person were made on a fair, flexible, and objective basis. In this plan every junior faculty member who is eligible for tenure or promotion is visited in class over a period of time by several senior members of his department or division. (The system is now being reconsidered to find a way for students to participate in the classroom observations.) The senior member must consult the junior member before the class to find out what is to be done and what has already been covered. The senior member must then stay for the full length of the period, have a conference with the instructor after the class, and write a fairly extensive comment on what was seen. A copy of this comment goes to the instructor, and a copy goes to the department or divisional chairman. The reason for this is simply to make sure that everyone understands the reasons for the senior member's judgment. Also, the senior member feels committed to say the same thing to his senior colleagues as to the junior member. These evaluations are often longitudinal and cumulative in nature: they outline the instructor's previous performance, his present situation, and his future plans; and usually the evaluations suggest specific ways in which the instructor can be helped. Thus, evaluations can be used as a decision-making device and can also provide a teacher with some specific ways in which he may improve throughout the year. Junior members may also visit the classes of senior members to witness the skills that senior faculty mention in their evaluations of junior members. Visitations by junior faculty members have a salutary effect on the senior members' evaluations.

Although this approach is subject to human frailty, it provides for a richness of clinical and statistical interpretation that other methods of faculty evaluation do not. A strong and diverse tapping of student views is essential, although no one advocates that students be the sole judge of faculty competence. Because student evaluations of faculty are usually in the form of heavily codified questionnaire returns, we may attribute too much weight to them, just as the ease of counting faculty publications leads us to think that we have a qualitative as well as quantitative measure. An integration of clinical and statistical information is needed for a fair, flexible evaluation system. Assessment systems must use many sources of information to get the attitudes of different groups and must find a way to put these data together. Certainly students and administrators have the right to be included in the faculty assessment.

Video tape, shown to be extremely useful in teacher training programs, is seldom used by college or university faculties. Here is a device that can publicize good teaching; yet it often gathers dust in the audio-visual room. A faculty member could use it, not only for instant replay discussions with colleagues throughout the year, but also could present some selected sections of classroom tapes as evidence for faculty evaluation. Such tapes could be useful to faculty groups as a source for developing the criteria to be used in classroom observations.

In some institutions, administrators hold undue power in the assessment of faculty largely because faculty members do not have the courage to open the door and go into their colleagues' classrooms. In fact, the college teacher is perhaps the only professional who performs in the total absence of other professionals. Surgeons are usually assisted by other surgeons; lawyers operate in the relatively open arena of the courtroom. The privilege of locking the door of the college classroom while the instructor is lecturing is a tradition that interferes with proper assessment.

I feel strongly that if college and university teaching is to be professionalized, we must rely in large part on the professionals to develop better criteria for the assessment of this act. As far as I can tell, the only conceivable way that college professors can do this is to get into the classroom, watch, and describe what goes on. The major virtues of this approach are that it encourages improved teaching and provides a means to establish criteria for assessment. Classroom observation by professional colleagues has its pitfalls, as does any other system, but I believe it must be used, in conjunction with student and administrator assessment procedures, if a legitimate assessment is to be made of a teacher's performance.

PART TWO:

New Settings for Learning

Almost everyone now realizes that, whatever the pressures on the college or the university, learning must be at the very center of its activity. This new attitude is significant; it enables us, finally, to go about creating the contexts that will put the learning process at the hub of these complex educational structures. The authors of the essays of Part Two envision an enormous potential for American higher education; but they point up the depressing side as well: a frightening chasm lies between our present settings for learning at the postsecondary level and the nation's needs during the crucial decades ahead.

5

The Other End of Sesame Street

Lawrence E. Dennis

I should like to begin this essay with the prediction that the President of the United States will proclaim the establishment of the University of North America, a confederation of several radically different regional higher education institutions and agencies that will have come into being during the 1970s in the United States, Canada, and Mexico. These new regional institutions will shape the course of events in higher education on this continent during the last quarter of the twentieth century. They will have originated in the late 1960s and early 1970s from the concept of the open university, a multimedia approach to continuing higher education. Pioneered in Great Britain and Japan, the open university will be brought into being in the United States in the next half decade through the combined efforts of national educational organizations (such as the American Association for Higher Education and the National Commission on Accrediting), national examining agencies (such as the College Entrance Examination Board and the American College Testing Program), national public broadcasting organizations (such as the Corporation for Public Broadcasting and the National Association of Educational Broadcasters), and regional consortia of junior colleges, colleges, universities, and public broadcasting stations.

In announcing the birth of the University of North America, the President will acknowledge a debt of thanks to the leaders of the Corporation for Public Broadcasting, who in 1970 began to ask these questions: What is at the other end of Sesame Street? Why can't broadcasting make learning just as exciting and meaningful for adults as that magnificent television program does for children? What should the Corporation for Public Broadcasting and other national educational agencies be doing to help colleges and universities transform continuing education into something truly excellent and worthwhile? The answers to these questions were there all the while. We in higher education had only to part the underbrush to put the answers together: at the other end of Sesame Street stood the open university, another idea whose time had come.

So much for prophecy. My purpose here is not to speculate about whether the open university will come into being over the next five years but, rather, to suggest how it can be brought about through the development of a series of regional models. In the 1970s, critics of our entire system of education tell us that society must produce new kinds of institutions of higher learning, relevant and responsive to the needs of the times. Students themselves are in the vanguard of critics; they see our educational institutions as outdated (from preschool through graduate school), our values false, our teaching dull, our priorities wrong. They perceive educators as being preoccupied with promotion and status, research grants, tests, rules, credits, admission requirements, academic jargon, footnotes, and government contracts. Students see barriers to college entrance, roadblocks to educational innovation, and a reward system based on the curiously inverted principle that the higher your rank and the more you are paid, the fewer students you are expected to teach!

The educational establishment, as the students and other critics quite rightly view it, has become a prisoner of its own rhetoric. In the name of excellence, we have sanctified trivia. In the name of democracy, we have stifled individuality. In the name of pluralism, we have exacted conformity. We pay lip service to diversity; yet our schools and colleges are dishearteningly imitative, one of another. High schools shape their demands to fit the specifications of the colleges; junior colleges imitate four-year institutions; colleges try to be universities; and all universities want to be like Harvard. The system makes poor black youth feel locked out, and middle class whites feel locked in. In short, the system is not working, and something has to be done about it. Specifically, we must back off and start over—or, at the very least, regroup and rearrange our forces. And while we seek to change the institutions we already have, we must turn our attention to creating new ones.

The open university and its regional models will be new kinds of institutions for the continuing education of adults. Let us consider the possibility of establishing the University of New England—an open university for the northeastern United States. The University of New England will not exist in one place or on one campus; it will be neither inner city nor suburban. It will not even be a single institution in the conventional sense. Instead, the University of New England will be a confederation of a selected group of junior colleges, colleges, universities (both public and private), and educational agencies and associations working cooperatively to add a new dimension to higher education through the medium of public broadcasting. The University of New England will use television as its principal teaching medium, supplemented by radio, correspondence study, films, tapes, programmed instruction, libraries, theaters, museums, tutorials, counseling centers, conferences, and short-term seminars at regional learning institutes. The faculty of the University of New England will include broadcasters, educators, laymen, professionals, students, and teachers. In the University of New England, the young will have a chance to teach the old; the blacks will be able to instruct the whites.

The University of New England will have a curriculum that will encompass courses on the environment, the arts, mass media, the cities, law, education, religion, human relations, international affairs, science, technology, public policy, the history of great ideas, and the lives of great men. The university will offer credits, administer tests, grant degrees, and charge a modest tuition. It will develop and distribute instructional materials. Anyone over fifteen may enroll, and there will be no other entrance requirements. For those who need it, the University of New England will offer remedial work in communications skills, mathematics, and other preparatory subjects. The University of New England will be a public interest institution: open to all who wish to learn.

Thus, as with England's Open University which is now underway, the University of New England would represent an integrated, multimedia approach to continuing education. Instructional television and radio, correspondence study, programmed learning, various audiovisual devices, libraries, counseling services, tutorials, and summer session seminars would be combined to make available to New Englanders a series of college level courses, planned and taught by faculty members from the colleges and universities in the region, with the cooperation of public television stations. Students desiring to enroll for credit would apply for admission; course materials would be provided; and examinations monitored. Special equipment (for example, language laboratories) would be accessible for independent study at the local learning centers where advisors and tutors would be available.

The responsibility for developing the University of New England would rest with a confederation including state commissions or boards of higher education, the New England Board of Higher Education, the New England Regional Commission, the New England Governors' Conference, the New England Center for Continuing Education, interested junior colleges, colleges, and universities in the region, and the public and instructional broadcasting stations in the Northeast. The consortium (or confederation) thus formed would provide various services, training programs, resources for course planning, and testing and evaluation materials. Similar models of the Open University could be developed in New Jersey, upstate New York, the Midwest, and so on. Finally, these experimental models would be linked together in a nationwide open university—the University of North America, which would include participating sister institutions in Canada and Mexico.

Given the importance of higher education, continuing adult education, and public broadcasting to the American society, the interlocking relationship that ought to exist among these three areas seems obvious: in the context of the present-day campus, continuing education should enjoy a status at least coequal with that of resident instruction, and broadcasting as a medium of teaching should be integral to both. Yet continuing education has always been more or less a stepchild in academic circles, and instructional broadcasting is still treated as an "add-on" on most campuses where it has been tried. In the scheme of things today, continuing education and instructional broadcasting are simply not in the main tent with the regular programs. Faculty members from the disciplines and the professions tend to regard these two areas as sideshows—something to do in one's spare time. The blue chips are still on research and on the teaching of graduates and undergraduates—on campus, in classrooms, in laboratories, and lecture halls. Innovation is not the name of the game, at least not yet.

Nowhere has the lack of concern for adult education and instructional broadcasting been more evident than in the priorities of national organizations and conferences concerned with higher education. How long has it been since the Association of American Universities, the Association of American Colleges, the American Council on Education, the American Council of Learned Societies, the American Association of University Professors, or the American Association for Higher Education has had anything to say about broadcasting as an educational medium? How much attention is paid to the field of adult education at meetings of the American Psychological Association or the American Association for the Advancement of Science? How many college presidents or deans highlight instructional broadcasting or continuing education as themes in their annual reports or convocation talks?

Institutional values reflect professional values. Administrators of extension programs and educational broadcasters are more often than not, treated as second-class citizens in the academic community. A large segment of the professoriate continues to view credits earned off-campus—whether by correspondence, television, radio, or at extension centers—as something less than the genuine article. But there are no objective data whatsoever to support this bias. With all the talk about new curricula, new teaching methods, and new institutional forms; with all the investment that has been made in experimentation, and with all the pressure for change and reform in higher education; the old myth endures: on-campus teaching is thought to be somehow superior to other brands of instruction. This entrenched methology, both institutional and professional, has made for slow going in the development of continuing education and instructional broadcasting in the past decade. This same mythology must be faced and dealt with squarely by the higher education community if the continuing education of adults through the broadcasting media is to achieve status in the academic enterprise.

Nationally, continuing education and instructional broadcasting need a new broker or a fresh advocate in the councils of higher learning. That role can and should be assumed, in my judgment, by the Corporation for Public Broadcasting. The Corporation could bring with it the determination to create a new dimension for higher education. If broadcasting could become a full partner in the educational establishment, the education of adults would be revolutionized. As the champion of the open university and as the cosponsor of the University of North America, the Corporation would be carrying out its mandate to serve the public interest and further the general welfare. The Corporation for Public Broadcasting could be the necessary catalyst for bringing together regionally and nationally those active in the academic community, in adult education, and in public broadcasting for the purpose of creating the first open university.

In order to build the new regional confederations essential for the establishment of open universities, we will need leaders, financial resources, credibility, research, and planning. The first problem is leadership. A cadre of leaders from the fields of higher education, continuing education, and public and instructional broadcasting should be convened as a national steering agency, with regular meetings to review plans, cut red tape, effect contacts, prepare proposals, and so forth. I believe the American Association for Higher Education and the Corporation for Public Broadcasting should bring such a steering committee together.

Financial resources is the second problem facing the open university. If the open university is to become a reality, whether regionally or nationally, the major educational foundations and federal agencies, the commercial networks, and private industry all must participate with financial support for regional pilot projects. The initial involvement of institutions and agencies in an open university confederation will be a new commitment for most participants; thus, outside funding will be basic to getting the projects planned and launched.

Credibility is the third problem of the open university. Whatever is done to bring about the development of the University of North America will need to be accepted both by the general public and by the academic and broadcasting communities. Obtaining this acceptance means securing a wide base of professional support from assorted agencies, such as the College Entrance Examination Board, the American College Testing Program, the Educational Testing Service, the National Commission on Accrediting, the Adult Education Association, the National University Extension Association, and others. Similarly, to involve the public in developing new regional universities without walls, advantage should be taken of the existence in almost every state of statewide councils on educational broadcasting, which include a broad representation of laymen.

The fourth problem facing the open university is research. Already some evidence has accumulated on visual literacy, which indicates that young people today are used to the new media and are unwilling to go without visual stimulation in their educational experiences. Young men and women who have grown up with the stimulation of movies and television will begin demanding curricula that include more visual stimulation. A person who is forced to learn only in a verbal environment is unable to learn as much as he could, if verbal learning were accompanied with tactile and visual experiences. Television demands the complete participation of the individual and involves visual as well as verbal stimulation. It has been said that education consists of exchanging time for experience. Television can change reality into images at the speed of light, which means, if it is properly used, that students can gain an enormous amount of experience in the same amounts of time without the need to decode. The establishment of regional open university models, such as the University of New England and others being proposed here, should be buttressed by the best possible educational research—something, alas, we have all too often neglected when initiating new projects within or among institutions of higher learning.

In addition to broadcasting, the field of adult education itself offers a goldmine for research. Mature and middle-aged students are venturing again into the world of schools and colleges. In order to prepare for them, either on campus or as enrollees in open universities, we must make concentrated research efforts in two areas: first, the nature of the learner; and, second, the content and methods of presentation of subject matter to the old learner. On the basis of existing studies, there is every reason to believe that old learners will successfully continue to expand their knowledge, whether it be through formal institutions, television courses offered by open universities, or some combination of both. It will be necessary, however, to structure the courses and curricula to take advantage of the proficiencies of the old learner as well as to compensate for his deficiencies.

Planning is the final problem that must be handled. Establishing the new kinds of institutions envisioned in this report will take time—time to develop a prospectus, time to build budgets, time to recruit staff, time to solicit support, time to create regional prototypes (such as the proposed University of New England), time to hold conferences, time to develop materials, and time to meld institutions and agencies within those regions where there is something like a critical mass in academic and broadcasting leadership.

Can the open university really come into being in the United States? Can an integrated, multimedia adult learning system be established in this country through a series of regional confederations? Can a new effective, on-going workable relationship be constructed, which involves the best talent there is from the fields of higher education, continuing education, and instructional broadcasting? Can the rigidities and obstacles present in academic institutions and organizations be overcome to make possible the development of regional models that will lead to the establishment of the University of North America? Can the external degree evolve rapidly to become the alternate degree (a term suggested by Jana Matthews of the Massachusetts State College System), indicating its integral relationship to the academic enterprise? Do we in higher education truly have the courage, the will, the daring, and the imagination to turn the system around in the next half decade —as we know we must? I think we will be able to give a positive answer to all of these questions. If we do not build the University of North America along the lines proposed here, then someone from outside the profession will do it for us. One way or another, the open university is going to be a fact of life in this country in the last years of the present decade.

6

A Plan for External Degrees

Jack N. Arbolino

If we really want to close the gap that now exists on the vast majority of our campuses betwen individual needs of students and degree requirements, we must first of all make some conceptual changes regarding time and money as they relate to the degree. We must also substantially increase the granting of credit by examination in our regular degree programs. If we do these things, we do a great deal; but something more remains. We must, in addition, establish a federally chartered national university, which will award external degrees and which will also grant joint external degrees with those colleges wishing to participate.[1] If this recommendation seems excessive, I can only assert my belief that we should reach for a major institutional reform—one that will enable us to generate humanistic and social incentive to

---

[1] J. N. Arbolino and J. R. Valley, "Education: The Institution or the Individual?" *Continuing Education*, 1970, 3(4), 6.

match our technological advances. If our reach does not exceed our grasp, we will close some gaps in the present system, and we will open a new way to the development of individual potential; we will deliver at last the equality of opportunity we have always promised.

In an address to the 1970 Columbia University charter day dinner, President William J. McGill said, "Reform in large institutions is possible only when people are running scared. Believe me, we in higher education are very nervous, and thus the next decade is likely to produce reorganization, curriculum reform, redefinition of professional life, and a variety of other innovations unlike anything seen in the last fifty years. Our survival depends upon it." McGill is right. There was never a more propitious time than the present for reform and renewal in higher education.

I will admit that I do not understand degree requirements. The liberal arts are hard enough to describe. For one, liberal arts meet inner needs, so that when you call on yourself somebody is home. For another, liberal arts are what do not enable you to make money. Or, as circumscribed by Jacques Barzun's aphoristic wisdom, the liberal arts can be taught mechanically and mechanics can be taught liberally. These thoughts, it is true, do not lead to a clear and easy definition of the liberal arts, but they do make sense. Our degree requirements, however, very often do not seem to make sense at all; they are like arbitrary curatives. Degree requirements seem to say to students, "I may appear strange to you; but that is because you have defects you do not recognize, and I will erase them." Within the profession degree requirements elicit a tacit exchange of tolerance: "We have a few quaint ones, and so do you; but, after all, we are all in this thing together." Only a few things about them are certain; they cannot be ignored, and they are usually presented with pride. The listing of requirements may state, "The founders of Halcyon College, valuing clear speech and serenity . . . ," and we read on to see that Calm Composition is required of all freshmen.

What does a degree mean—both by itself and when it is compared with other degrees? The holder has racked up 120 or more points. But do these points represent acquaintance with the major branches of knowledge or the ability to move with understanding within only one field of learning? Does a degree indicate a state of being that will be forever lighted by the glow of learning, or does it represent the ability to swim one hundred yards? Does a degree indicate all or any of these things? What about the qualities a student must have in order to see himself through? This does not mean the courses he must pass but the character traits he must display—patience and stamina. What about time and money as well? These are degree requirements too; but concessions to these requirements are rare, and the admonitions are clear. Stay the course; serve your time; pay your fees; stay in line. To these requirements our colleges and universities seldom yield. Ironically, this is the area in which we should yield the most.

We must, without fear or favor, examine our higher educational system and ask Harold Howe's question, "Do our institutions meet the needs of individuals, or is it the reverse?" We might be forced to admit that although we do bend a good deal in the matter of course requirements, when it comes to the other kinds of requirements, we are extremely rigid. A fourth semester of French can be cleared, but time and money are waived for no man.

If we really want to close the gap between individual needs and degree requirements, we should recognize that degree requirements consist of more than courses and subjects. We should also recognize that the term degree requirements is often a euphemism for institutional needs: the residence requirement, for instance, is of far more interest to the bursar than the director of residence. Moreover, we create a false antithesis when we put the needs of the individual in opposition to the needs of the institution, but we have often made that dangerous antithesis. We assume that if one is helped, the other is hurt.

If we really want to close the gap between individual needs and degree requirements, we would have to make conceptual changes regarding time and money as they relate to the degree; substantially increase the granting of credit by examination; and establish a federally chartered national university that will award external degrees. We already possess the key to these changes. It is the College Level Examination Program (CLEP)—a young College Board program which, with the generous support of the Carnegie Corporation of New York, is starting to make an impact on higher education. Three institutional uses of the program may be cited as examples.

The University of Iowa authorizes CLEP general examinations as an alternate way to meet degree requirements. Between the fall of 1966 and December, 1969, 1,235 out of 1,531 matriculated students who took the tests did well enough to receive a total of 5,124 hours of credit. The University of Nebraska at Omaha last year graduated 800 students who averaged 20 semester hours of credit by examination on the basis of CLEP tests. The University of Texas announced that the

CLEP American government subject examination would be accepted in lieu of required courses and had to quell a small riot when test tickets ran out one day last November. More than 5,000 students took the test last fall, and now the University of Texas is contemplating the use of the American history test. The saving in instructional costs alone should be significant. Through the national program that serves the public, examinations are available to unaffiliated students once a month at sixty centers located in large cities throughout the country. At the moment more than six hundred colleges will give credit on the basis of CLEP tests; and, although the program is not yet a pervasive force in higher education, it is growing steadily as its uses are understood.

CLEP is the College Board's newest, most exciting way to help colleges grant placement and credit by examination. It is also the key to the flexibility we must have. We can help students and help ourselves too; but to do both, we must make concessions. We must recognize that there are other ways to learn, other ways to measure, other ways to keep time. We must ask ourselves how much longer a faltering system sanctified by outworn custom, besieged by shock, and led by less than superhuman men can continue. Maybe forever, but I do not think so. We should start asking how to close the gap. How do we move better to serve students and institutions? How do we preserve our profession and ourselves? We can begin by acknowledging that there are several kinds of degree requirements and by recognizing that credit by examination is the key to flexibility for individuals and institutions.

A working system of credit by examination within a college can open the door to functional programs of independent study and to the conservation of the time and resources of both students and colleges. Credit by examination can lay the groundwork for a movement that will truly open education to all our citizens. There is only a small step from the development of a substantial number of institutional external degree programs to an operating national university that will award external degrees. A national university would be a sound supplement to our present system of higher education by alleviating some of the pressures on our established institutions. Such a university, even if it did not engage in instruction (and, incidentally, I do not think it should), might seem to threaten our established institutions. Perhaps the answer to that threat, if it is real, lies in the establishment of joint external degrees, where some of the requirements are met through the national university and some at those colleges choosing to participate in a joint program.

Of the three kinds of external degrees mentioned—the institutional external degree, the national external degree, and the joint external degree—the first two have obvious weaknesses. If we had only institutional external degrees offered by two or three hundred colleges, we would risk proliferation, confusion, fragmented effort, and duplication of validating instruments. If we had only national external degrees awarded by a chartered national university, we would risk the strictures of the monolith. The best plan might be a combination of the last two approaches—national external degrees and joint external degrees. This plan would give us a new institution, a national university that would award degrees by examination, and a joint program in which colleges wishing to participate would award degrees completed in part by examination. (The participating colleges would, of course, continue to award regular degrees as well.)

I began this discussion by saying that credit by examination is the key to flexibility for individuals as well as institutions. This flexibility is essential if we are to reconcile individual and institutional needs. We cannot and should not avoid recognizing some form of the external degree. A national university with the power to grant joint awards with participating colleges seems to be the best plan. If we shape this part of our future and do not let it shape us, we may one day see as providential the problems that now afflict us.

7

A New Interdisciplinary Curriculum

George A. Morgan

In the fall of 1969, after two years of intensive discussion and planning, Hiram College launched a new integrated curriculum that emphasizes interdisciplinary studies and increased student freedom and responsibility.[1] All the traditional discipline-oriented graduation requirements were eliminated in favor of several types of new interdisciplinary programs and student electives. In this paper, I will review the first year and a half of this innovation and attempt to draw some conclusions, which I hope will be helpful to other educators.

Our experience at Hiram is valuable in two ways. First, I believe that the Hiram curriculum provides a specific example of a successful implementation of several goals that are now coming into

[1] The curriculum has been supported in part by planning and development grants from the National Endowment for the Humanities and the George Gund Foundation and by an evaluation grant from the Office of Education.

acceptance in higher education. Therefore, a description and critical evaluation of the curriculum should be of interest. Second, our experience should provide encouragement to educators who hope to make significant academic changes at their colleges. The Hiram program provides evidence that substantial innovations, more than just tinkering or gimmicks, can take place at typical (that is, moderately selective, nonexperimental) colleges that have fairly traditional faculties and student bodies. Furthermore, our experience indicates that such changes can win widespread student and faculty support. Curricular changes can have a generally positive impact on student achievement, attitudes, and satisfaction, and can be operated with little additional staff or cost. Despite the fact that we face the enrollment and financial problems of most small private colleges, we have this year a balanced budget and the largest freshman class in our history.

The Hiram program has several major objectives. First, we encourage students, starting in the freshman year, to take on more responsibility for planning and conducting their own education. To implement this goal, we have greatly reduced the number of graduation requirements and provided the opportunity for individualized major areas of concentration. Although students have more freedom of choice than is typical at most colleges, freshmen are supported by close relationships with the faculty and a strong advisory system that is built into the course structure. Second, we try to make education integrated and holistic by developing many topical and interdisciplinary courses and by encouraging cross-disciplinary majors. The college graduation requirements are all interdisciplinary in nature. Third, the entire college emphasizes effective written communication and open, articulate discussion. Fourth, we place the rational discussion of contemporary society (its heritage, problems, and future) at the thematic center of the curriculum. Fifth, the curriculum encourages faculty to use new content and new approaches to teaching, to respond to students more individually, and to try cooperative teaching efforts. Finally, the focus of the Hiram curriculum is on the freshman year because of its importance in the development of student attitudes toward education and because it was previously the weakest part of our (and most) college programs.

Students of Hiram usually take three concentrated courses each quarter. A typical freshman program would be arranged as follows: mid-September—institute; fall quarter—colloquium I, twentieth century, an elective; winter quarter—colloquium II, twentieth century, an elective; spring quarter—an elective, twentieth century, an elective. You can see that the freshman year is composed of four electives and six new curriculum courses. The institute and colloquia courses are small in size, while the Twentieth Century course is common to the whole freshman class of four hundred. During the ten days before the opening of the regular school year, the freshman institute provides all freshmen an extended academic orientation to college and an intensive program of study and practice in written and oral communication skills. About one-third of the Hiram faculty members, representing most academic departments, take part, each working with a group of about thirteen students. One unusual feature of the institute is the use of film as a means of expression. Besides viewing and discussing several carefully chosen commercial films, each group of thirteen students plans and produces its own 8 millimeter movie. Both students and faculty agree that the institute has been very successful in meeting its goals.

When regular classes begin in the fall, each freshman continues his small group learning experience by meeting in a freshman colloquium with eleven other freshmen and a professor-adviser. Student preference determines membership in the colloquium groups. Among the sixty-eight colloquium topics offered this year are evolution and modern man; history and fiction; science and human involvement; modern music; noise, pollution, or art; and self and society. Students select two such colloquia, one in the first quarter and another with a different professor and group in the second or third quarter. There is general agreement among students and faculty that colloquia are interesting, valuable, and effective in meeting the four common goals of improving communication skills, improving advising, dealing seriously with substantial academic topics, and exposing students to humane, moral, and aesthetic concerns. Freshmen praise the informality of the colloquia and suggest that there is better student participation than in most courses.

The Twentieth Century and Its Roots is a fifteen credit-hour course for all freshmen and lasts all year. It is designed to help students critically examine, from many perspectives, the major issues of our society (the search for meaning, the uses of technology, the individual and the state, planet survival). Three or four times a week the freshman class meets as a whole for lectures (often by outstanding visiting speakers), films, plays, debates, concerts, and so forth. Once or twice a week, freshmen meet for discussion in small groups, led by upperclassmen or faculty. Students are encouraged to attend the sessions and read widely, but, with the exception of required position papers, they are free to get what they want out of the course since there are no exams and no penalties for lack of attendance. Student evaluations of the Twentieth Century course indicate that it has been moderately well received, being rated about the same as the average freshman course had been under the old curriculum. As such, it was apparently the least successful and most problematic of the new freshman programs. The freshmen themselves agree that they do not respond as well to the freedom and demands of personal responsibility as had been hoped.

Our emphasis on the holistic, interdisciplinary approach to education is not limited to the freshman programs. We further implement this philosophy by offering a variety of upperclass interdisciplinary courses. Some credit is given for active participation in a wide range of activities outside the usual course structure, and students are encouraged to develop individualized topical or multidisciplinary major areas of concentration.

We are thoroughly evaluating the curriculum and its effectiveness. As part of this evaluation, we have studied the impact of the new curriculum on the general satisfaction, achievement, and attitudes of students. We are still collecting data, but the preliminary results are encouraging. Freshman satisfaction with various aspects of the college is sampled in September and again in May. We have completed results for the last freshman class to enter under the old curriculum (1968–1969) and the first class to enter under the new curriculum (1969–1970). In September, both groups of freshmen gave high and very similar satisfaction ratings. During the 1968–1969 school year, there was a large drop from the expected satisfaction indicated in September to actual satisfaction recorded in May on almost all the rated aspects of the college. Comparisons with satisfaction at other colleges indicate that this drop was probably no greater than the common failure of most colleges to live up to freshman expectations. However, last year, with the new curriculum, there was significantly less disillusionment and more satisfaction with almost all aspects of the college than in the previous year.

This finding was supported by results from the second part of the ETS College Student Questionnaire. In May, 1970, freshman satisfaction with the Hiram faculty, administration, and other students, was significantly higher than in May, 1969. Whereas the year before Hiram freshmen had rated the faculty and administration only about average, last year freshmen rated their satisfaction with both these groups higher than did students at more than 90 per cent of the colleges in the national norm group. Since students in the new Hiram curriculum do not take the traditional freshman English courses, it seemed important to measure their ability to write clear effective English at the end of the freshman year. The freshmen under the new curriculum scored significantly higher on the College Board English Achievement Test (relative to their high school scores) than did the 1968–1969 group, which had had the presumed advantage of two terms of freshman English under the previous curriculum. Finally, scores on the attitude scales of the College Student Questionnaire indicate that students under last year's new curriculum changed significantly more during their freshman year than did students under the old curriculum. These changes were toward becoming liberal, socially concerned, and culturally sophisticated.

Although I personally feel that the positive findings were largely due to the new curriculum, other factors may have influenced the results. For example, it is well established that most innovations work at first. Also campus turmoil and the rapidly changing world probably had some effect on student ratings. However, the contention that the high satisfaction scores resulted from the curriculum change is supported by the fact that satisfactions were concentrated in areas that should have been affected by the new curriculum; in other words, there were large increases in satisfaction with the faculty, freshmen courses, graduation requirements, and the adviser, and only small increases in satisfaction with the town, social life, and college facilities. We are now repeating the above evaluation with 1970–1971 freshmen. In addition, we are measuring achievement and attitude changes more broadly than we were before. But even though some aspects of the curriculum have been highly successful, others have been less so.

It is perhaps somewhat surprising that the Hiram freshman institute has been such a successful part of the program, given the general difficulty colleges have with orientation programs. The institute is a good orientation in large part because it is only indirectly an orientation; that is, the institute is really a course to which both faculty and students come with expectations for hard and meaningful work. The fact that the goals of the institute are clear, attainable, and short range helps make the program rewarding. The success is probably due, not so much to the specific planned lectures, films, and discussions (these were rated rather ambivalently), but to the general feeling that the whole life of the college is focused for these ten days on the freshmen, attempting to get them ready for college—academically, socially, and personally. The usual orientation lectures and social events seldom seem to provide this feeling. No doubt, freshmen are also motivated by the prospect of not having to take English composition, if they are successful in the institute.

In both the colloquia and the Twentieth Century course, freshmen have been given extensive freedom and responsibility for their own learning. Although there has been some faculty concern about academic rigor in the colloquia, most students and faculty have adjusted well to the informality and the grading system (pass or no credit). This adjustment has been facilitated by the close contact and support of the professor-adviser. However, in the Twentieth Century course, many freshmen have found themselves unable to cope with the responsibility of working without the threat of exams, required attendance and so on.

We hoped that the relevance of the topics and the rich mixture of visiting speakers, films, and the like would make up for the large size and relative passivity inherent in the Twentieth Century course. As stated, however, there has been only moderate satisfaction with it. In retrospect, placing freshmen so much on their own in a large Twentieth Century course was probably a mistake, but perhaps the struggle and partial failure to seize the opportunity for learning will be an important lesson with positive long-term effects on the students. Because the Twentieth Century course deals with the problems of our society, many students have felt that it should involve direct social action rather than listening, reading, analyzing, and discussion. I think the course has been less successful than we hoped partially because of the gap between unrealistic expectations and the reality that a course cannot provide the solutions to the world's problems.

Our early experience with the Twentieth Century course and upperclass interdisciplinary courses makes me pessimistic about the possibilities for successful team teaching, or even successful individual teaching, in cases where the syllabus is designed by others. I think the Hiram colloquia work well not only because they are small and informal, but also because each professor picks his own topic, the only restriction being that he work toward a common set of goals. (It should be emphasized that the intimate nature of the popular colloquia is made financially possible by the large lecture format of the Twentieth Century course.) Both faculty and students seem to prefer courses taught by a single person. However, faculty certainly learn from each other when they work together, and students learn important lessons about the complexity and multifaceted nature of reality when associating with more than one professor at a time. Unfortunately, I do not have a solution to this dilemma of individual versus team teaching, but we are working on it.

Although the Hiram curriculum is not a radical or revolutionary one, we feel that it is a significant move toward regenerated vitality in American higher education. I think few people would dispute the fact that we have been able to make bigger changes than most colleges. There are, in fact, large differences between Hiram's present academic program and the program of several years ago. Over 20 per cent of the Hiram courses are new, not only in title, but also in general content and methodology. To list some of the factors that have enabled Hiram to make these changes, I would say, first, that Hiram has a relatively young, flexible faculty and a history of innovation. (The single course study plan of the 1930s to 1950s is an example.) Second, there was a general awareness that the old distribution requirements were not accomplishing what had been hoped. Third, Hiram had a new president who encouraged the faculty to make a major change without trying to determine its form. The only guidelines set by the president were that the changes should be imaginative, educationally sound, and cost no more to operate than our former program. The president also pressed hard to come up with a proposal within a year's time. The resulting proposal had support from the top administrative officials but did not have the stigma of being imposed from the top.

The fourth factor that helped Hiram make changes was that a small task force of twelve carefully selected faculty members formed the outline of the curriculum. This group represented a balance of disciplines, ages, and educational philosophies, but all members were receptive to reasonable change and had the respect of a sizeable segment of the whole faculty. It took six months of long, weekly meetings before this group became cohesive and really began to communicate with each other.

Several other factors facilitated change. For one, there were no students on the task force. From today's perspective, this may seem strange, but I suspect that perhaps this made the proposal seem acceptable to some of the traditional faculty members. However, most of the faculty and a number of students were included on committees that filled out each component of the program by following the general outline drawn up by the small task force. This greatly broadened the base of support for the program and probably also improved the quality of the final results. Finally, a detailed model was developed in response to questions about how the programs could be staffed and how they would affect departmental offerings. The model served to base the necessary changes on data rather than personal considerations and, thus, helped us avoid most of the internal divisions that often result from major changes. The staffing model was important not only in answering faculty questions prior to the approval of the curriculum, but also served as a clear, if tacit, agreement of faculty commitment to the new program. I believe that this planning has been an important factor in the success of the curriculum and our ability to continue to staff the program adequately.

We have found that it takes a tremendous amount of energy to get a major change started and to sustain it. There is always the possibility of slipping back into traditional ways, but we are working hard toward effective, comprehensive innovation. We feel that we have an effective and workable curriculum that meets the needs of contemporary students through its increased flexibility and interdisciplinary emphasis on general education.

8

Community College: Organizing for Change

David S. Bushnell

⸎⸎⸎⸎⸎⸎⸎⸎⸎

The phenomenal growth of community and junior colleges during the last decade, represented by a national increase in enrollments of almost 300 per cent attests to the popularity of these remarkable institutions. Ten to fifteen years ago, community colleges were pressed with the need to establish themselves as educational institutions of worth. This is no longer a major concern. Enthusiasm for community colleges is demonstrated by the recommendation of the Carnegie Commission on Higher Education that a comprehensive community college should be within commuting distance of every potential student by 1980. At this time of optimism and unprecedented growth, W. K. Kellogg Foundation decided to fund a stock-taking project to determine where the community college movement is headed, how likely is it to achieve its objectives, and what alternative strategies ought to be considered, if any. These issues represent the central concern of Project Focus. Edmund J. Gleazer, Jr., executive director of the American Association of Junior Colleges, was asked to head the one-year study. He accepted and took a leave of absence from the Association. I was hired as research director, and about six months ago the enterprise was launched.

The time is coming for a reappraisal of the community college movement. Frank Newman's *Report on Higher Education* sums up the dilemma of the nation's community colleges as follows:

The public and especially the four year colleges and universities are shifting more and more responsibilities onto the community colleges for undertaking the toughest task of higher education. Simultaneously, the problems we have already identified—the poor match between the student's style of learning and the institution's style of teaching, the lockstep pressure to attend college directly after high school, the over-emphasis on credentials—are overtaking the community colleges and rendering them increasingly ill-equipped to perform the immense task they have been given. The two year institutions are not yet set in concrete, but the molds are being formed. . . . There is time—but not much time. Graduating Ph.D.s, unable to find jobs in universities and colleges and now moving into the junior college market, will add to the trend toward the conventional academic format. Enrollment pressures are forcing abandonment of the concept of the intimate campus. States are eagerly beginning to plan for "their" junior college systems, and the federal government is under increasing pressures to finance the junior college movement through state-formula grants—a mechanism guaranteed to replicate the junior college scenario across the nation. What is needed are community colleges that fulfill the promise of their name—colleges organized to meet the specific needs of the students they serve.[1]

My quoting this passage should not be taken as a blanket endorsement by me of the Newman report. Many of its comments on community and junior colleges are patronizing at best. One wishes that a document of this importance (important, that is, to the extent that it will shape HEW policy concerning higher education) might have

[1] F. Newman and others, *Report on Higher Education*. Washington, D. C.: Department of Health, Education, and Welfare, 1971, pp. 71 and 75.

been more thoroughly researched. Fault could be found with the implications of the data that show only 20 to 25 per cent of the freshmen
enrolled at two-year public junior colleges graduating within a two-
year period. Many who do enroll in our public two-year institutions
never intend to graduate in the first place, since they seek vocational
training requiring less than two years. Other students enroll on only
a part-time basis. Another problem with the Newman report is that
state agencies serving community colleges are singled out as being
dominated by the higher educational establishment, but little docu-
mentation is provided to support this observation. In general, however,
many of the issues raised by the report warrant serious consideration.
In this paper I will cover three important topics. First, I would like to
examine the expectations and needs of students to be served by community colleges. Second, I would like to make a brief assessment of
how well these needs and other goals of community colleges are being
served. Third, I would like to indicate what I perceive as the implications of the trends of community and junior colleges in the future.

Let us begin by asking: Who is the community college student,
and what are his needs? Leonard Koos has helped to answer these
questions in his recently published book, *The Community College
Student*.[2] Koos brings to our attention an array of research literature
dealing with the psychological and physiological developmental tasks
of later adolescence. Those who have surveyed the problems and concerns of college age students generally agree that seventeen to twenty-
four year olds face three important challenges. First, these youths are
struggling to achieve a sense of independence from parental authority.
Second, they must achieve a level of social and economic status commensurate with the individual's expectations. Third, they need to
develop an internalized set of values and a sense of control over their
own destinies.

The following description is a summary of Koo's findings on
the community college student. Today's college student is the product
of a shrinking world, a world made small through television and travel.
Access to foreign cultures and exposure to the real life dramas of war,
racial bigotry, and poverty have produced a generation of students
who are intolerant of inequality and of mores that can be ignored or
adhered to depending on place or time. The student of today wants

---

[2] Leonard Koos, *The Community College Student*. Gainsville, Florida:
University of Florida Press, 1970.

a lasting, harmonious set of values and a life philosophy to help him establish a consistent standard of conduct toward others.

Never has a younger generation been so affluent or so aware of its potential power. Youth between the ages of fourteen and twenty-four now comprise 20 per cent of our total population. With few fears about where the next dollar is coming from and with a sense that physical wants will be met, the modern generation is concerned with commitment to socially significant activities. Adolescents today are undergoing a shift from passive tolerance to an aggressive concern with the shaping of their own destinies. It is fair to describe our younger generation as tolerant of change and optimistic about the eventual triumph of science over all social ills. Advances in technology, from the H-bomb to the power mower, from the electric guitar to heart transplants, have given this generation an increased sense of control over man's destiny. A belief in the empirical and a desire to discover have led students to observe and question events around them. They have a desire to know, to be involved, and to have an impact.

Many of the younger set are more open and honest in their relationships than were previous generations. They have a high regard for individual worth and are less apt than others to be hypocritical in their actions. In effect, adolescents have committed themselves to leading more meaningful lives and are less willing to accept compromise than their elders. With increasing urbanization and a large number of person to person contacts, students feel a need for the development of interpersonal skills. Unless we develop the skill to reach out and relate to others in a mutually rewarding fashion our mobile society can create in each of us a sense of alienation.

What I have painted is perhaps too rosy a picture of the needs and perceptions of students now enrolled in our colleges and universities. The community college student, while he shares some of the values of his counterpart in other higher educational institutions, is apt to be at the far end of the continuum. He is unsure of himself and his future career interests. He has a high school record that bars him from enrolling at a four-year institution. He cannot afford to go away to college; and, while he says he is interested in transfering to a four-year program, he is not likely to do so.

Such characteristics—if even partly true—have profound implications for the organization and administration of colleges. For one, in their approach to students, faculty members need to be more honest and humanistic than in the past. Decisions about curriculum offerings and instructional procedures should be made in a democratic way, with careful attention to the real involvement of students in the decision-making process. Colleges must be oriented to the real world and should be responsive to local, state, and national priorities. For too long a time, college administrators have justified traditional practices on the basis of tradition alone. College students are challenging these timeworn procedures and demanding that teaching methods and the learning environment be shaped to the requirements of students and not designed just for the benefit of the institution. Programs centered on faculty must give way to programs centered on the learners.

The vitality and rapid growth of community and junior colleges during the last decade attest to the general appeal of this option to higher education. Not all observers of the junior college scene give it their unalloyed endorsement, however. Rather than accept the claim that the rapid growth of community colleges is due primarily to widespread appeal and accessibility, some observers point to insidious forces at work. Christopher Jencks and David Riesman in *The Academic Revolution* [3] argue that the popularity of the community college movement can be attributed to proximity, low cost, and a backlash against national institutions of higher education. Much of this backlash represents the anxiety of adults over the increasing emancipation of the younger generation on residential campuses. Lower middle-class parents, according to Jencks and Riesman, resent the snobbery and the selectivity of the universities and seek to give their own children access to higher education at a low cost and without the steep requirements of most four-year institutions. Jencks and Riesman contend that community colleges appeal primarily to the marginal student of modest ability and uncertain plans.

Let me turn now to the goals and the present state of the community college movement itself. A growing concensus among junior college administrators indicates six purposes for the existence of comprehensive community colleges. First, a full range of academic course offerings should be provided closely paralleling the lower division undergraduate programs at four-year colleges. Such courses are fully transferable upon completion of an associates of arts degree and should be equal in every way to university based courses. Second, all enrollees should be provided with a broad general education, analagous to the

---

[3] Christopher Jencks and David Riesman, *The Academic Revolution.* Garden City, New York: Doubleday and Co., Inc., 1968.

traditional concept of a liberal education. One major benefit should be the development of learning skills and independent study habits that will aid the student beyond his formal years in education. The basic and intermediate level arts, humanities, and sciences should be studied with the intent of developing a full range of intellectual skills. Third, occupational training opportunities should be offered, which match the industrial and business needs of the community as represented by local trade and apprenticeship advisory committees.

Fourth, the adult education and community service functions of the community college should clearly be geared to the special needs and interest of the community. Most junior colleges recognize the community need for generalized educational opportunities by providing college level courses during evening hours, career development or retraining programs, and special events of a cultural or aesthetic nature. Fifth, all of these functions should be linked to a counseling and guidance program serving the total student body. The guidance function should serve the student from registration to graduation and provide him with knowledge about career opportunities appropriate to his skills and interests. Finally, the open door concept should insure that a wide variety of students with differing interests, motivations, and abilities be served. Most institutions limit entrance qualifications to a high school diploma or equivalent, and most require little or no tuition. Coordinate with this openness is the notion that the junior college faculty should be oriented to the needs of students rather than to the requirements of a particular discipline.

The junior college is expected to bridge the gap between high school and the four-year college or between high school and a job. The junior college has its historical roots in an eclectic mixture of the academic and the vocational. Even though many two-year colleges compete with and duplicate the efforts of area vocational schools and local high schools, the idea of a comprehensive educational program is a strong drawing card. As an organization, however, the junior college is in many ways dysfunctional. This is mainly an outgrowth of the forces that shaped the junior college during its formative years and the constant societal changes and pressures that go beyond the community college as an institution. Institutions that are not well tuned to student and community needs frequently respond to pressures for change in spasmodic and unplanned ways. This is not to disparage the devoted and often brilliant efforts of the teachers and administrators of the two-year institution, but, as with most educational institutions, the disparity between current practice and stated goals is readily apparent.

One example of the disparity between goals and actual practice may be seen in the attitude of those faculty who are oriented toward the university transfer program. Such faculty members have negative attitudes toward occupational programs. They have been educated in the tradition of the liberal arts, and their courses are geared to college transfer. The organization of academic departments are also along traditional lines. As a result, the occupational training programs have only a secondary emphasis and are held in low esteem by many of the faculty.

Perhaps the most glaring gap between goal and practice is in the area of general education. Little, if any, emphasis is placed on interdisciplinary studies; little effort is made to develop a broad set of problem-solving skills or to integrate various fields of study. Furthermore, ambiguity and conflict characterize the counseling and guidance function in the junior college. Most junior colleges allocate extensive resources to this function, both in terms of staff and space. Yet several studies have indicated that students benefit very little from counseling in its present form.

Community services and the extended day program often operate in an auxiliary fashion. There is meager financial support for such efforts (most evening instructors are paid on an hourly basis and do not enjoy tenure), and resources for community service programs are often limited or the first to be cut in a budget crunch. Until recently, many programs had little relevance to community needs or interests. In fact, the community needs have tended to be limited to the special interests of middle-class business and professional groups that exert pressure on the college. As for serving the students, the junior college is at best limited in its ability to accommodate a diverse set of needs and interests. Instructional procedures and curriculum content are clearly oriented to the above average student. Although there is currently a growing interest in remedial education, few of these programs have gone beyond the demonstration stage. Little provision is made for differentiating between the verbally skilled and the nonverbal student, between the self-starters and the other directed students. A high drop-out rate still persists, particularly among those from disadvantaged backgrounds.

Policy decisions are frequently a result of expediency rather than planning. Because of external pressures, many who occupy key roles are resistant to change. There is clearly a mandate for change, but the goals and practices of the community college will not be aligned merely by changing the organizational structure, rearranging class-rooms, or appointing new investigative committees. Basic changes dealing with the values, career interests, and attitudes of the staff are required. A coordinated, holistic approach to educational reform is needed to resolve the conflicts that exist.

At this point, let us turn to a consideration of the scope and nature of Project Focus. This one-year study of the nation's community and junior colleges is being done under the auspices of the American Association of Junior Colleges (AAJC) and funded by a grant from the W. K. Kellogg Foundation. The study has a twofold purpose: first, to examine the long-range goals and present practices of the com-munity and junior colleges and, in the process, to identify the social and economic trends that will influence their future role; and, second, to study the AAJC itself in terms of its stated functions and long-range goals. The study is examining how these institutions change; we want to know the directions of change, the facilitators of change, and the impediments to change. Through face-to-face interviews and survey questionnaires administered to a sample of one hundred community and junior colleges, we are examining the changes in the student populations served; the changes in how these students are served; the changes in organization and governance; shifts in financial support (who pays and who should pay); and the trends in community rela-tions or services.

To date, Gleazer and other members of the team have met with board members, community representatives, students, faculty, presi-dents, deans, and department heads in fourteen institutions located in some ten different states. We have also conferred with state per-sonnel and members of state legislatures. When asked what goals our community colleges should serve, almost all respondents spoke of helping the disadvantaged, offering occupational preparation, provid-ing retraining programs, providing education beyond the traditional college age, and being a community service. Occasionally, a respondent voiced the opinion that community and junior colleges should con-centrate their efforts—that the two-year colleges were being spread too thin. In general, however, it was felt that enrollments should include more students and older students than at present and that the colleges should serve students with wide-ranging abilities and interests. In short, the responses indicated that there is clearly no natural drift towards an integration of academic and occupational programs. If there is value in integrating these two fields, then deliberate and organized measures must be taken toward that goal.

Project Focus has also shed light on the position of the disadvantaged student. Faculty members themselves feel unprepared to teach disadvantaged students. Counseling in both the community colleges and in the high schools, as perceived by students and faculty and even counselors themselves, appears to be inadequate in helping the disadvantaged student. He cannot see realistically what his chances are likely to be if he should attempt various career commitments. Most minority group students avoid the occupationally oriented courses. The study also pointed out that community colleges are often comprehensive only in the sense that several discrete functions are contained under one roof. We witnessed some exciting new strategies for learning. However, in the responses to our questionnaires, very little mention was made of Benjamin S. Bloom's concept of the mastery of learning. Moreover, community colleges do not utilize to any great extent the Job Corps approach to training. There is little evidence of a curriculum approach that takes advantage of skill clusters or commonalities between related fields.

Project Focus indicates that the locus of power at two-year colleges is changing. State agencies and legislatures are becoming conscious of their responsibility for the financial viability and quality of local community colleges. They are beginning to ask questions about benefit and cost and who should be held accountable for results. Although most staffs insist upon the value of local decision making, they recognize that legislative mandates are calling for direction by the state agencies. In addition, local boards are insisting upon involvement in policy issues and in the review and evaluation of the output of the local institution. Although a full range of community interests are not yet represented on such boards, there is a concerted effort in that direction. Our study suggests some evidence of rising faculty power, but the role of unions is as yet ambiguous. None of the institutions visited so far had adopted a union shop, although two or three had considered the idea and rejected it. There is little evidence of any significant growth in student power, although most institutions have made token gestures in that direction. The transient and/or part-time nature of the community college student explains why students do not participate actively in campus affairs. A means needs to be developed to enable students with leadership capabilities to participate in campus affairs.

Our study shows a clear trend towards state financing, usually by means of a formula allocation. Two-year colleges in both Florida and Washington receive full support from the state. Texas is moving toward financing instructional costs at the state level, while financing building and maintenance costs at the local level. Eliminating local tax revenues reduces the flexibility of the local institution in raising its own funds. Increasing state support, however, may offset this disadvantage, but competition for funds is steep, since state officials must consider other pressing social needs such as welfare costs. Few of our interviewees, however, advocate raising tuitions in order to meet revenue requirements. Some respondents advocate expanding student loan programs and outright grants, which would give students greater autonomy than they now have.

Project Focus indicates that community services are expanding at a rapid rate. District programs are reaching beyond the campuses into satellite centers. Newly planned structures tend to be small in size and have adopted the concept of a service center for the administration of satellite operations. Recreational facilities on many campuses are being used year round by the community. One board member in Oregon stated that youth will actually become a minority group to serve, and the community college will be primarily a community service institution. Classrooms will have to move from campus to where the people are.

Our study also leaves us with a few random impressions of two-year colleges. For one, it is no longer accurate to refer to students as kids. One-fifth of the enrollment in Phoenix, Arizona, is women over twenty-five years of age. At another institution, the president of the student government is an Air Force veteran of thirty-seven. The average age at several institutions is twenty-six or twenty-seven. Another impression concerns the qualities needed for educational leadership. People are now describing the community college president as one who should understand the dynamics of change and who should know how to work with political pressures. A final impression is that few junior college districts seem to be working closely with local high schools or nearby universities. Joint planning and problem solving is almost nonexistent. There is, however, growing acceptance of more sophisticated planning and budgeting procedures.

Since Project Focus is concerned with developing alternative strategies for change, our efforts are necessarily focused on how community colleges should change. This, of course, implies dissatisfaction with the way community colleges operate today; yet we do not in any way wish to negate the tremendous impact that community and junior colleges have had and will continue to have in the future. Our interest is to bring about an alignment of goals and practice for the ultimate benefit of those served by our institutions.

PART THREE:

Exits and Entrances

The phrase exits and entrances *comes from Dylan Thomas, a poet who made no attempt to hide his disrespect for the academic world. His hostility was directed toward the establishment in general, but at least part of it arose from his experience with the university as a low-risk enterprise. It is an institution that characteristically undertakes nothing that is not perfectly safe. The poetic irony of the title "Exits and Entrances" sets the theme for the essays of Part Three, which ask how higher education—a low-risk enterprise—is responding to pressures to accommodate the high-risk student.*

9

College Admissions: A Systems Perspective

Alexander W. Astin

Much of the controversy about open admissions and special programs for disadvantaged students has been unproductive because the adversaries tend to talk past each other. The proponents of open admissions typically speak of the need for equalizing educational opportunities and aiding minority groups, whereas the opponents usually speak of the need for maintaining academic standards and for conserving our dwindling institutional resources. Whether these various objectives are indeed incompatible will be difficult to determine as long as there is no common basis for discussion. In this paper, I should like to discuss some of these issues in the broad context of what the entire system of higher education is trying to accomplish. Some of my arguments will be based on recent results from our research program at the American Council on Education. Other arguments will be mostly a matter of theory or personal opinion. Whatever the validity of these arguments, my main hope is to provide a rational basis for debating the issues.

One of the problems for any college that is trying to examine its admissions policies is what might be called institutional myopia. The faculty and staff of most individual institutions tend to regard any proposed change in admissions policies only in terms of how the institution will be directly affected. The educational consequences of any change in admissions policies would be more easily assessed if an institution would make an effort to see its own admissions decisions in relation to the larger systems to which the institution belongs. For example, policymakers should ask: What is likely to happen to the rejected applicants? Are they likely to go to some other institution? If so, where will they go and to what educational end? What about the applicants who are accepted? Where might they have gone had they been rejected? Would any of them have fared better in some other type of institution? The point is that, if the institution is trying to be of maximum benefit to its constituency, then it must ultimately regard any decision to accept or reject a particular student in the light of the other options that are open to the student.

Regarding the admissions decisions of individual institutions in this large context requires a systems perspective. This approach is illustrated in Figure 1. Let us assume that the principal purpose of the system of higher education is to improve the general level of intellectual performance in our society. Let us further assume that curve (a) in Figure 1 represents the distribution of intellectual performance for the total population of potential students that could be served by the system. (I have made the distribution normal in shape, but there is no necessary reason why the actual distribution of raw scores could not assume some other shape.) Two major cutting points on this score distribution have been identified: borderline literacy, at the low end of the continuum; and Ph.D. level performance, at the high end. Note that only a very small fraction of the population is performing at the Ph.D. level prior to entering college, but that a substantial proportion is performing at or below borderline literacy. The desired educational output (the goals of the higher educational system) can be specified in terms of changes in the characteristics of the distribution. (Higher education can influence many outcomes other than intellectual performance. I have chosen this particular distribution simply for the sake of example.)

Although an almost infinite number of changes might be desired, curves (b), (c), and (d) in Figure 1 are examples of only three basic types of changes. The solid lines in each of these three curves show the desired shape of the distribution (the educational objective) after four years of college. The dotted lines that are superimposed on each curve show the same distribution as curve (a)—in other words, the potential population before it is exposed to college. The first of these hypothetical changes in the performance distribution, curve (b), involves an upward shift in mean performance only. Note that the population as a whole has improved its performance and that the shape or dispersion of people remains unchanged. One might refer to this as a sort of democratic or egalitarian plan. Note also that, in order to implement this plan, it would probably be necessary to expose all members of the potential population to some form of higher education. Obviously, if certain individuals are excluded from the system, it would be unrealistic to expect them to show improvements in performance comparable to those of individuals who are admitted. We do not know at this point whether equal increments could be achieved more economically by means of a track system rather than by some other type of institutional arrangement, but at least there would have to be some attempt to provide educational opportunities to every member of the population.

Curve (c) portrays the next alternative educational outcome. Here, the proportion of students performing at or near the Ph.D. level has been substantially increased, while the scores of those at the low end of the distribution remain almost unchanged. This type of plan is concerned primarily with maximizing the number of very high-performing students and might be characterized as elitist, in the sense that the greatest share of the resources would be invested in those who are initially high performers. In an elitist system, there is relatively little concern with improving performance at the low end of the continuum. This particular type of educational plan has been implicit in the American higher educational system in the past and in the higher educational systems of Western Europe. To implement this plan, it would not be necessary to admit to higher education people at the low end of the distribution.

The third alternative outcome, shown in curve (d) of Figure 1, is primarily concerned with minimizing the proportion of low performers. Here the number of persons performing at or near borderline literacy is greatly reduced, but the number of performers at the high end of the distribution changes only slightly. Since this plan is concerned primarily with eradicating illiteracy, it might be labeled a remedial plan or, possibly, a social welfare plan. In order to implement this last plan, it would be necessary to admit the low performers into some form of postsecondary education. However, it would probably also be necessary to devote a disproportionate amount of the higher educational resources to the education of these low performers. This type of resource allocation is precisely the reverse of what is done now.

Each of the three alternative models for the distribution of intellectual ability has contrasting effects on the *variation* in performance within the population. Note that in the elitist model, curve (c), exclusion of low-performing people from the system and massive investment of resources in the education of exceptionally high performers will tend to increase variability. The remedial model, curve (d), which calls for investing a disproportionate amount of resources in the education of low-performing individuals, will tend to have the opposite effect and, therefore, decrease variability. It would be interesting to speculate on how such alternative schemes would differentially affect societal problems such as racial tensions. Some advocates of the elitist plan for higher education argue that it is essential to invest a disproportionate amount of our resources in the education of the exceptionally bright in order to promote scientific and technological progress. Some of my elitist friends have referred to this approach as the "let's not lose the Third World War" plan. Advocates of the remedial or social welfare plan might argue that low-performing members of the society represent the biggest drain and, in the long run, the biggest threat to the general welfare of the society. According to this argument, substantially improving the competence of these low performers might ultimately have enormous societal benefits by alleviating poverty and crime.

In short, the three alternative models pose some interesting questions of value for educational planners. Does a given increment in performance at the high end of the distribution have the same value to the society as an equal increment in performance at the low end of the distribution? What about increments in the middle ranges of the distribution? What personal value do given increments have to the individuals themselves? Although this is not the place to debate such issues, one thing seems certain: the educational system cannot hope to enhance the performance of individuals at any point on the distribution if they are excluded from the system altogether. Nor can educational systems hope to recruit, retain, and influence the performance of individuals unless sufficient financial support is provided and programs appropriately geared to initial levels of performance are developed.

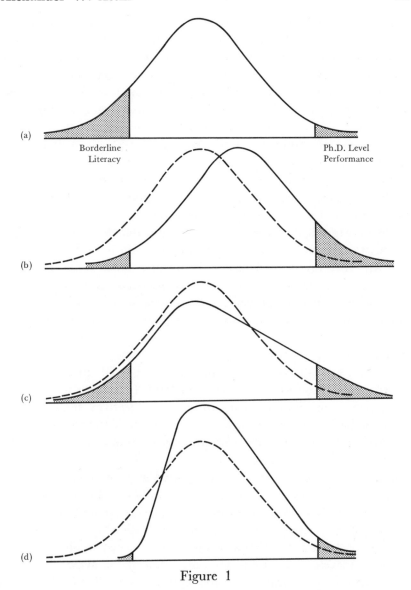

(a)

Borderline
Literacy

Ph.D. Level
Performance

(b)

(c)

(d)

Figure 1

Hypothetical Distributions of the Intellectual Ability in the Population of College-Aged Students. (a) distribution of intellectual performance for total population of potential students; (b) egalitarian model for possible output of educational system; (c) elitist model for alternative educational outcome; (d) remedial model. Originally presented in A. W. Astin, "Measuring Student Outputs in Higher Education," in *The Outputs of Higher Education: Their Identification, Measurement, and Evaluation.* Bolder, Colo.: Western Interstate Commission for Higher Education, July, 1970, pp. 75–83.

Even if it were possible to achieve some degree of agreement on the desired outcomes of higher education, the question remains as to which system is needed to bring about any particular outcome. There are at least two aspects to this question. First, it is important to understand what kind of system we already have; second, we must determine whether certain changes could be introduced to make the system effectively achieve the desired outcome. Our research program at the American Council on Education has been concerned with both of these problems. I would like to present briefly some of the relevant findings. Let us look at some of the characteristics of the current system. In our studies of college characteristics, we have determined that one of the most important institutional attributes is the average academic ability of the undergraduates who enroll—a variable that we call institutional selectivity. Selectivity is highly correlated with an institution's prestige and with such diverse variables as the faculty-student ratio, the size of the library, faculty salaries, endowment, research contract funds, the amount of academic competitiveness among students, and even the political orientation of the institution. Selectivity is, in fact, probably the best single measure of the perceived academic quality of an institution.

Table 1 shows how the population of 2,319 institutions was distributed with respect to selectivity in 1968. (Although minor variations occur from year to year, institutional selectivity tends to be a highly stable institutional trait.) The mean aptitude test scores of entering freshman classes have been grouped into eight intervals. In addition, there is a category which includes 854 institutions for which no direct estimate was available. Data to be reported in a forthcoming publication of the author suggest that virtually all of these 854 institutions have very low selectivity scores and can be regarded as falling in the bottom two levels of selectivity. Note that the distribution shown in Table 1 follows a market positive skew, with the bulk of institutions scoring at the lowest levels of selectivity and only a few at the highest levels. In fact, when the no estimate available institutions are dividend between levels 1 and 2, the distribution takes on a "J" shape.

Some observers have likened this institutional arrangement to a kind of track system, where students are grouped into various types of institutions on the basis of their abilities. Although there is some truth in this conception of American higher education, it is perhaps more accurately described as a status system than as a track system. What

Table 1

Selectivity Levels of Higher Educational Institutions, 1968 [a]
(N = 2,319)

College Selectivity Level	Corresponding Range of Student Mean Scores		Institutions	
	SAT V + M	ACT Composite	Number	Per-cent
8	1320 or higher	30 or higher	27	1.2
7	1236-1319	28-29	43	1.8
6	1154-1235	26-27	85	3.7
5	1075-1153	25-26	141	6.1
4	998-1074	23-24	342	14.7
3	926- 997	21-22	331	14.3
2	855- 925	19-20	273	11.8
1	854 or lower	18 or lower	281	12.1
No Estimate Available	854 [b]	19 [b]	796	34.3

[a] Includes all institutions listed in Part Three of the 1968 edition of the U.S. Office of Education's *Education Directory,* with the exception of those institutions that require prior undergraduate credits for admission.

[b] Estimates of the average test scores of students entering institutions in this category were based on evidence reported in a forthcoming publication by the author.

are considered the best institutions are, of course, those in the upper track; the good institutions are those in the middle tracks; and the poor or mediocre institutions are the many small private colleges and two-year colleges in the lowest tracks. That this arrangement represents a status hierarchy more than a planned system of ability tracking is revealed by the fact that the institutions clearly fall into a pyramid shape, with a few highly selective centers of excellence at the top. Another indication of the status implications of this system is that variability in student ability is closely and inversely related to the level of ability; thus, even the least selective institutions—those at the bottom of the pyramid—do not turn away the few bright students who apply. These institutions clearly do not attempt to maintain the homogeneity in student ability that a track system would require. For that matter, most institutions at the bottom of the hierarchy and virtually all of those in the middle covet the same commodities that characterize top institutions—bright students, highly trained and prestigious faculty, and money. In short, the track system in American higher education is not part of a conscious plan based on educational theory but rather the outcome of a competitive system in which the spoils are drawn from a finite pool of student and faculty talent.

Although some educators have developed elaborate rationales for this hierarchical arrangement of institutions, it is probably safe to assume that the system is perpetuated, not for educational reasons, but for reasons of competition and status. Professors support selective admissions because they feel that bright students are more fun and easier to teach than slow students. Indeed, even within a given institution or within a given classroom, professors probably favor their brightest students. Alumni, legislators, faculty, administrators, and probably a great many students support selective admissions because bright students enhance the prestige of the institution. Many college administrators probably support selective admissions because a good input of highly motivated, talented students will almost guarantee a good output of distinguished, possibly wealthy alumni in years to come. Secondary schools support the track system that results from selective admissions because they see it as an incentive system for motivating their students; teachers and guidance counselors frequently tell their students to study hard so they can get into a good college.

But what are the educational justifications for the institutional hierarchy? Is there any validity to the notion that a hierarchical arrangement will yield a better overall educational outcome than some other sort of arrangement? Perhaps the most common justification for ability tracking is the assumption that the student will develop better academically if he is grouped with students of similar ability than if he is grouped with students of varying abilities. There are several important corollaries to this assumption. One is that the bright student needs the stimulation and the competition of other bright students if he is to realize his full potential. Another corollary is that the bright student will become bored and lose motivation if he is grouped with students of low ability. The third corollary is that the slow student will become intimidated and discouraged if he is forced to compete with students of high ability. To date, little research has been done to test these assumptions, but the available evidence suggests that there is little or no intellectual value added for students who attend highly selective colleges. By the same token, the bright student does not appear to suffer intellectually by attending a college of average or even below average selectivity.[1] Although these studies have relied on standardized tests of achievement administered to college seniors and cannot be regarded as the final word on the effects of selectivity on intellectual development, they do suggest that some of our cherished assumptions need to be reexamined. More important than this, these findings suggest that segregating students into separate institutions on the basis of their academic ability may not really benefit either the bright or the dull students.

We have also tried to look at the effects of selectivity on the grades that students receive. In order to explore this question, we employed one-year longitudinal data from a national sample of 26,806 students who entered college in the fall of 1967. Using the student's freshman grade point average as the dependent variable and a variety of precollege measures as predictors in a multiple regression equation, we developed an expected freshman GPA for each student based on his precollege data. (As you might expect, a student's high school grades and scores on college admissions tests carried by far the most weight in predicting his freshman grades.) This expected GPA was then compared with the student's actual GPA to determine how he performed during his freshman year in relation to his background characteristics.

Table 2 shows the mean actual and mean expected freshman GPAs for students attending colleges at seven different levels of selectivity. (The top two levels of selectivity were combined for this analysis.) Looking only at the mean actual freshman GPAs, one might be led to conclude that college selectivity has a positive influence, since these actual means go up regularly with increasing levels of selectivity. However, when these means are considered in relation to the expected GPAs, a totally different conclusion emerges. Thus, even though the least selective colleges award low grades, these grades are actually higher than would have been expected from the characteristics of the entering students. Similarly, even though highly selective colleges tend to award relatively high grades, they are not as high as would be expected from the background characteristics of the entering freshmen.

[1] For discussions on these points see: A. W. Astin, "Undergraduate Achievement and Institutional 'Excellence'." *Science,* 1968, *161,* 661–668; R. C. Nichols, "Effects of Various College Characteristics on Student Aptitude Test Scores." *Journal of Educational Psychology,* 1964, *55,* 45–54; and D. A. Rock, J. A. Centra, and R. L. Linn, "Relationships Between College Characteristics and Student Characteristics." *American Educational Research Journal,* 1970, *7,* 109–122.

Table 2

Actual and Expected Freshman GPAs for
Students Attending Colleges in Different Levels of Selectivity
(N = 26,806 students)

Level of Selectivity	Number of Colleges	Number of Students	Mean Actual Freshman GPA	Mean Expected [b] Freshman GPA	Actual Minus Expected Freshman GPA
1 [a]	20	2,156	2.44	2.32	+.12
2	12	1,088	2.49	2.31	+.18
3	27	3,536	2.51	2.47	+.04
4	45	7,030	2.56	2.55	+.01
5	26	4,280	2.55	2.62	—.07
6	21	3,714	2.63	2.71	—.08
7 and 8	28	5,002	2.75	2.84	—.09

[a] This level includes unknown selectivity.
[b] These expected GPAs were based on a prediction formula utilizing nineteen student input variables (R = .58).

In short, a given student is likely to get somewhat lower grades if he attends a highly selective institution than if he attends an institution of low selectivity. Somewhat surprising, however, is the small degree of difference that selectivity makes. There is only about one-quarter of a letter grade difference in mean actual GPAs between the most and least selective colleges.

Many of the proposed changes in current admissions policies have been motivated by a concern about the racial segregation that typically results from selective admissions policies. It is important to determine if college selectivity has effects on the academic performance of students of different races. To explore this possibility, we sorted our sample of 26,806 students into four categories by race and sex and compared the mean discrepancies between the predicted and actual freshmen GPAs. The results of these analyses are presented in Table 3. All four groups of students—black men, black women, nonblack men, and nonblack women—appear to be affected similarly by college selectivity. In each case, selectivity has the same type of negative effect on academic performance that was observed for the combined group. Nevertheless, there are some differential effects of selectivity by race and by sex that are worth noting. In the colleges at the lowest selectivity level, black and nonblack students alike show very similar discrepancies between actual and expected performance. At the higher selectivity levels, however, the blacks perform relatively poorly in comparison with the whites. Since a disproportionate number of blacks attend colleges in the lowest selectivity level, the overall performance of blacks does not differ from that of whites. In the more selective colleges, however, blacks of both sexes appear to perform below their white counterparts. This means selective colleges that contemplate recruiting larger numbers of blacks should probably not expect these students to perform at the same level as white students with similar background characteristics. The data in Table 3 also suggest that selectivity affects the sexes differentially. Women at the low selectivity levels perform better than men, and men at the high selectivity levels perform better than women. These sex differences appear to apply to both black and nonblack students. What this finding means, in effect, is that the negative effects of college selectivity on freshman grades are more pronounced for women than for men.

Table 3

Mean Actual Minus Mean Expected Freshman GPAs of Black and Nonblack Students as a Function of College Selectivity Level

College Selectivity Level	Men		Women	
	Nonblack	Black	Nonblack	Black
1 [a]	+.09	+.05	+.15	+.14
2	+.17	−.04	+.19	+.15
3	+.03	−.07	+.04	−.19
4	.00	−.06	+.03	−.21
5	−.09	−.22	−.06	−.26
6	−.08	−.18	−.06	−.38
7 & 8	−.06	−.33	−.12	−.39

[a] This level includes unknown selectivity.

One alternative to open admissions is the establishment of racial quotas as a means of integrating the student body. In essence, this practice amounts to the use of double standards of admissions for whites and blacks (and sometimes other selected minorities). While such double standards are probably the most straightforward means of integrating student bodies, there are certain undesirable side effects that should be taken into account. For example, in contrast to a simple policy of open admissions, the use of double standards tends to accentuate differences between the races in academic ability and past performance. The reason for this is that the pools of black and white applicants already differ in past academic achievements and in performances on academic ability tests. Simply applying a merit criterion at admissions, without regard to race, would have the effect of admitting proportionately fewer blacks than whites, although those blacks who are admitted would not differ appreciably from the whites in terms of academic ability and past performance. However, if double standards of admissions are employed, the criteria for admitting blacks would have to be lowered, while the criteria for admitting whites would be raised. The net result would produce a class of entering students in which the correlation between race and ability is accentuated. If the criteria for blacks are reduced substantially (or eliminated altogether, as in the case of some institutions), the resulting freshman class would include a substantial number of blacks whose level of academic preparation is substantially below that of the white students. Since the subsequent academic performance of these black students is almost certain to be below that of most white students, the potential for increased racial tensions and hostilities is very great. Open admissions could remedy this situation through the possible advantage that the students who enroll at the institution will not form dichotomies related to race. On the contrary, a substantial number of nonblack students will enroll whose ability and past performance is comparable to that of the typical black student. In this sense, then, a policy of open admissions has less potential for racial conflict than does a policy of double standards.

The most carefully considered arguments against either open admissions or double standards of admissions for disadvantaged students center on the question of academic performance. Perhaps the most persuasive promoter of such arguments is Julian C. Stanley of Johns Hopkins University.[2] Stanley's argument runs somewhat as follows: since high school grades and test scores predict college grades for disadvantaged students as well as for advantaged students, disadvantaged students who are admitted under special criteria will tend to perform below the level of regularly admitted students. If the argument

[2] See J. C. Stanley, "Predicting College Success of the Educationally Disadvantaged," *Science*, 1971, *171*, 640–647.

is extended to the open admissions concept, Stanley would be concerned that students with relatively poor grades and low test scores who elect to attend a previously selective institution are likely to do poorly academically. As the argument goes, why subject such students needlessly to the humiliation, frustration, and disappointment that will accompany their academic failure?

In examining such arguments it is important to grant several points from the start. First, if previously selective institutions opt for open admissions or for double standards of admissions without also establishing special educational programs for their less qualified students, the academic performance of these students will be below par and their failure rate will be somewhat above that of other students. But since grades and test scores are far from perfect predictors of academic performance, only a few of the specially admitted students are likely to fail completely, while a few will perform outstandingly. How many of these specially admitted students will fail and how many will succeed is primarily a matter of the discrepancies between the test scores and grades of disadvantaged students and of other students. A second point that must be conceded is that, if the specially admitted students are selected on the basis of race or economic criteria without regard to past performance or academic ability scores, then we must face the fact that the more selective the institution, the larger these discrepancies in academic performance are likely to be.

Stanley cites a good deal of evidence suggesting that tests of academic ability predict equally well for the disadvantaged students as for advantaged students. While our own research data would support this same conclusion, I do not feel that the predictive validity of admissions criteria is necessarily relevant to the basic issues. To defend selective admissions on the grounds that aptitude tests and high school grades predict performance is perhaps to miss the main point of education. Even if students learned absolutely nothing as a result of their courses in college, these tests would have the same predictive validity. Indeed, if we were to administer college admissions tests to high school seniors, put the students in cold storage for four years, then thaw them out and give them a set of final examinations, the college admissions tests would still have validity in predicting performance on the final examinations. The point is that the predictive validity of college admissions tests and high school grades may be largely irrelevant to the educational objectives of the institution. To be sure, if it could be demonstrated that the value added by virtue of college attendance is greater for the high-scoring than for the low-scoring student, one might argue that college admissions tests are appropriate criteria for selecting college students, but the available evidence clearly does not support such an assumption.

Perhaps the most important assumption underlying a faith in the predictive value of test scores is that a student's grade point average reflects what he has learned. Indeed, the concept of flunking students is based on the assumption that students who get low grades are not profiting from their educational experience. There is, however, little evidence to support this assumption, and some recent evidence actually contradicts it. One of the most provocative studies conducted in recent years was reported by John Harris of the Institute of Higher Education at the University of Georgia.[3] This study involves the administration of the College Level Examination Program (CLEP) tests to freshmen when they first enter college. In order to measure gains in intellectual performance, the same battery of examinations was readministered after the students had completed their first six quarters of academic work. Students were sorted into several comparison groups on the basis of the academic grades they had received in various courses. The groups were then compared to determine if grades were related to differential changes on the CLEP. As it turned out, virtually all groups showed significant positive gains on the CLEP, indicating that some learning was taking place regardless of course grades. In certain fields, the course grades appeared to reflect the amount learned. For example, students with the highest grades in physical science courses showed substantially larger gains on the CLEP natural science test than did students with poor physical science grades. A similar result occurred with grades in history courses and gains on the CLEP social science-history test. In both of these instances, however, even students with grades below C showed significant gains on the CLEP. In other fields the situation was quite different. For example, students who obtained D or failing grades in mathematics courses actually showed slightly higher gains on the CLEP mathematics test than did students who received A or B grades. Students with D or failing grades in English literature showed larger mean gains on the CLEP English tests than students in any other grade category.

Although Harris' study was conducted at one small southern

---

[3] John Harris, "Gain Scores on the CLEP—General Examinations and an Overview of Research." Paper presented at the Annual Meeting of the American Educational Research Association, Minneapolis, March, 1970.

college and clearly needs to be replicated, his findings could have profound implications both for admissions and for grading practices in higher education. Is it possible that grades are a poor reflection of a student's progress? Is it possible that college grades simply rank the students in the same relative manner as do high school grades and test scores and fail to reflect what students actually learn? Is it possible that many students who are flunked out are in fact showing significant progress, although at a lower level of performance than students who receive high grades?

It is probably a serious mistake to assume that all disadvantaged students should ultimately catch up with the other students; this is a matter of individual capacity and motivation. The criterion for determining whether an educational program is effective, however, should be: Does the student continue to acquire skills and knowledge that are valuable to himself or to society? In other words, the decision to retain a student in an educational program should not be based only upon his ability to reach an arbitrary standard of performance within some specified period of time; rather the decision should depend upon whether he continues to show significant progress and growth.

Some critics of open admissions argue that abandoning traditional meritocratic criteria in admissions will make it impossible for colleges to perform their selecting and sorting function. There seems to be little question that colleges have traditionally performed such a function. By rejecting less able applicants for admission, colleges can be reasonably sure that the products they turn out four years later will be of high quality. Flunking out those students who perform poorly provides added insurance that the high calibre of the graduate will be maintained. The more stringent the initial selection criteria and the more severe the grading practices that are applied to those who are admitted, the higher the quality of the product at the other end.

Graduate schools, professional schools, and employers rely heavily on undergraduate colleges to perform this sorting and selecting function. If the initial selection criteria used by the undergraduate school are stringent enough, a prospective employer or graduate school can virtually ignore any other information about the candidate and still be reasonably confident that he is bright and highly motivated. That this selecting and sorting function has proved to be useful is difficult to argue. What has not been considered, though, is how the college's educational function is affected when it engages in selecting and sorting. For example, when a college fails to admit a student or when it chooses to discharge a student with poor grades, the possibility of having any further educational impact on the student is precluded. By selectively screening out the low performing student, the institution implicitly takes the position that educating these students is not a worthwhile enterprise.

We must ask if there is any necessary reason why higher education, rather than some other agency in our society, must perform this role of selecting and screening. If one tries to put himself in the position of an employer who is interested only in finding the most talented persons, one wonders what difference it should make as to whether a student attended a particular college. What would really matter is the candidate's level of competency at the time of graduation. Reliance on undergraduate admissions criteria freezes students in their relative order of performance at the time of graduation from high school. Not only is such information outdated and of limited value to the employer or graduate school, but it also penalizes the late bloomer and gives unfair advantage to those students who go downhill during the college years. As long as sufficient information is available at the time of college graduation, undergraduate admissions information seems to be of limited value and, possibly, even misleading. In short, the sorting and selection function of undergraduate admissions practices appears to be of dubious value to employers or to graduate and professional schools.

It is sometimes said that a policy of open admissions will inflict undue burdens on colleges and universities. Such arguments ignore the fact that several of the largest state systems of higher education have for many years been operating what is essentially a policy of open admissions. Several hundred private institutions have traditionally enrolled students in the low ability ranges, and many of the great state universities have been accommodating students at all levels of ability without any apparent ill effect. To be sure, such institutions have instituted a kind of track system within their curricular programs, but the fact that the programs have operated within a single institution has blunted many of the social and political problems that result from an institutional hierarchy based on selective admissions. Accommodating a wide range of student ability within a single institution can be accomplished by establishing curricular programs similar to the ungraded primary system found in many elementary schools. Confining these programs to a single institution also facilitates easy and rapid transfer of students across and within various curricular tracks.

An argument that is commonly used to support the concept of selective admissions is that academic standards are somehow determined by admissions standards. If this were indeed the case, it would not be necessary for colleges to award grades or degrees or even to assume any responsibility for educating the student. Colleges would simply serve as talent scouts and certification agencies for business, industry, and the graduate and professional schools. Academic standards ordinarily refers to the absolute level of performance that the student is required to exhibit in order to pass courses or earn a degree. Consequently, the college is free to set any performance standards it wishes, independent of the abilities of the students it admits. Educators who might be concerned about maintaining academic standards should probably support the idea of national certification examinations. This concept has already been adopted at the secondary school level with the use of national examinations such as the American College and the College Entrance Examination Board tests. There is no valid reason why colleges and universities could not adopt similar national standards and, thereby, ultimately eliminate the necessity for awarding grades and degrees.

Perhaps the strongest argument in favor of a program of open admissions is that selective admissions is one sure way for colleges to avoid any responsibility for educating the student. If only the brightest students are admitted at one end, then the high quality of the final product is virtually guaranteed. What happens in between—the quality of the educational experience itself—need not be of concern, since the employers and graduate schools are suitably impressed with the high quality of the graduate. Converting to a program of open admissions imposes certain new responsibilities on the institution. One obvious responsibility is that the institution must develop educational programs that are geared for students in the low ability ranges. While many unselective colleges have already developed such programs, the selective institutions may be forced to undergo certain severe transitions in faculty and curricula before they can adequately deal with students in the low ability ranges.

A sometimes unrecognized problem for institutions that adopt an open admissions policy is that the responsibility for matching students with colleges falls into the hands of the student. Under traditional selective admissions criteria, institutions can avoid the problem of mismatches by eliminating what are considered to be the unqualified students. However, if the admissions decision is placed in the hands of students, then the institution must assist prospective applicants in making informed choices. One obvious mode of assistance would be to provide the prospective applicants with definitive information about the academic demands and requirements of the institution.

The argument against open admissions that is perhaps of most concern to administrators has to do with the cost of developing special programs for underprepared students. It is argued that the limited resources of the selective institution will be squandered and the existing program diluted, if disadvantaged students are admitted. There is little question that additional resources will be required if colleges are to develop programs appropriately geared to such students. However, many highly selective institutions could institute certain practices that might free funds to invest in special programs. For example, is it really necessary for highly motivated students to take the traditional four years of undergraduate study in order to complete the baccalaureate degree? Some institutions are already employing methods of acceleration such as the Advanced Placement Examination and the College Level Examination, but the extent to which such tests are used is a drop in the bucket when compared to their potential use with highly gifted students. In short, many students who now spend four years to obtain the baccalaureate degree could greatly accelerate their progress, and the savings in institutional resources could be devoted to students whose undergraduate education should be protracted.

In summary, I would like to stress my fundamental point that the issues of open admissions and of special programs for disadvantaged students cannot be resolved without a careful consideration of the desired objectives of the higher educational system. Should we strive for outcomes that are egalitarian, elitist, or remedial? What are the long-term implications of these various types of objectives for the society? I have also tried to point out that, whatever our objectives may be, the existing hierarchical arrangement of institutions in American higher education may not be the most effective means of achieving these objectives. There is some hope, I think, that ongoing research on institutional impact will soon provide clues as to how existing institutions can become more effective than they now are. I have raised certain questions about the relevance of current grading practices, primarily because there is evidence that grades may be reflecting, not what students are learning, but merely how they are performing in relation to one another at some point in time. Under these circumstances, we may be well advised to consider replacing our current grading system with some other form of assessment that will reveal changes in the student's performance. As long as the student continues to show evidence of progress and growth, one can make a case for retaining him in the system, regardless of how he performs relative to others. Finally, I have argued for greater flexibility in the matter of credits and certification of students. If institutions can become flexible both in their programs and their requirements, it would be possible to permit the new student to enter at his current level of performance and to progress at his own rate. Educational resources that would be conserved by accelerating the progress of the more able students could be used to support the protracted education of many other students. In this way, we free the high performer from the four-year lockstep of traditional undergraduate education and relieve the disadvantaged student from the burden of unreasonable expectations.

❦ 10 ❧

The Policy of Open Admissions

Amitai Etzioni

The decision to open admission to some of our institutions of higher learning is one which will have pervasive effects on the next generation of Americans, the economy and culture of this society, the quality of its sciences as well as its humanities, the extent to which social justice will be realized, and the overall rate of social change. Unlike scores of other decisions we make that are chiefly important in their own right (such as increasing traffic safety), opening the system of higher education to all Americans wishing to enroll in it is not only important in itself but is of far reaching importance for all parts of the societal system. Despite its significance, open admissions and its effects have been little studied; the program itself is poorly understood, and many of the crucial questions about its far reaching implications have not yet been studied. I shall comment here on nine aspects of the policy of open admissions, moving from issues better known to less known ones.

Open admissions or expanded admissions? The term open admissions is misleading; completely open admission to a higher education system has never existed, and it does not exist now. No system of higher education admits all those who belong to the age cohort or even all who would want to attend. Currently, those colleges in the system of higher education that are open, in effect, are undergoing an expansion of the criteria by which individuals are admitted into the system. While the criteria of academic achievement at a particular level are being waived as the basis for admission, there remain other characteristics of the potential student that are unaffected by the removal of the academic requirements. Specifically, economic forces remain as powerful barriers. Even with the open admissions policy, the individuals entering higher education tend to be those who can afford the educational experience—that is, those individuals who can live without incomes for long periods of time and who are not responsible for the support of their families. Even if an educationally disadvantaged student is admitted to a college or university, he or his family must still meet the costs involved, which cover not only his subsistence but also the financial loss to his family that is incurred by his attendance, since he no longer works. In removing the academic barriers, the economic ones appear as yet another set of factors, which limit attendance in institutions of higher learning and thus limit the scope of the open admissions policy.

If we intend to make open admissions truly open, we must affect the basic life conditions of the educationally disadvantaged, not only by removing tuition and fees, but also by providing economic assistance. Although in some parts of the country experiments have been carried out to test the implications of such support, this is not part of the routine program in New York City, New Jersey, or the Midwest (where the oldest open admission schools are located). Until broad economic aid is provided, students from disadvantaged backgrounds will continue to be disadvantaged, and to enroll less and drop out more frequently than other students.

A minority program? Since a genuinely open program of admissions does not exist, it may be more accurate to describe what has been happening as expanding admissions. We come now to one disturbing feature of this policy: the character of the ensuing programs. The tendency has been to view these programs as programs for blacks or other disadvantaged minority groups. In New York City, admissions officers, deans, faculty members, and others connected with the open admissions programs have consistently described these programs in ethnically or racially particular terms; for example, courses in Swahili and soul music were recommended. However, roughly two-thirds of the students admitted under the new programs are white, many of them from lower middle class and working class families. Thus, the program of expanded admissions must take into account not just the needs of minority groups, but also the needs of the majority of students admitted.

An expanded program of admissions must reach majority students in order to help bring them into the twentieth century educationally and must offer a relevant curriculum that may help prepare them for the twenty-first century. It may seem strange that in the last third of the twentieth century, there are segments of the general population who have not been exposed to the values that are communicated in the course of a liberal arts education. They especially lack the experience of seeing the multifaceted aspects of our society; they have a parochial, limited, and essentially backward view of society. They constitute one potent force retarding the transformation of contemporary society into one that is committed to the principles necessary for just and humane social relations. While the liberal arts experience is no panacea for the closed mind, it does offer each individual involved in it the opportunity to broaden his outlook. The expanding admissions policy is recruiting an ever larger number of students from those groups whose life experiences are not liberating, not forward looking; it enables the colleges and universities to share with these students the kinds of insights societal members must possess if the society is to be innovative and truly committed to the future.

Maintenance of academic standards. A dilemma posed by the policy of expanded admissions is that of maintaining the existing academic standards, while academic achievement has been waived as a criterion of selection. Several leading educators (among them Albert Bowker, while he still was the Chancellor of the City University of New York) have stated that no dilution of academic standards would take place. A similar position has been taken by William F. Birenbaum, president of Staten Island Community College. He has suggested that the quality of education has benefitted rather than suffered from the policy of open admissions. According to him, the literary productions of the new students, while poor in grammar, syntax, vocabulary, and style, are extremely rich in emotive materials and life experiences. I am not suggesting that open admissions has nothing to offer to the quality of traditional academic experience; it may well enrich higher education in the sense of broadening its existential and expressive base. But as Birenbaum himself admits, there has been a lowering of standards, unless one values raw experience as more important than command of the English language.

I find this position untenable on logical grounds. As I see it, the present form of expanding admissions must result in a dilution of academic standards. This does not mean that we should not proceed with the programs or that we must be content with present ways of judging academic success. As Alexander Astin and others have maintained, there are other ways of measuring achievement that may be more accurate than the ones being used now. Also, one of the prime functions of any educational system is to take the underprepared individual and to attempt to help him catch up with others in the system. However, it is unrealistic and, in the long run, harmful to assume that the injection of underprepared students into a student body whose general achievement is high can have no effect on the standards or quality of an academic institution. Whether this dilution will continue or be temporary is a problematic question, which cannot be resolved on the basis of current experience. What is of prime importance is that educators and concerned individuals throughout American society maintain a sense of reality and not close their eyes to the real problems that result from expanded admissions. Maybe some institutions have had to do this in order to appease excessively vigilant legislators. I, as a social scientist concerned with the effects of this program on the societal level, cannot do so.

One realistic solution to this academic dilemma is the modification of the traditional features of our educational institutions. Many students from minority groups fail to do well academically because the institutions attempt to adapt the student to their standards, while ignoring the student's particular background and life experiences. There is no reason why the institutions cannot be made to adapt themselves to their students, at least to some extent. However, there are also wrong ways of adapting. Some would advocate the substitution of ethnic history courses for mathematics courses, which may prove to be overly difficult, and some would replace lectures with "rap sessions." There are those who advocate completely restructuring the educational institution so that the educationally disadvantaged will perform better. Formally, this is one possible solution. If the university is reshaped in the form most congenial to the disadvantaged students, then their lack of preparation will not show. However, such a redefinition of the university in the image of the underprepared student carries serious consequences for the rest of the students and does not seem to be truly responsive to the desires or needs of the disadvantaged students themselves.

Most of these students have demanded an adaption quite different from that demanded by some of the highly vocal advocates of adapting the university to the disadvantaged. As a group, disadvantaged students can be characterized as wanting to be genuinely prepared. The Federal City College in Washington, D.C. is a case in point. There students voted, with their feet, against programs that were set up to be easy, choosing to go into programs that followed traditional academic structure. When they were given the option between a newly devised rap session and a genuine course in history or literature or other academic subjects, the overwhelming majority—more than 80 per cent —chose to take those courses that are academically demanding and that would better prepare them, both as individuals and as professionals, for life and work in American society. The institutions of higher education must respond genuinely to the needs, deficiencies, and talents of the disadvantaged students; they must not offer poor substitutes for the real academic goods to be obtained in these institutions.

Let me assert again that I am not against institutional changes. The educational institutions in many areas need to be much more responsive than they have been. Nor do I believe that every change in the academic curriculum or the method of teaching is—even if it is aimed at the disadvantaged—a dilution of academic standards. Numerous changes may indeed increase the effectiveness and viability of universities. More options should be given to students, and ethnic offerings (such as courses in black studies) are valuable additions to the usual curriculum. Differential certification also gives the whole system much greater elasticity and relevance than it now has. However, the solution to the dilemma of academic quality cannot be found in abolishing academic standards or in providing automatic promotions that pass everyone from grade to grade. The solution does not lie in the "high schoolization" of higher education.

The experiences of schools in Japan and Israel make it possible to predict the reaction of various sectors of our own society if a trend toward dilution of standards were to continue. Industry, government, and other important segments would institute their own certification and selection systems. The certification of the student by the university or college would carry no weight, and students would be awarded a degree without a societal or economic value.[1] Students who had studied for years, would react violently to this waste of their time and effort. If the integrity of our educational institutions is to be maintained and their role of certifying the prepared is to remain, then some standards of quality must exist, and some effort must be made to certify genuine achievement in a field of endeavor. One can remove the colleges' ability to certify, but one cannot remove the society's demand for certification.

Compensatory education. Given that some standards, however revised and adapted, must exist and given the mass entrance of underprepared students into the educational system, some form of compensatory education must be introduced. In reviewing the findings of about 150 different studies of various systems of compensatory education, I have concluded that evaluating the effects and benefits of this approach is an extremely difficult undertaking. No piece of evidence with which I am familiar supports the notion that, by putting disadvantaged students through a few courses, seminars, weekend workshops, or summer sessions, one can remedy the effects of four hundred years of discrimination or of the four or five years that separate disadvantaged students from their academically prepared classmates. One does find in the literature the cases of three students here and eight students there who have benefitted from such programs; however, the main conclusion from the same body of literature points to the need for reaching the disadvantaged student as early in his academic career as possible. If we are to take compensatory education seriously, and that is exactly what I think we should do, we must start early and must continue with the programs on a broad basis during the greater part of the student's academic career. In addition, an effective program of compensatory education must take into account all the relevant characteristics of the individual by combining academic assistance with personal counseling and concern for the student's adjustment within the academic institution. Only if this multiphased approach is utilized, only if the necessary staff to fulfill the special needs of the underprepared students are trained, and only if we are constantly aware of the complexities involved, may we then move in the direction of providing all students with a viable, effective liberal arts education and profes-

[1] This subject is carefully explored in a report prepared by Murray Milner, *Effects of Federal Aid to Higher Education on Social and Educational Inequality.* New York: Center for Policy Research, 1970.

sional training. Only through a rich system of compensatory education can we avoid awarding meaningless degrees or promoting the failure of students who find themselves educationally frustrated, thus compounding the already existing stigma.

While much can be done to insure the success of a college program, one must realize that there are often powerful institutional forces that overload the college by transferring too many burdens onto it. Many of our high schools are often miserably behind as educational institutions; they fail in their function, thus retarding the student and passing onto the university a tremendous burden. Kenneth Clark has pointed out that, if higher education is to become workable, the high schools must be made to assume their share of the responsibility. We should all be more active in demanding that they will do their job. However, the responsibility does not lie completely with the high schools; future high school teachers are at the moment in our colleges. If we are reluctant to challenge our high school teachers to do their jobs, we are even less willing to ask ourselves why we are not preparing better teachers. If the training of high school teachers is effective, if high schools are improved, and if a realistic and responsible program of compensatory education is instituted in colleges, then we may be able to construct an over-all educational system which will expand rapidly with little loss in quality.

The societal matrix. Even if all the above conditions were met, education is not that fantastic a lever; it cannot redo society on its own. Among the various levers available for societal change, education may well be one of the weakest. Our cultural upbringing in American optimism has tended to make us believe that education can remedy everything that went wrong in a variety of social institutions, from law to economics.

There are many factors in the creation of social injustice that exist in a society, and the extent to which any one program of compensation can remedy this is problematic. We must point out that when a child comes from a neighborhood in which there are few success models, in which the father is unemployed or underemployed, in which the housing does not provide a place to study, and in which the child does not receive adequate medical care, the chances for the effectiveness of education are lowered. As long as these societal conditions persist, the system of education will be unable to perform its function. We are led to ask what else has to be changed in the societal fabric. If we do not ask this question, three or four years from now a new

Coleman report on open admissions will tell us that the programs have had no discernible effect of educational enrichment on the students involved. Both educators and social scientists must be constantly aware of these other factors in the social fabric and demand that society improve the noneducational conditions of the underprepared, as more education is provided.

Differential admissions. A program of differential admissions would solve the dilemma posed by the expanded admissions program— that is, the problem of admitting underprepared students into institutions with a high ratio of highly prepared students. Differential admissions calls for a new way of thinking about educational experience; presently the thinking is in terms of a zero-sum conception. That is, one is considered to be either in or out of college, either a freshman or a sophomore. I favor a new way of thinking about the college positional placement. An admission to a college could be fragmented so that a student could be a freshman in English and a sophomore in some other academic field, while not being admitted to mathematics. That is, a student might qualify in some areas and not in others; the completion of one's studies might take longer or shorter than the present four years. If admissions and promotions were broken down into steps by subject area, I believe that the educational system could go a long way toward the desired goal of an effective academic program for students of a variety of achievement levels.

Two or four years? There are two other reforms besides differential admissions in the college system that I would favor. However, I must admit I am not particularly optimistic that these reforms will come about because of the strained financial situation. We must face the fact that for the time being we have a limited amount of public educational resources. We should and must demand that they be rapidly expanded, but the probability of receiving an additional $20 billion next year or of having the resources to double the size of our faculties seems very low. Hence, one must unfortunately order the various innovative programs in some priority ranking. Basically, we must ask: Where should the resources go first? While it is more appealing to say that everything is of the same priority, we must (and in fact we do) make priority decisions. Given the limited amount of resources available, new public funds must be used to support the first two years of higher education, either by supporting junior or community colleges or by supporting the first two years of four-year colleges and universities. Until every young American who wishes can obtain an effective, viable two years of education, we should not use new public resources to fund full four-year educations. It is simply a question of allocative justice. If there are some who have not had a viable two-year program, why give others four-year programs? So, by focusing new resources, talents, and manpower on the first two years, we are in effect producing a system that tends to approximate a standard of social justice. Once everyone is provided with two years of education, then a third year can also be considered. (I am not certain that a fourth year is necessary at all.)

The liberal arts. While on the issue of expanded admissions I suggested some possible solutions to the dilemmas that this policy poses for the higher educational system. However, on the extent to which a balance needs to be established between liberal arts and professional and vocational education, I have been unable to find an answer that satisfies me even in theory. The forces or conditions under which this issue will be resolved are even more unfathomable. Part of me is convinced that liberal arts should be the focus of our educational system, that every young American is entitled to two years of enrichment in liberal arts and the intellectual values conveyed by this particular form of education. The liberal arts experience has an intrinsic value for the disadvantaged student. There are no possible grounds to argue that some members of society are not entitled to spend two years in a curriculum that will enrich the rest of their lives, no matter what they finally choose to do. Liberal arts gives the disadvantaged student a chance to open himself to the central values of our culture, thus enriching and broadening his world view and making this a better society. The other half of me is much more practical. If we will not give disadvantaged students vocational and professional training, then we will be helping to promote a system in which such persons may have more enriched mental lives but will still be hungry and unemployed. Along with the enrichment, one must also consider (if one's recommendations are to be realistic) that certain skills are needed that will enable the individual to earn a livelihood in our highly technological society. One of the best ways of reallocating income is to give previously disadvantaged persons a semiprofessional or professional training.

It is easy to say that both should be done; but the educational system cannot do both, especially in view of the limited resources available. The dilemma is also faced by the individual student who must decide whether he is going to take only thirty points of liberal arts and concentrate in the preprofessional curriculum. The educator has the responsibility of providing meaningful liberal arts courses; he must decide whether a course in English literature will be a "snap," a "Mickey Mouse" offering, or whether it will genuinely convey the great cultural ideals. I have no certain answer to this dilemma; however, I would recommend that any commitment to liberal arts or to an applied curriculum must keep the realities of the present situation in mind. Over emphasis of the one to the exclusion of the other could have disastrous consequences, not only for the individual student, but also for the system as a whole.

A new teacher. I would like to close on a more hopeful note about a phenomenon of which I have first-hand knowledge. Our universities are beginning to produce a new generation, which will take the mission of teaching seriously and which will be willing to rethink the traditional emphasis on research as the prime role of the university professor. This new trend has great significance for the policy of open admissions, since the new entrants require a dedicated faculty, willing to work wholeheartedly with the students. If the policy of expanded admissions is to be a success, a new type of university professor will be needed—one more concerned with his students than with his research. I am not saying that every graduate who comes out of every graduate school has this motivation, but I believe there is a new wave of serious social consciousness, which is finding its expression in this new generation of university teachers. Even in such traditionally conservative and research-oriented institutions as the medical schools, one sees increasing concern for the individual and his problems. This new generation could provide junior and community colleges with individuals who want to teach and who do not want to turn these institutions into minor imitations of Princeton, Yale, Harvard, or Columbia.

To further promote teaching we should deal with the complex problem of rewarding the good university teacher. I learned from personal experience how much emphasis is placed on research as opposed to the teacher in colleges. Recently, I was considered for the presidency of one of the colleges with an open admissions program. In the course of my visit with the institution, I was surprised that, at an institution whose main purpose was teaching, the overwhelming ambition of the faculty (at least of those chairmen and professors I met) was to publish. Undue desire to publish is regrettable even in the major research institutions. The unfortunate result of this ambition is to fill academic periodicals and libraries with marginally useful materials and to overload the computers and other data retrieval systems. In a college whose main institutional emphasis has been on expanded admissions, this insatiable desire is disastrous, since the prime mission of such an institution and others like it must be teaching. There are difficult problems: how to recognize and reward the good university teacher and how to replace the prestige of research with social honor for the good teacher. However, it seems for the first time that the conditions are favorable for resolving these issues. Our universities are producing graduates who are dedicated to teaching as their prime concern. It is time that we meet them, by finding ways to make teaching (and particularly the teaching of the new students who are coming in now) their first and foremost obligation.

❧ 11 ❧

The Case Against the Wisconsin Voucher Plan

Russell I. Thackrey

The report of the Wisconsin Governor's Commission on Education, recommending the adoption of a student voucher system for public financing of higher education, presents a timely opportunity to examine one proposed solution to the problems of financing higher education in the United States. An examination of the report reveals that the voucher system is not a very desirable solution. Instead of meeting present and future needs, the system proposed by the Commission looks backward considerably more than a century, to a point in time when public support of education was limited to those who took a pauper's oath.

Despite its imaginative and forward-looking concept of an open education system the thrust of the report is aimed toward saving money by freezing public support of higher education at approximately the present level. The Commission says bluntly, "The Higher Educational Opportunity Program has been designed by the Commission to have a minimal impact on the state budget." Individual need would, in theory, be the basis for public expenditure for undergraduate education. The philosophy is that of a welfare program. There is nothing wrong with this, as such, but it should never dominate our policies in financing higher education.

Society makes available services that are considered essential by supporting institutions to provide these services. The institutions and services are paid for by public taxation and are available to all. That is the basis of support for public libraries, schools and colleges, parks, fire departments, police departments, and so on. The question of who should pay is determined by the tax laws, not at the point of use. A somewhat similar philosophy is involved in private philanthropy. Donors make possible partial subsidy of the over-all cost of education, and uniform tuition fees are charged. The general societal value of this is recognized through substantial tax concessions.

The welfare principle of aiding individual access to essential commodities and services is also widely exemplified in our society. It includes direct support of low-income families, subsidized food and health-care programs, and special scholarships and other aids in the field of education. In each case this aid is for purposes considered to be so essential to the individual or of such prime importance to society, that special individual assistance is justified. The Wisconsin Governor's Commission declares that higher education primarily benefits the individual, rather than society: "The Commission has concluded that those receiving a higher education are major beneficiaries of it, and should pay the costs of instruction consistent with their ability to do so." By this remarkable fiat, the Commission justifies eliminating direct public support for undergraduate education in Wisconsin's colleges and universities.

Having stated that the individual is the primary beneficiary of higher education, the Commission argues the case for public subsidy on the basis of individual need. This, of course, is wholly inconsistent with the stated premise. If higher education is primarily an individual economic benefit (which it is not), rather than a major benefit to society (which it is), what is the case for public or private support either of individuals or institutions? Inadvertently, no doubt, the Commission plays into the hands of the small but vocal group of economists who argue that higher education should be placed in the same class as automobiles, color television, shares in the stock market, and speculation in real estate. The thesis is that society should take no action in financing higher education except to make long-term credit available to those who cannot pay cash.

The Commission's specific recommendations are inconsistent with its basic philosophy in other ways. No doubt, pragmatism or conscience intervened. While direct instructional support would be abolished, public financing of plant operations and facilities construction would continue. But the report says that the latter would be minimal, as enrollment growth in Wisconsin's public colleges and universities is not expected under the plan. State appropriations would remain at the present level, except for a possible 10 per cent increase in enrollment in the state's institutions as a whole. If inflation persists, as it always has, the state's contribution to higher education would steadily decrease in real terms, as time goes on.

Funds saved by abolishing support of public undergraduate education would be used to finance tuition vouchers. The Commission recommends, again inconsistently with its ability-to-pay thesis, that each college student receive $500 toward tuition. Further aid would be based on family income but limited by a total college attendence requirement. (The suggested amount was set at $1,800—$1,200 being a tuition component and $600, or $66.66 a month, going for board, room, books, supplies, and incidentals.) Of this $1,800 all students would be expected to supply $400. Beyond the $500 grant, the most needy students would get a maximum of $900. Seven hundred dollars of this would be earmarked for tuition aid, leaving $200 as the state's maximum contribution to nontuition costs for the disadvantaged! From these amounts, federal aid would be deducted. The proposed program is wholly supplementary to other programs. If the Federal government increases aid to needy students, Wisconsin will reduce it.

Vouchers could be used in any Wisconsin public or private institution. The $1,200 suggested as the maximum tuition aid component is based on the average undergraduate instructional cost in all Wisconsin public institutions of higher education. Private institutions could continue to raise or lower their own fees. Whether public institutions could charge more—or less—than the set amount is not clear. A member of the Commission assures me they could; however, an illustration in the report as to how the plan would work assumes a charge of $1,200 (maximum amount of the grant) at the University of Wisconsin. The report also says students would pay the same wherever they went, except in private institutions with high tuition charges.

The point is that average undergraduate instructional costs average a wide range of costs which vary according to specific levels and fields of instruction. In Ohio, for example, the average cost for all public institutions runs in a ratio of 1.0 for lower division instruction, 1.5 for upper division, and 2.0 for undergraduate professional curricula. An institution whose student body includes a high proportion of students in upper division, science, and professional curricula might face financial disaster by charging a fee based on average instructional costs of all institutions at all levels. Conversely an institution offering instruction only in low-cost fields, or having a preponderance of lower division students, might achieve sudden affluence with a subsidy based on average instructional costs at all levels in all types of instruction. If Wisconsin's public institutions are in fact permitted to charge tuition on the basis of their own instructional costs, rather than on a statewide average, the fiscal impact on many individual students may be substantially different than that suggested by the Commission. This, however, is not suggested in the report.

Let us consider what would happen if large numbers of students in low-cost programs in public institutions transferred to nonpublic institutions. This would leave the public institutions with a concentration of students in high-cost scientific, professional, and upper division programs. The savings anticipated by the Commission would not exist. Average instructional costs in public institutions and the permissible tuition subsidy available for use elsewhere would both rise sharply, regardless of the actual costs of the programs involved.

A desirable outcome of the tuition-voucher system as seen by the Governor's Commission is the enhancement of diversity and variety in higher education. This, however, is an erroneous notion. It is possible to argue that the voucher proposal would render essentially identical all the state's institutions (whether public or private) at the undergraduate level. All institutions would have the same sources of support; the student would be the direct source, while the state would be the substantial, indirect source of support. Title IV of the Civil Rights Act, which bars discrimination in public institutions on the basis of race, religion, or national origin, defines a public institution as one "operated by the State or a subdivision of a state" or "operated wholly or predominantly from or through the use of governmental funds or property, or derived from a governmental source." The source of funds, not the method of channeling them, is the key.

While it is impossible to predict the nature of future court decisions, one may note that federal courts have consistently held that tuition-voucher plans for elementary and secondary education in the South are unconstitutional, since they are designed to use public funds indirectly for purposes (in other words, segregation) for which they may not be used directly. A few court challenges to actions by private colleges have hinged on the question of whether the influence of the state (through direct and indirect support) was substantial enough to make the institution an arm of the state and subject to constitutional and other legal provisions applicable to public institutions. The idea that using a voucher system to finance higher education will preserve or enhance a dual system of public and private higher education is mistaken. The requirements of the Federal constitution and laws (including the definition in Title IV of the Civil Rights Act) and the responsibility of the state for accountability in the use of its funds will sooner or later place all similarly financed institutions on the same basis of regulation. The idea that institutions can have it both ways by channeling funds through the student rather then directly to the institution is, I believe, an allusion.

Other comments are prompted by the recommendations of the Governor's Commission. Let us explore the question: What is the cost of education, and who pays? The Commission, under its private benefit theory, says students should "pay the cost of instruction consistent with their ability to do so." Students now pay, on the average, nationally, about 75 per cent of the true economic costs of higher education, according to the distinguished economist and president of Claremont Graduate School, Howard Bowen. This amount includes foregone income (estimated to average $2,000), tuition, books, supplies and incidentals, but not board, room, or clothing. Since research is included as part of the cost, the estimate is conservative as applying to undergraduates. Society's subsidy from public and private sources thus runs about 25 per cent. If we really believe that the primary beneficiary of higher education is society rather than the individual, the 25 per cent contribution seems too small rather than too large. Since the loss to society of the potential contributions of economically disadvantaged students is great, we should also provide the additional, individual support necessary to give these students genuine equality of opportunity. The cases for general support and for individual aid rest on the same basic philosophy of primary benefit to society.

Another question raised by the Commission's report is: What are the implications of full cost pricing? The idea that some students, or all students, should pay the full cost of their education has been little analyzed. To mix metaphors, it is a Pandora's box, which few have cared to open or examine. We assume that the uniform tuition fees now determined by trustees involve a substantial subsidy to all students. Most institutions do subsidize their total teaching and research programs from nonfee sources; but costs of particular programs and levels of instruction vary widely. At current tuition levels in some institutions, some students pay well above the cost of their own instruction; through the uniform fee they help subsidize instruction of other students or research. If higher education ever really goes to a full cost basis, students can and will insist that the price charged not exceed the cost of services provided. On a cost basis, uniform undergraduate tuitions will disappear. Some students (particularly in science and engineering and other professional programs) will pay far higher fees than others. Some may pay well under present fees.

Graduate study is another subject touched upon by the Commission report. Under the Commission recommendations, graduate students would receive no subsidy for the first year. They would be subsidized for the second and third year but not the fourth. State subsidies would be supplementary to federal funds. Those who studied outside Wisconsin could borrow and would be forgiven an amount equivalent to the second- and third-year subsidy if they returned to the state for a specified period. Ironically, the Commission stresses the need for reform and improvement of teacher education, but it would deny aid for first-year graduate students, many of whom are teachers seeking master's degrees.

Parochialism is another area of concern. The Commission's plan would undoubtedly increase the tendency toward parochialism in Wisconsin higher education by boosting nonresident charges and establishing quotas. Under the plan, with public support eliminated and private support discouraged, prices would go up. Enrollment of nonresidents would be discouraged, except for the affluent and those with strong ties to particular institutions. Both public and private institutions would tend to be limited to subsidized Wisconsin residents.

There is a marked dichotomy between the Commission's stress on freedom of choice and market determination and its stress on the need for improved planning and coordination in higher education. Graduate students would have freedom of choice of institutions and programs, but the State would subsidize them only in programs of high quality and in fields where need is determined to exist. Undergraduates would have free choice of programs and curricula in public and private institutions, but public institutions, particularly, would be encouraged to specialize in their offerings and develop distinctive identities. In short public institutions would be encouraged not to let consumer choice prevail.

The Commission also suggests that market competition can be relied upon to keep colleges and universities from making undue price increases. Yet with public support eliminated and private support discouraged, all institutions would clearly be dependent on increasing student charges to meet rising costs, to retain outstanding faculty members, and to satisfy employee demands for a rising standard of living. This suggests that prestige institutions will be under special pressure to charge whatever the market will bear. Other institutions may be driven to compete on other grounds, perhaps including lowered admissions standards and academic requirements. In any event, the potential for consumer (student) and faculty-employee conflict of interest is clear.

Under the Commission proposal the State Higher Educational Aids Board would administer funds approximated by the state or allocated by the federal government for student financial assistance, for construction of facilities, or for other purposes in which both public and private institutions may participate. In short, most of the state and federal funds going into higher education in Wisconsin would be administered by this board. The composition of this board is interesting. Twenty members would be named by the governor, five by the proposed State Education Board (appointed by the governor), and five by Wisconsin's private colleges and universities. Public colleges and universities would not be represented. The Commission's attitude toward the University of Wisconsin is ambiguous to say the least. It is described as a "state university of international stature" and a "remarkable resource to be retained and refined by (policies) that cherish the particular characteristics essential to an eminent university." But elsewhere the report states that the "primary mission of the University and the Wisconsin State Universities" are "growing more alike" and that the first order of business for the proposed all-encompassing State Board of Education should be to "consider the merger of the two systems!"

The problems faced by the several states in financing higher education are indeed great, as are the fiscal problems of both public and private institutions of higher education. Recommendations of the Wisconsin Commission by no means represent the worst solutions to these fiscal problems; but the Commission's report is far from being a good or desirable solution. It is not necessary to destroy the public principle in education to save private higher education, nor to make private higher education public. Diversity and variety of support are important to the integrity of higher education. Nor should the obvious societal importance of higher education be denied, merely to justify a reluctance to appropriate public funds. There are better solutions to the problem of financing higher education than the plan put forward in Wisconsin by the Governor's Commission on Higher Education.

❧ *12* ❧

Women in Higher Education

Ruth M. Oltman

When the University of Michigan opened its doors to women in 1870 after fifteen years of painful debate and soul searching, it was regarded as "a very dangerous experiment . . . certain to be ruinous to the young ladies who should avail themselves of it . . . and disastrous to the institution." [1] President Henry Tappan had written a few years earlier that "men will lose as the women advance, we shall have a community of defeminated women and demasculated men. When we attempt to disturb God's order we produce monstrosities." Yet in 1870 coeducation already had been in effect for thirty-three years at Oberlin and for eighteen years at Hillsdale and Antioch Colleges. The original statute that established the University of Michigan in 1837 stated that "it shall be open to all persons who possess the

[1] See Dorothy Gies McGuigan, *A Dangerous Experiment.* Ann Arbor: Center for Continuing Education of Women, 1970, p. i.

129

requisite literary and moral qualifications." [2] Women, apparently, were not regarded for some time as persons in the academic world, any more than they were so regarded under the Fourteenth Amendment for many years thereafter. Meanwhile, however, a few women's colleges had been established, and later separate women's colleges were created such as Radcliffe (1879), Pembroke (1891), and Barnard (1893). Even then it took fifteen years for Radcliffe to become a degree-granting institution, and Harvard diplomas were not given until 1963.

Much has happened in the hundred years since the first woman, Madelon Stockwell, entered Michigan to become, as she described it, "the target of curious stares and pointed fingers." [3] The community was hostile at first. Finding a room to rent was difficult for women students, and initially they were not even welcome at the local churches. The history of women's education and of the women's movements in general has been closely tied to some of the major social causes of the century—slavery, civil rights, welfare, and laws on marriage, divorce, property, abortion, and the like. The renewed emphasis on humanistic values in modern society and the forces that challenge authority and relevance are creating a catalytic climate for the second revolution.

Today, through the legal efforts of organizations such as WEAL, Human Rights for Women, and National Organization for Women (NOW), a major attack has begun against sex discrimination at the institutions of higher education. These academic cases have not had the backing of an Equal Rights Amendment; they have had no protection under the Civil Rights Act of 1964 and little support from prior court testing of the Fourteenth Amendment. The cases had to be prosecuted by the Department of Health, Education, and Welfare, under Executive Order No. 11246 of 1967, which obligates government contractors to comply with the principle of equal pay and with the prohibition against sex discrimination. Forces from many diverse groups are creating pressures that are building up to necessary action. It will take time to change attitudes; but there are very obvious differentials and inequities that need to be remedied at once. Possibly, changes in academic structure can in themselves create new attitudes. However, as long as the organization and policies of higher education support discriminatory practices, attitudes are unlikely to change greatly, for there is no channel through which to route new behavioral approaches.

The growth during the past two years of women's caucuses,

[2] McGuigan, pp. 15–18.
[3] McGuigan, p. 29.

commissions, or committees among professional associations has been phenomenal. One might call it a revolution within. These groups are achieving some amazing results and are taking their parent associations along with them—sometimes with considerable support, both financial and otherwise; sometimes with some reluctance or even hostility; and frequently with differing views among women members themselves. Nonetheless, the growing awareness among professional women of the lack of professional acceptance and recognition in many areas has created some strong mutually supportive groups. The resolutions that are passed at annual conventions offer some evidence that professional women are being heard. The increasing number of women elected or appointed to governing bodies, the research monies granted, and, finally, the reactivation of the committee on the status of women (Committee W within the American Association of University Professors—AAUP—itself) are further evidence that women are being heard.

The fall, 1970 issue of the AAUP Bulletin carries a well-documented paper by Ann Sutherland Harris, of Columbia University, entitled "The Second Sex in Academe." The objective data contained in this paper is a powerful indictment of what higher education has done to women—as undergraduate and graduate students, as faculty, and as administrators. The role that the AAUP committee sees for itself is one of active participation in the formation of association policy and in the developing of data and information. Committee W and Committee A of the AAUP have just released a very strong statement against existing nepotism regulations.

Organization of the different women's groups varies from a separate association related to, but not a part of, a parent group (such as the Association of Women in Psychology), to a commission, subcommittee, or section within the association (such as the Coordinating Committee on Women in the Historical Profession), to caucuses organized independently but attempting to work within the association (such as the Women's Caucus of the American Political Science Association—APSA). At its convention last December, the American Sociological Association (ASA) established an ad hoc committee on the status of women in sociology, as well as an academic section on sex roles in society. The caucus, which previously acted as a lobby of members, now has become a separate organization known as Sociologists for Women in Society.

There is some male support for the work of these groups and, in the case of the Modern Language Association, the committee's research has been financed by the association. In fact, several committee members are men, and their panels at convention have been well attended by both men and women. Many resolutions have been given sound support, but all have not been translated, as yet, into the policy of the association. Newsletters and journal articles are spreading the information and fostering the exchange of ideas and projects. It is interesting to note developments in two organizations that are predominantly female—the American Library Association (ALA) and the American Speech and Hearing Association (ASHA). Seventy-five per cent of the membership of ALA is made up of women; yet of the eighty-five presidents only sixteen (including the present one) have been women, and only 47 per cent of the council are women. When the ASHA caucus was formed at convention last November, there were no women on the executive board, and only one-fourth of the legislative council were women, despite the fact that 74 per cent of the members are women. Remedying the problem of representation, therefore, is one of the major functions of these two groups.

The mathematics and science groups have been the last to organize, perhaps because of the smaller proportion of women in those associations. The Association for Women in Science has had particular concern for the identification and recruitment of women for major appointments in the health sciences. The Association of Women Mathematicians is developing a roster of its women members and promoting new areas of employment. The new caucuses in the American Physical Society and the American Society for Microbiology are still in the process of identifying their problems. Graduate Women in Science, organized in 1921, functions more like the Association of Women Lawyers in relation to the American Association for the Advancement of Science (AAAS), rather than as a caucus. AAAS did have a lively symposium on Women in Science at its 1970 meeting and elected its first woman president for 1971. The American Chemical Society has had a Women's Service Committee since 1927, which has promoted retraining opportunities for women and an annual award to an outstanding woman chemist. Each group representing professional women has attempted first to determine the facts and then to define programs. For example, the APSA Committee on Status of Women in the Professions has been conducting a survey of its members to: determine potential supply and recruitment of women in the profession; develop socio-economic data, comparing men and women; assess effects of competing social roles of women; identify limitations on opportunities as factors affecting performance of women; ascertain self-perception of women as related to their professional role choices and perceptions of those roles; and determine satisfactions and material and psychological rewards. (The APSA committee is also holding hearings on campuses and at professional meetings.) Armed with the facts, these groups can then seek support for: relevant changes in curriculum; active recruitment of women in the profession; equitable distribution of graduate stipends; equitable policies on promotion and salaries; day-care centers on campus; abolition of nepotism rules; new policies on maternity leave and part-time status; and special courses on the role of women in our society. (Many of these courses are being taught during 1970–1971, most for credit, in the departments of history, psychology or sociology.)

One should not overlook the studies of professional women on individual campuses—notably Columbia, the University of Minnesota, the University of California, SUNY at Buffalo, Pittsburgh, and many others. These studies have also made substantial contributions to improvements in the status of women in academe. Female students, too, have joined the force, as the Intercollegiate Association of Women Students (IAWS) has formed its own commission to examine the roles of women students in the academic community. Where the traditional self-government organizations of women have been abolished, women's lib groups have sprung up to further the cause for their special needs as students. It is to the credit of the women working in this movement that they have been quite objective in their approach to the problems of discrimination. They are establishing research committees, developing facts, and then presenting their cases. This is a long way from the general notion of women's libbers as bra burners, men haters, or Lesbians.

In this spirit of inquiry about what was really happening to women on campus, we began our American Association of University Women (AAUW) survey a year ago, tapping areas that would provide a comprehensive picture of women at all levels in academe—students, faculty, administrators, and trustees. Our Committee on Standards in Higher Education recognized that very little data is available to document the role of women in higher education and that if any improvement is to be achieved much information must be obtained. The need for such data is made evident by the great activity within the professional groups and campuses that we have just described; yet surprisingly few government and educational organizations include data analysis by sex in the statistics they publish, thus obscuring facts that would be evident if such differential data were given. One of the recommendations of the President's Task Force on the Status of Women was that "all agencies of the Federal Government that collect economic or social data about persons should collect, tabulate, and publish results by sex as well as race." [4] In January, 1970, the AAUW questionnaire on the role of women on campus was sent to the 750 colleges and universities that hold institutional membership in AAUW. Questions explored participation of women in decision making; personnel policies affecting hiring, promotion, maternity leave and nepotism; special programs designed for mature women students; utilization of women's abilities in major offices and committees, as department heads, principal administrators, and trustees; and the general attitudes of administration regarding women. Of the 750 institutions surveyed, 454, or about two-thirds, returned the questionnaire. Those replying are broadly representative of the nation's colleges, although the AAUW sample has a large percentage of public institutions and schools with enrollments over 10,000 and a small percentage of private and public schools with enrollments under 5,000.

In evaluating the findings, one must keep in mind that women students in the fall of 1969 comprised about 41 per cent of the total student population in four-year colleges and universities. Almost 2,400,-000 women were enrolled in degree-credit programs in 1969–1970. Nationally, women comprise about 18.4 per cent of all faculty (last figures from 1965–1966 NEA report), although the percentage was 25 per cent in 1950 and 28 per cent in 1940. Only 9.4 per cent of women faculty hold the rank of full professor, however, as compared to 24.5 per cent of the men. The percentage of women faculty increases sharply as rank decreases (for example, 34.8 per cent of all women faculty are instructors, as compared to 16.3 per cent for men). Women faculty are particularly absent at some of the prestige institutions and often are employed in nontenured or part-time positions. Moreover, there is a conspicuous lack of women in administrative positions or as trustees in higher education. Results of the survey add to the increasing accumulation of data that women do not have equal status with men in academe. At every level—student body, administration, faculty, and

[4] President's Task Force on Women's Rights and Responsibilities, *A Matter of Simple Justice*. Washington, D.C.: U.S. Government Printing Office, 1970, p. 24.

trustees—women are insufficiently represented or placed in positions with little power in decision making. This is particularly true in the large public institutions. When women are represented, more often than not it is in small colleges or women's colleges where there is a shortage of men or where women have special skills in specific areas that have sex stereotypes, such as dean of home economics, and the like.

Opinion or policy does not always equate with fact. For example, 90 per cent of the schools surveyed state that their promotional policies are the same for men and women faculty; yet in thirty-four schools (all coeducational) there are no women department heads, and the mean number of women department heads in all schools is less than three per institution. Ninety-two per cent of the schools stated that they do include women in top-level administrative positions; yet women administrators are seldom employed in positions involving critical decision making and are not actively recruited at higher levels. In this period of increased student involvement in campus governance, 43 per cent of the schools indicated that women students are represented in proportionately smaller numbers than men on student-staff committees. Forty-six per cent of the responding institutions indicated that during the past year they had had no programs related to the special educational needs of women on campus.

The study was necessarily a very general one, attempting to define the extent of women's involvement on campus and to create an awareness of discrimination where it may exist. Results point to a number of issues that need further in-depth study. (Maternity policies for faculty women is an example.) The data illustrate in a rather dramatic fashion the sex inequities on American campuses and suggest many areas in which the utilization of women could be increased. Our study indicated that immediate action is needed for the development of opportunities for women students in genuine leadership positions and participation in campus governance; the development of good counseling programs and programs specifically designed to meet the unique educational needs of women students; the recruitment and employment of women in administrative positions on campus and participation in higher level policy making; the appointment or election of women trustees, particularly in coeducational schools and the large public institutions; the improvement in recruitment of women for faculty and in promotional policies for faculty women and the examination of institutional policies that may contribute to covert or overt discrimination; the elimination of regulations against nepotism in hiring and adoption of clear policies of employment on the basis of merit and training; the establishment of clear maternity policies for all faculty women; and the development of professional statistics by all government agencies and educational organizations, showing clear designations of data for men and women.

Other areas not covered by the study but which need examination are: the recruitment of women for graduate schools—necessitating a close look at how women are motivated and counseled in their undergraduate years; the incentives offered to women in the form of stipends for graduate study; the quotas or limitations placed on admission of women to graduate schools; the employment of college women after graduation—breadth of opportunity, training, salaries; and the establishment of criteria related to the full participation of women on campus in the accreditation of institutions of higher learning. Jo Freeman's dissenting statement in the University of Chicago report on women at that institution expresses very succinctly the core of the problem:

As long as the University does not concern itself with the variety of life styles prevalent among academic women and the many needs they have that differ from those of men, it will inevitably discriminate against otherwise qualified women. The life styles of the population of intelligent, highly educated women are much more heterogeneous than those of intelligent, highly educated men. The University is geared to serve the needs of the latter and those of the former group who most closely resemble these men or who can organize their lives, however uncomfortably, into the environment created for intelligent, highly educated men. Failure to realize that women as a group have a wider diversity of life styles than men as a group will result in an exclusion of those women whose life styles least resemble those of men.[5]

Once that diversity of life styles is fully recognized and institutional policy and organization adapted accordingly, higher education as a whole will benefit greatly. The needs are clearly established. Courageous leadership is imperative in assisting women in higher education to realize their potential and to make their maximum contribution to the academic community. Then it can no longer be said (as stated in 1959 by Theodore Caplow and Reece McGee in *The Academic Marketplace*) that "Women scholars are not taken seriously and

---

[5] University of Chicago Senate, *Women in the University of Chicago.* Chicago: University of Chicago, 1970, p. 113.

cannot look forward to a normal professional career . . . not because they have low prestige but because they are outside the prestige system entirely." [6] Improvement in the role of women has thus become one of the major aspects of the humanistic concerns of modern society. It is hard to understand why it has taken so long for women to be recognized as individuals, since the problem is so entwined with social developments and political structures. It is particularly difficult to understand why higher education has not taken a position of leadership in this movement or why government action has been needed to force compliance with the law and with the spirit of fairness and dignity of human relationships.

[6] T. Caplow and R. J. McGee, *The Academic Marketplace.* New York: Basic Books, 1950, p. 111.

13

Disadvantaged Students and Survival in College

Fred F. Harcleroad

A useful definition of educationally disadvantaged students was developed by the Florida Community College Inter-institutional Research Council for its 1970 study of compensatory education practices in twenty-four Florida community colleges. This study concerned students "considered to be educationally disadvantaged because of either one or a combination of the following conditions: low ability, low achievement, academic under-preparation, psycho-social maladjustment, cultural or linguistic isolation, poverty, neglect, or delinquency." [1] Office of Education, in its division of Student Special

[1] See: M. I. Schafer, E. Boddy, and W. T. Bridges, Jr. *Implementing the Open Door: Compensatory Education in Florida's Community Colleges, Phase I: Questionnaire Analyses.* Florida Community Junior College, Inter-institutional Research Council, 1970.

138

Services, identifies disadvantaged students according to five general factors: low income, migrant background, recipient of welfare or vocational rehabilitation benefits, resident of innercity public housing or model cities programs, and black students. These specific criteria were employed at the University of South Florida in developing a special plan for counseling and assisting culturally disadvantaged students. Other writings have often referred to disadvantaged students as students from ethnic minorities with limited cultural and environmental backgrounds. Much of the literature describing efforts to assist disadvantaged students basically describes assistance to black, and occasionally Chicano, American Indian, or Puerto Rican students.

Defining the term survival also poses a problem. The Carnegie Commission's 1971 report, "Less Time, More Options," presents a generalized model of college student success and attrition (it does not recognize AA degrees or vocational/technical education certificates) and reports that 53 per cent of entering college students will survive to a bachelor's degree. This is an extremely limited model of educational survival. As the concept is used in this paper, it includes other forms of success, such as achieving an associates of arts degree or a vocational certificate or completing the freshman year in any type of higher education institution. A number of specific services are critical to increasing the incidence of survival in all forms of higher education. Recent research studies conducted by the American College Testing Program indicate that almost any student wishing to enter higher education can be successful if guided to an appropriate institution. Julian Stanley urges that each student attend a college geared to his level of academic competence. He argues that not many colleges in the United States are highly selective; there exist at least 2,000 that can accommodate most levels of developed ability and achievement.[2] A study by Donald Hoyt provides information on almost 1,000 nonprofit collegiate institutions and can be extremely helpful to students who wish to learn the differences in academic demands made by various colleges.[3] Clearly, analysis of institutional demands is a first step in improving survival rates of educationally disadvantaged students. For example, in 1970 the College Career's Fund of Westchester, New York, reported that they try to fit the college to the person, not the other way around. Prospective students were found by combing lists of high

[2] J. C. Stanley, "Predicting College Success of the Educationally Disadvantaged," *Science*, 1971, *171*, 640–647.

[3] Donald P. Hoyt, "Forecasting Academic Success in Specific Colleges," Research Report No. 27. Iowa City, Iowa: American College Testing Program, August, 1968.

school dropouts, checking with local police departments for chronic troublemakers, and recruiting students standing on street corners in the slums of southern Westchester. Volunteers tutored some of these students in a special summer school program. Counselors helped students select appropriate campuses and later made trips to the campuses to visit their students. In three years the program has sent 123 students to more than fifty colleges. Eighty per cent of the students have remained in school or graduated, and during the 1969–1970 school year the retention rate was 91 per cent. Certainly, this is survival far beyond the normal expectation. The tutorial and followup programs are extremely important in the success of this private effort, but the initial selection of colleges that seem to be appropriate for the students is the first and most important step.

In the next decade, it is exceedingly important to work toward results of this type. The current reports of the U.S. Census Bureau have included a number of facts that bear on this problem. For example, during the last five years of the 1960s, the number of black students enrolled in colleges more than doubled. In 1960, 63.7 per cent of the white students in high school graduated from high school; and by 1970, 58 per cent of the Negroes and other minorities had graduated from high school. However, in 1970 a clear disparity could be seen between whites and blacks finishing college in the twenty-five to twenty-nine year old age group. In this group only 10 per cent of black students and other minorities had completed college as compared with 17.3 per cent of the white group. Thus, although the number of black and other minority students entering college increased during the sixties, the percentage graduating (surviving) was appreciably lowered.

The Carnegie Commission's special report of December, 1968, indicated that "the proportion of Negroes in the American college population is less than half of the proportion of Negroes in the population as a whole, and half the Negroes in college attend predominantly Negro colleges." [4] Allan Cartter reported in his perceptive studies of future minority group enrollments that the total freshmen enrollment entering colleges and universities in the fall of 1970 would have been increased only between 50,000 and 75,000 if the percentage of non-

[4] Carnegie Commission on Higher Education, "Quality and Equality: New Levels of Federal Responsibility for Higher Education," a special report and recommendations by the Commission. New York: McGraw-Hill, 1968. Readers may also wish to see the supplement to this report, which appeared in 1970.

white and white high school graduates had been essentially equal.[5] Cartter cites further the estimates of the effect of open admissions on the City University of New York for September, 1970, in which only 7,500 additional students entered the freshman class, with less than one-third of them nonwhite. Nevertheless, large numbers of black and other minority students will enter our colleges and universities in the coming years, and extensive efforts will be necessary in order to make this a challenging and worthwhile experience.

Disadvantaged students of many differing ages are also taking advantage of the open-door opportunities in colleges and universities, particularly in community colleges. Essex Community College in Newark, New Jersey, is a good example. Only 38 per cent of the applicants for admission to the first freshman class were young and just out of high school. The remaining 62 per cent represented all age groups within the college area, and approximately 50 per cent of the students were enrolled on a part-time basis. Many of these were working full time and had enrolled in order to increase their skills or to move into a new field of occupational endeavor.

Hundreds of colleges and universities have made conscious efforts to recruit educationally disadvantaged students from minority groups. Many of these institutions would be considered academically the most difficult of any in the United States. For example, the University of California at San Diego has established its third college, and less than half of its first class of 130 students failed to meet the standard criteria for admission to the university. In addition about thirty freshmen have been selected and admitted at both Revelle College and Muir College without meeting the normal criteria for admission. The large majority of the students are from disadvantaged neighborhoods and most of them are from minority groups. The third college is described as one designed to provide a good, fitting academic environment for youngsters from minority schools and neighborhoods and to create environments that these students can relate to. Another objective is to encourage more minority group youngsters to go into the professions such as medicine and law.

The University of Iowa has specifically recruited students in its educational opportunity program (EOP) and finds that on normal measures of academic potential the typical EOP student needs spe-

---

[5] A. M. Cartter, "Faculty Manpower Planning." In G. K. Smith (Ed.), *The Troubled Campus: Current Issues in Higher Education 1970.* San Francisco: Jossey-Bass, 1970.

cialized assistance. The university provides special help through tutorial and counseling and guidance efforts, plus special financial assistance. Thomas Sowell, a black professor at the University of California at Los Angeles, has indicated that some colleges and universities are bending over backwards to select black or minority group students, who are authentic ghetto types. In some cases black students who are competent or equipped to be successful are not admitted, even though they often still require special help in order to make up for gaps in their education.

Colleges and universities are making special efforts to overcome the deficiencies of many past generations. In doing so, they must realize the special problems that exist for students moving from culturally deprived environments into the seemingly hostile and foreign culture of the college or university. Harry Edwards has described in some detail the April, 1969, confrontation at Cornell, and he concludes that white faculty members and students alike were unable to understand the emotions and feelings of the small black group of students. In his analysis, Edwards states that "The strange inability to understand ones fellowman reflects a peculiar form of racism, attributing as it does to blacks a different kind of humanity from that of whites. As long as these attitudes persist, communication between black and white at the university will remain difficult." [6] Similarly, Van Allen of the Southern Regional Education Board, speaking at a workshop for counselors held at Jackson State College in March of 1970, said that the manner in which the law has been applied to blacks has had its influence in shaping the black culture. Because for so long any white person could and did to some extent take the law into his own hands in regard to blacks, children of black families living in our urban ghettos learn very early to be evasive and protective of the members of the family, and they carry this feeling and behavior pattern into college. Van Allen stresses the difference between white and black cultures, and he believes that unless we accept the concept of two cultures, we will continue to make the mistake of treating two patients having different symptoms with the same medicine. He further believes that the difference between successful and unsuccessful counseling will come from understanding the motivations of the students. White counselors will have to make a real effort to "think black." This simply means that the white counselor should familiarize himself with the

---

[6] Harry Edwards, *Black Students*. New York: The Free Press, 1970, p. 183.

black students and plan activities and make decisions on the basis of understanding the motivations that are operable in the black experience.

Frank Cervantes in discussing the problems of Chicano students as they go on to college education indicates that, "the Anglo-American school system and the Chicano culture clash head-on and the loser is the Chicano student and his society." [7] Southwestern colleges have less than a 2 per cent representation of Chicanos in their student enrollments, despite the fact that the college age population in the area is almost 20 per cent Chicano. San Diego State College has increased the number of Chicano students to 2 per cent during the years from 1968 to 1970, but the percentage of Chicano students in San Diego County is from 12 to 14 per cent. According to Cervantes, one of the important reasons for part of this problem is "the family-cultural background. In Chicano society, the family is usually placed before the individual. Therefore, the individual is expected to stop being a financial burden of the family as soon as possible and begin helping to support the family." Due to this pressure, financial aid is absolutely critical to the Chicano student.

Even among the academically talented students in minority groups, there are definite problems in making a move from high school to college. Alfred E. McWilliams, Jr., indicated in his recently completed followup study of academically talented black high school students in Denver, Colorado, that "educational counseling for black students is very poor and that high school counselors of black students must become interested in their students and more aware of their needs and aspirations." [8] McWilliams primarily studied black students in the top 10 per cent of their graduating class, but he indicated that the educational counseling for the average and marginal black high school student was exceedingly poor or even nonexistent. McWilliams recommended that counselors create an interest and a desire for their black students to go on to college. Moreover, counselors are not going to succeed in this goal by waiting in an office for the students to come in and seek advice; the counselor must go to the students.

Gordon D. Morgan's very complete study entitled "The Ghetto College Student" also emphasizes the problem of two cultures. Accord-

---

[7] Frank D. Cervantes, "Chicanos and the Economic Problem of a College Education," in *Financing Equal Opportunity in Higher Education.* New York: College Entrance Examination Board, 1970, pp. 22–23.

[8] Alfred E. McWilliams, Jr., *A Follow-up Study of Academically Talented Black High School Students.* University of Northern Colorado, 1970.

ing to Morgan, the black student attending college "is required to learn in a new and different culture, one which has little relevance for him, while the white student is learning in a familiar culture, which has a relevance he accepts and understands. While the white student is only extending his knowledge, the black ghetto student must learn the new culture, keep up in it, and be evaluated by it at the same time that he operates from a new base." [9] Morgan further indicates that there are two basically different approaches being taken by college and universities in assisting students to meet these problems. He calls the first the remedial approach, and the second, the cultural difference approach. In the latter approach, black culture and urban problems are often stressed, and field experience in the community is often part of the courses. The students are taught by persons intimately acquainted with the problems of the culturally different group and with the use of methods based on language technology and experiences close to the students.

A study of over 4,000 colleges and universities by Edwin Gordon attempts to go even further in determining collegiate compensatory programs for disadvantaged youth. Initial findings indicate that a majority of the institutions (universities, four-year colleges, junior colleges, and nursing schools) do not have any special programs. Over 50 per cent of the universities responding do have a special program for the disadvantaged already in operation, while only about 30 per cent of the four-year colleges and junior colleges report such special programs. Special programs for black students, and particularly those students from large urban ghettos, must place heavy emphasis on language training and improvement of communicative skills. However, valuable compensatory programs include activities such as tutorial programs; special counseling on an individual or group basis; special financial aid programs, including workstudy, loans, and scholarship grants; special field trips; preparatory summer courses; special medical services; and special housing and classroom facilities. The most important characteristic of any of these programs is the relationship between the faculty and the students. Understanding the cultural shock incurred when moving into the college is a basic necessity for a successful program.

A number of specific programs have contributed greatly to the

---

[9] Gordon D. Morgan, *The Ghetto College Student: A Descriptive Essay on College Youth from the Inner City.* Iowa City: The American College Testing Program, 1970.

survival of black and other minority group students in college programs. The Upward Bound program, in particular, has had many successes. In 1970, Upward Bound was reported to have sent 72 per cent of its enrollees on to college; about 65 per cent of the enrollees remained in school—a slightly higher average than the national average for the retention of students. This program recruits sophomores and juniors in high school and carries them through the summer prior to their entry into college. The program tries to provide sustained support and encouragement to all of the participants to help them maintain their college aspirations and to motivate them to go on to higher education. It develops basic skills necessary for survival in college through intensive summer and after school tutorial programs, enrichment activities, and meetings between secondary teachers and college faculties. A special relationship is established between the enrollee and the specific college the student may attend. The personalized relationships built up through this program, plus the remedial skills that are provided, have definitely assisted in making this precollege program highly successful.

There are many differing special programs at the college level. As stated previously, a recent study of the Inter-Institutional Research Council of The Florida Community Junior Colleges has provided data on the extensive compensatory education practices in twenty-four of these colleges. Fourteen of the twenty-four institutions had less than 10 per cent of their enrollment from disadvantaged student groups; six institutions had 10 to 20 per cent of their students from disadvantaged groups; and four institutions had more than 25 per cent of its students classified as disadvantaged. The Afro-American student group composed 8.5 per cent of the total enrollment, and over one-half of these students were classified as disadvantaged. The Spanish-American group composed 6.8 per cent of the total enrollment, and 18 per cent of these students were disadvantaged. Of the remainder, almost all were white, 9.5 per cent of which were classified as disadvantaged. In classification by community background, 12 per cent of the urban students were considered disadvantaged; 25 per cent of the rural students were so classified, while only 8.7 per cent of the suburban students were disadvantaged. Of the total group of disadvantaged students, 58.3 per cent were white; 31.3 per cent were blacks; and Spanish-American or Oriental-American students made up the rest. Teachers of the disadvantaged students were predominantly white with some specialized training of a workshop type and possibly college course work or experience with in-service training programs at the college itself. Sizes of special classes averaged around twenty-two students. A wide variety of instructional methods were used by individualized, tutorial instruction, and individualized programmed instructions were in use in most of the institutions. The success of this series of programs is still being evaluated, and the results should be known in the near future.

The California State Colleges recently reported a fairly extensive program involving 3,150 students in the Educational Opportunity Programs. These students were from minority and impoverished groups and were admitted to college despite low grades if they indicated some aptitude for college study. The percentage of students who were still in college after two years was 60.1. Over one-half of those who dropped out had left in good academic standing and were eligible for return. Forty-eight per cent of the students in the program were black; 36 per cent were Mexican-American; 13 per cent were Caucasian; and 3 per cent were listed as Asian-Americans. High survival rates of this type mean that such programs can be extremely successful in helping educationally disadvantaged and impoverished students.

At Stanford University, a select group of twenty-one black students were admitted in the fall of 1965 as a result of what is described as an intensive program to increase minority enrollment. The students' scores on entrance exams were low, and some had been dropouts or poor disciplinary risks; but a faculty group determined that the group had good university potential. By August, 1970, all but two of the twenty-one had graduated. Special attention, of course, was given to selecting students with drive and motivation, and special assistance was given in making it possible for them to succeed. Survival rates for specialized universities of this type, however, further indicate the importance of choosing an appropriate institution.

The Project Success Program of Northeastern Illinois State College was started in 1968 with research and financial assistance from the American College Testing Program. It provides another striking example of the value of special educational assistance programs for high risk students. In this program a pilot group of thirty, normally unadmissable students were admitted in the fall of 1968. Of the thirty admitted, twenty-seven attended the fall, 1968, trimester, and twenty-four had grade point averages of C or above. Three of the remaining four had grade point averages between 2.6 and 2.9 (barely below the C average). Twenty students started the third trimester in the fall of 1969, and by March of 1971, sixteen were still in college. Fourteen of these students were in Northeastern Illinois State College. In other words, approximately 60 per cent of the original entering group was still in college making progress toward degrees, when under normal circumstances none of the students would have been admitted to college. The program was so successful that a second comparable group of thirty students was enrolled in the fall of 1969; twenty-five of these students entered the second trimester with satisfactory grades. A third group of ninety-seven students was admitted in the fall of 1970 with even lower qualifications than the preceding group. At the end of the 1970–1971 fall trimester, three students had averages above 4.0; thirty-one students had grade point averages between 3.0 and 3.9; and forty-seven were on probation with averages between 2.0 and 2.9. Of the eleven students who had low averages, some had remained in college because they felt they were just getting use to the collegiate situation.

What accounts for this high survival rate? The students were provided with preadmission counseling, financial aid programs, and registration programming for twelve and thirteen credit-hour schedules of regular classes. Faculty members in the classes did not know the students belonged to this specially admitted group. These are standard services available to every student. Northeastern Illinois provided academic, vocational, and personal counseling by a coordinator who was a black, male social worker experienced both personally and vocationally in intercity life. In addition, Northeastern Illinois provided individualized tutoring beyond the regular departmental services in such areas as reading, math, and composition; this type of tutoring was provided by minority group members who had been successful in achieving advanced status at the college. Specialized facilities in the campus union also provided for the group as a whole a general workroom and gameroom space where the students could be tutored, study, or could share experiences. More importantly, this area served as a retreat from the foreign community of the college itself. In addition, the coordinator and an additional black counselor provided opportunities for the students to visit other colleges and to gather as a group for mutual consideration of their college experiences.

The survival rate for high risk students at Northeastern Illinois State College is not quite as high as the phenomenal survival rate at Stanford University but closely approximates the survival rate in the California State Colleges. The additional cost of the specialized programs in 1968–1969 was less than three hundred dollars per student beyond the regular basic budget of the college. This is a very modest amount to spend for the tremendous increase in the potential benefit to the student and society. Undoubtedly, Stanford's costs per student were much higher than the costs at Northeastern Illinois, but the gain in human potential and in individual human welfare from this expenditure is almost incalculable. Personal discussions with the people involved in these projects indicate that coordination and direction of such programs need to be in the hands of understanding, concerned members of the minority groups involved. It helps immeasurably for the involved students to work with coordinators, counselors, and tutors who can provide differing role models from a variety of backgrounds. Disadvantaged students can clearly survive at college in far greater numbers than has generally been considered possible in the past. Experience at a wide variety of institutions provides enough methods and results to encourage every institution to provide specialized personnel and specialized counseling services in establishing programs for students with limited backgrounds.

PART FOUR:

Paradoxes in Decision-Making

The future of the new teaching and the new learning is intimately tied to decisions being made at this very moment—decisions taken not only by professors and students but by everyone who shares in the governance of colleges and universities. To many observers (including a large number of faculty members), campus power games appear senseless—indeed, absurd. But anyone who has participated in them knows how deadly serious they are. No one, inside or outside the academic world, can afford to make light of them. The essays of Part Four analyze and clarify the nature and processes of academic decision-making.

❧ 14 ❧

Governing Boards:
A Redefinition

Morton A. Rauh

Although the legal power of trustees has not changed, the application of this power has been drastically altered. The complexities of the contemporary university have created a whole new set of educational managers, and changes in attitudes about governance have created new seats of power in faculty and students. We may wonder then what is left to the trustees but to play meaningless games according to rules barely understood by anyone. It is the purpose of this paper to answer that question. I shall confine my discussion to four basic responsibilities: selecting the president and evaluating his work, planning and maintaining institutional purpose, preserving the assets, and acting as the final court in the resolution of issues.

The enabling legislation or corporate charters of colleges and universities are specific in charging governing boards with the respon-

151

sibility of naming the chief executive officer. Although the manner in which this function is discharged varies widely, the responsibility for the final choice remains with the board. What happens after the selection of the president is what most needs redefinition in terms of the trustee role. I argue that the responsibility that follows selection is evaluation.

In my recent book [1] I joined the throng of writers who recite the apocryphal story of the wise trustee who says, "The first item on the agenda of every board meeting should be 'Shall we fire the president?' " The story should be removed for, unfortunately, it creates the totally false impression that the alternate to hiring is firing and that the function of evaluation is merely to decide when the incumbent must be removed from his post. Actually, evaluation should be a continuous process based on the assumption that an employee—at whatever level of responsibility—is a human being and, as such, will be endowed with a full array of strengths and weaknesses. A college president is assuredly no exception.

Boards tend to shy away from performing this kind of evaluation lest it lead to disenchantment and ultimately to the recruitment of a new president—a prospect that is viewed with horror. To avoid this prospect, boards are likely to back the president with uncritical fervor or, far worse, to restrict their reaction to petulant criticism. Neither approach constitutes effective evaluation, and neither serves the president or the institution.

The proposition I make, therefore, is that the essential extension —or redefinition, if you will—of the responsibility for selecting a president is the evaluation of his performance. Ideally, this function should be continuous; that is, the operation of the board should provide each trustee with a firsthand, valid impression of the president's strengths and weaknesses. A less desirable alternative than this is a formal evaluation process, which takes place at stated intervals. Significantly, Kingman Brewster's insistence on such a process is so uncommon that it has received special note in most of the news media. The assumption I make is that informed, sensitive, and constructive criticism assists the president in recognizing his weaknesses and in improving his performance. An important by-product of the evaluation procedure is that the constituents of the university are assured that the board is monitoring the president. The attitude of evaluation, rather than the process,

[1] M. A. Rauh, *The Trusteeship of Colleges and Universities.* New York: McGraw-Hill, 1969.

is what counts. It tells everyone that there is some middle ground between the act of hiring and firing.

The second responsibility of trustees is to see that the purpose of the institution is maintained. This is easier said than done. The stated purpose in the instrument of trust is usually so vague that it offers little guidance to those who act as trustees. If we assume that the purposes and forms of education are and should be responsive to contemporary needs, then a responsibility of the trustees is to see to it that evolutionary changes in education take place according to some sensible plan. In this role, trustees have not earned very good grades. Let me give some examples.

For one, trustees have failed to take the initiative in adapting the purposes of their universities to the needs of underprivileged individuals. Second, trustees have failed to consider the need for providing more options for education beyond high school. Whether they will now respond to the findings of the Carnegie Commission in this regard remains to be seen. In addition, trustees have steadfastly fought to preserve parietal rules that are totally out of gear with the mores of young people today. And finally, trustees have shown little sympathy or support for the administrator who is obliged to deal with campus violence and disruption, without any prior experience. In summary, I suggest that trustees must stop looking backward to the original purpose of the institution. Instead they must look forward in order to meet the responsibility of maintaining a relation between the purpose of their own institution and the needs of society in general and of their clientele in particular.

A third basic responsibility of trustees is to assure the preservation of the assets of their institution. In its broadest form this responsibility states that the special quality of educational institutions—as differentiated from foundations or business corporations—is the presumption of perpetuity. Boards wholeheartedly assume this responsibility in terms of endowment investments and the physical properties. But the very willingness to define assets in the restrictive sense of physical assets suggests a redefinition of this role.

Trustees must begin to think about human assets, about the quality of education, and about the relevance of the educational program to the university's clientele. These aspects of the university assets are at least as potent in assuring perpetuity as a portfolio of stocks or a new dormitory. An investment counsel retained by the university should be able to do a better job of portfolio management than a trustee investment committee operating in its spare time. Moreover, the university should have on its staff personnel fully qualified to deal with problems of plant management. The university needs people who will raise questions such as whether the new dormitory should be built at all in the face of student demand for living arrangements that are less artificial and more to their personal choice than dormitory living. In short, the university needs trustees who will be concerned with the preservation of human assets, who will ask questions about personnel policies, evaluation procedures, and the competence of the middle management.

In addition, trustees are needed who will question the catalogue verbage that says, "You name it; we've got it." Persons are needed who will assist the college in realistically determining the nature of its clientele and how its clientele can best be served. Perhaps most important, the trustees must recognize that the job of preservation is not all long range. There are instant pressures of public opinion and political expediency against which the board should erect solid barriers. We could use some of the protective postures that boards displayed in 1954 when Senator Joseph McCarthy and his crew set out to dismantle the hard-won structure of academic freedom.

The fourth basic responsibility of the board of trustees is to act as the final court in the resolution of issues. This is a function more commonly abused than used. It is proper that this role be infrequent, for when an issue escalates to the board level normal processes have usually failed. Unfortunately, however, too many boards assert their right of ultimate authority in situations where the process has not broken down. When the regents of the University of California elect to nullify one out of thousands of personnel decisions, they are, in my opinion, abusing or at least misusing their legal prerogatives. The reappointment of Angela Davis, for example, should not have been an issue for trustees. One must assume that in the vast array of personnel decisions including renewals, terminations, promotions, and salary determinations, all sorts of questionable judgments had been made. For the board to exercise its power to negate only one of these judgments serves only to weaken its responsibility as the seat of ultimate judicial power.

In general, the typical board is poorly equipped to adjudicate specific issues. Trustees are usually too remote from the university community to have a reliable sense of what disputes are all about.

What then is needed for a redefinition of this responsibility of acting as a court of last resort? I would suggest several components be added to this redefined role. First, there must be firm resistance to accepting the position of referee in campus disputes. Second, if it is impossible to avoid the judicial role, the board must make sure that it does not pre-judge the case from the administrative point of view. Third, the board must have enough insight into the university community that it under-stands the background against which controversy is set. Finally, and most important, the constant attention of the board should be directed to those policies and decisions that minimize the possibility of unre-solved issues.

Let us now ask what these redefinitions of the trustee role say about the composition of the board. First of all, these roles suggest that trustees shall act as trustees and not as managers. The trustee's function is to inquire, to support, to criticize, and to evaluate. If we can accept this concept of the role, then we can rid ourselves of one of the pre-occupations that has dictated the composition of our boards. In other words, we can do away with the notion that trustees must bring to the institution business expertise otherwise lacking on its staff. If we can also accept the fact that trustees simply do not give very much money to their colleges (68 per cent gave less than two thousand dollars per year) and that they spend little time getting other people to do so (78 per cent spent twenty hours or less per year in fund raising), then we will have opened the door to a whole new array of trustee candidates.

New trustee candidates will be from fields other than business or law. They will be younger, and they will not be overwhelmed by other civic demands. New candidates may be women or members of minority groups. We are at a point in time when boards are making ill-conceived responses to the criticism directed against them. When it is said that trustees are too business-oriented, the suggestion is made to add a member of the faculty. When it is charged that trustees are too old, it is suggested that a student be added. This is not the time to hit the panic button. It is the time to seek trustees from the wider pool of talents, which has scarcely been tapped.

❦ 15 ❦

Creative Tension
and Home Rule

W. Joseph Dehner, Jr.

T he university is today, as Clark Kerr has said, like an amoeba
in an unfriendly environment. Students, faculty, administrators, trustees, alumni, government officials, and the general public tug and pull
at the university, generating tensions that seem to threaten the very life
of higher education in America. But tensions imply opportunity as well
as danger, interest and concern as well as disgruntlement. It is precisely
because of the university's triumph that so many groups and individuals
demand different things of it. Our focus in this essay must be on how
tensions can operate creatively rather than destructively, how a university can be governed so as to further the goals of higher learning.
The basic question is: Who should decide who makes which decisions
for the overall governance of the university? This question has two
aspects: how those with formal authority delegate decision-making
power, and how university home rule can be achieved and organized.

Funding sources are going to decide the shape of higher education and the general uses to which funds are put. Since government outlays for higher education are a matter of priority among competing needs, government will and should decide the general extent of its funding among fields of knowledge and research, public and private universities, undergraduate education and graduate studies. Beyond general allocations and specific research assignments, however, government should let universities decide how best to put funds to specified uses. A revenue-sharing plan applied to higher education might be ideal. More government funds should be channeled through institutional grants rather than narrowly drawn project grants. Government officials do not and cannot know enough to develop detailed plans for funding uses. Moreover, higher education should not be a production line operation but a handicraft enterprise with considerable flexibility and local control.

An exception to the university control of government funds should be noted. When government specifies a need for research and knowledge that only the university can provide, it should make sure that universities are prepared to cope with that need. For example, in the area of environmental control, hard thinking, new strategies, and training are essential. Before granting funds for environmental studies or establishing new universities or institutes, the government should require changes in university departmental structures, if it is clear that a proper attack on ecological problems can only be mounted through a coordinated effort of faculty and students from various disciplines brought under a single roof. The institute approach is essential to a worthwhile response of the university to the environmental crisis; and, if universities do not so shape themselves, they should receive little or no funding for work in this area. Here, government must force changes in traditional notions of faculty organization to achieve results that society requires for its very survival. This principle applies equally to urban problems.

Beyond this important exception, funding sources should not decide who makes university decisions. Granting such powers to the funding sources would severely damage the university's morale and capacity to respond to the task of education and research. Some private sources of money can likewise do a distinct disservice to the universities and the nation by withholding funds because of a disagreement with current university policies.

Boards of trustees and regents are formally constituted to decide questions of university governance. Trustees and regents are legally responsible for the university's operation and must insure that the law and essential purposes of the university are not violated. Their role in university governance should not go beyond guarding against violations of the law, the essential purposes of the university, and the procedures for university home rule. Governing boards should let university residents govern themselves. This means that boards should not decide who makes what decisions for the overall governance of the university, except to guarantee that administrators, faculty, students, and staff are all assured a role in the decision-making process and that particular decisions are made by those who are most directly concerned and most knowledgeable. Governing boards should ensure that procedures developed by resident community groups are followed and should not overrule decisions unless the procedures, central purposes, or laws of the university are violated. Although governing boards have a primary role in gathering financial, moral, and political support for higher education, they should not set up a specific system of governance. Trustees are not close enough to the day-to-day life of the institution; they do not represent a cross-section of either the American public or the university community; and thus they could not satisfactorily tell university residents how to govern themselves.

All members of the university community should decide who makes what decisions for the overall governance of the university. Although alumni and governing boards are part of the university community, they are generally not residents of that community. Faculty, students, and a president as leader should have the overwhelming influence in questions of university governance, with lesser degrees of impact accorded to staff, alumni, and the public. A university should enjoy home rule because only home rule can turn tension to creativity and transform conflict into progress.

The procedures that a university uses to decide how to govern itself are partly a matter of history. Many universities have gone through the initial stages of student-faculty home rule and have developed a variety of procedural systems. All thorough reforms toward control by faculty and students occurred through a review by a committee of administrators, faculty, and students whose recommendations were made unanimously. The success of such efforts emphasize the validity of the assertion that those persons who are most directly concerned and who know most about particular decisions should make those decisions. This is a principle of democratic community control of universities, but it does not imply the one-man-one-vote idea that administrators and faculty members rightly find abhorrent. The principle also does not stand for participatory democracy in the sense that anyone making sufficient noise should be pacified with a decision-making role. It simply means that those who are directly affected or who have positive contributions to make should have the primary responsibilities for making decisions. Precisely how control should be allocated among students, faculty, administration, alumni, and staff is important, but a matter of secondary importance. This sense of democracy means that the influence of various groups will be relative to the decision being made. Students, for example, should have the primary responsibility for setting student social rules. Faculty should have the primary role in setting curricular policies. General university decisions (such as university relations with the military or campus demonstration policy) should be made by all members of the university community, with faculty and student sharing equal amounts of responsibility.

The principle of democratic community control envisions a heightened sense of community on campus; it asserts the common goals of university members, while not ignoring the diversity of interests among administrators, students, and faculty. The principle does have the connotations of a happy family, where the president and faculty discipline or control students who do not know better. Rather, the aim is toward a sense of community participation among students, faculty, and administrators as equal partners in deciding the future of the university. In this sense, the principle of democratic control approaches the ideal of the university as a community of scholars rather than a battlefield of the generations.

Behind this idea of democratic community control is an educational philosophy that focuses on the students' interests and needs. In the early days of higher education, decision making by a strong college president and small faculty (with significant controls exercised by governing boards) upheld an educational philosophy that sought to equip upperclass children for upperclass, cultured lives. The recent organization of decision making through strong faculties in independently minded departments is based upon the meritocratic aims of twentieth century education and the specialization of knowledge forced upon us by the scientific revolution. The principle of university decision making outlined here embodies a belief that students should decide their own educations. Higher education today is preparation for an unknown future not for predefined positions that are amenable to specialized channels of training. Students, as the future public, must be able to exert strong pressures on the content and form of their education. Furthermore, students as the future body politic must be able to exert significant controls over the university's educational make-up, to ensure that universities respond to the needs of society. The greatest failing of the faculty is not recognizing that the university has public responsibilities. Students can be the motivating force in getting universities to accept their social responsibilities.

The precise implementation of a plan for university home rule must vary from institution to institution. Several common features, however, should be found. First, a review of governing procedures should be made by a representative group of administrators, students, and faculty, and the recommendations of this group should be decisive in reforming the university's governing system. Second, university administrators should open up decisions before they are made, so that the opinions of university residents can be considered. Third, when university representative groups are organized, they should be public and visible, especially in times of crisis. Two examples will demonstrate how decision making can be organized so that tensions are creatively resolved through home rule.

For the first example, imagine a university council that is chaired by the president and composed of seven administrators, eighteen faculty members, fourteen undergraduates, eight graduates, four alumni, one librarian, one research staffer, one nonacademic staff member, one secretary, one professional technical staffer, and one janitor. The council meets once a month, has several standing committees, advises on all aspects of university policy, and decides all rules applicable to all university members. A crisis occurs: say, the president of the United States orders the invasion of a foreign country. Students are shouting "Strike!"; faculty members are incensed; and the university has visible ties with the U.S. military. The council's executive committee formulates proposals to respond to the situation and keep the university open. The council meets in a large auditorium, open to all university members, and decides on a response. The council has only the power of recommendation, but its plan is accepted by those with formal authority. Because all groups in the university were involved in the decision making and because the council's deliberations occupied central attention, the university responds as a community. No destruction occurs; the university remains open, and a coherent and wise response is made to the crisis.

For a second example, imagine a committee on priorities, which reviews the current university budget early in the academic year, reviews all plans for university development in advance of final decisions, and recommends to the president increases and decreases in the following year's budget. The committee is composed of three administrators, six faculty members, four undergraduates, two graduate students, and one staff member. It meets twenty or more times in the fall term, issues a lengthy report to the president and community on the budget, then fights for the acceptance of its recommendations. The president accepts the report and forwards it with his approval to the trustees, who accept the committee's recommendations. When a committee of this sort is faced with a severe financial squeeze, then representatives from all sectors of the university community have participated in the decisions, say, to decrease the budget, to raise tuitions, or to grant no increases in faculty salaries.

These examples of home rule decision making procedures are not merely conceptions on paper. These procedures have been in operation for two years at Princeton University. The university council provided guidance and stability during the Cambodian crisis, while other universities suffered. The Budget officials claim that the priorities committee is the best thing to happen in years and that decisions are better made and much better accepted than ever before. Community control over the budget in this manner has created widespread discussion and understanding of the university's financial plight and has obviated the distrust and antagonism that tuition and budget hikes have been known to cause.

Tensions will always exist in university decision making, as in all forms of human organization. University tensions can be creative forces for progress if members of the university community realize their common purposes. Higher education would suffer if students did not challenge irrelevant educational substance and form, if faculty members did not assert their views on proper teaching methods, or if administrators did not lead as well as listen and respond. To establish a process of creative tension, the members of the university community should decide who makes what decisions for the university's over-all governance. Home rule by students, faculty, and administrators means good governance. Home rule ensures more widely considered decisions and better acceptance of decisions than any other kind of governance. Home rule is a means of putting people back into control of the institutions that affect them; it is an infusion of democracy into university affairs that ensures that people who are affected by decisions will have something to say about those decisions. In short, it is community control over community decisions.

❧ 16 ❧

Resolving Conflict Through Mediation

Phyllis E. Kaye

W hat techniques will be utilized in the 1970s to resolve the conflicts that arise in the university community? Recent data from the Campus Governance Program of the American Association for Higher Education confirm the widespread belief that students, faculty, administrators, and trustees on the same campus have markedly different perceptions of campus problems and different judgments as to who should define problems or place them on a priority list. The study predicts that these varying perceptions and the resulting conflicts will not go away in the 1970s. If anything, they will increase.[1] It is imperative that college and university officials with the power to take affirmative action recognize and accept the existence of these conflicts as a basis for improvement rather than as an obstacle to be removed. It is also im-

---

[1] Morris Keeton, "The Disenfranchised on Campus," in G. K. Smith (Ed.), *The Troubled Campus: Current Issues in Higher Education 1970*. San Francisco: Jossey-Bass, 1970, pp. 116–117.

perative that those with the power to veto affirmative action do not block constructive change.

Much of the efforts of universities to resolve conflicts during the 1960s were ad hoc. The resolution of conflict focused on developing responses to specific events and dealing with the visible issues. Unfortunately for the university, the issues in question were often symptoms rather than causes and their resolutions did not get to the heart of the conflict. The process of mediation can often succeed in this respect, where other means fail. The mediator is not a contender in a given conflict but serves as a facilitator in conflict resolution or in problem-solving processes. The mediator can help lower the barriers that often prevent useful conflict from resulting in positive change.

Mediators have been helping groups resolve their problems for thousands of years, by involvement in international disputes, labor management disputes, and community disputes. The question is, however, whether the mediator can succeed in campus conflicts where relationships are often unstructured and where the situation often appears to lack rationality. The fact is that the process has worked on a number of campuses. It is important to make clear at the outset, however, that the campus mediation process is very different from the mediation process used in the sophisticated field of labor management. All that can be said is that mediation comes closest to describing the role the third party has played in facilitating the resolution of campus conflicts.

The attitudes of the parties involved finally determine the success or failure of solving problems through dialogue, discussion, and negotiations. If in fact either or both of the parties do not want to reach an agreement or if they adopt a closed attitude toward a settlement, then there is little a mediator can do, aside from determining more accurately than those directly involved in the conflict whether an attitude is indeed unchangeable. A conflict often escalates to the point of crisis because the process of communication breaks down. The mediator can help bridge this gap, by assisting parties to create an atmosphere in which conflict can be resolved. He is an expert in conflict management and is dedicated to the relationship of the parties.

The strength of the mediation process lies in its voluntary nature. Each party has the right to say yes or no to any suggestion the mediator might make, and each has the right to ask the mediator to leave. If a mediator is to be successful, he must be acceptable to both parties, and they must trust him and feel free to talk with him.

All must realize the confidential nature of whatever is said to the mediator. Because of this confidential relationship, the mediator can help parties clarify their own positions, and he can show parties how their posture is perceived by others. He can help the parties identify the central issues. The mediator, because of his objectivity, can also see solutions that the parties have overlooked. For example, at one school the parties faced a problem concerning what role the college president was to play in expelling a student for disciplinary reasons. The mediator was able to prevent an impasse by making a specific suggestion to the parties: the proposal was that when a discipline case results in a final order of expulsion, the student be given the option of submitting his case to arbitration—the arbitrator to be appointed by an impartial agency, the National Center for Dispute Settlement (NCDS). This procedure was acceptable to the parties and a recommendation that the board of trustees authorize this approach was included in the agreement that was finally reached.

In the past two years the NCDS—a division of the private, nonprofit American Arbitration Association—has provided mediation services to several universities, colleges, and high schools. The center has helped these schools handle specific conflicts and develop procedures to deal with conflicts that might arise in the future. The discussion that follows is based on some of these experiences.

As stated previously, the complexities of the conflicts that face the education community and the general lack of an acceptable structure within which conflicting parties agree to work make the campus mediation process somewhat different from the mediation process generally utilized in labor-management relations. In many campus situations the third-party mediator is a relationship facilitator. On campus, the mediator may have to determine parties to the conflict as well as find those persons who have the power to implement the agreed changes. Unlike the mediator in a labor dispute who enters a situation by the invitation of all the parties or in accordance with state or federal statutes, the campus mediator may enter a situation at the request of just one party. Once invited, the mediator might have to meet with a number of parties to sell them on the process and on his ability to resolve conflict. He might have to identify the power sources and get the parties he is dealing with to understand the extent to which a meaningful agreement may be reached without bringing into the process those persons with the power to implement the agreement.

The campus mediator may also be an issue finder. In labor

disputes, the parties generally present the mediator with a set of un-
resolved issues, and these issues are usually a fairly clear indication
of the subject of the dispute. The issues in a campus conflict may not
be clearly defined. The practical issues in dispute may be rooted in
philosophical differences, which cannot and should not be mediated.
The mediator must help the parties identify concrete issues, separate
philosophy from practical problems, and separate issues that can be
resolved through mediation from those that cannot be resolved. The
campus mediator may have to make formal public recommendations
for the settlement of specific conflicts—an option the labor mediator
generally does not exercise. The campus mediator may also be in a
position to prevent the development of a crisis by helping the parties
identify problems that have yet to take the form of overt issues. Thus,
the campus mediator can be of assistance even in the absence of an
impasse or overt hostility.

The exact role a mediator plays depends upon the specific
dynamics of conflict at a particular university or college. The mediator's role depends upon the existing relationship between the
parties; the extent to which the parties perceive their relationship as
being interdependent; the relative strength of the parties as perceived
by themselves and by each other; the extent to which the parties have
clearly identified the real issues among themselves and conveyed this
to the other side; and the extent to which the parties have thought
through these positions and have separated the philosophical considerations from the practical problems. In short, the role of the
mediator depends upon the people involved, and mostly on the extent
to which the parties want to reach agreement and are willing to assume
the responsibility entailed.

At this point it is appropriate to examine how the mediation
process has been utilized in four specific campus situations. The first
example involves a coeducational, rural college of about 2,600 students.
A few days before the mediator was invited to come, there was a fight
on campus involving two students—one black, the other white. Normally a fight would be handled through existing disciplinary procedures, but this fight was different. At the time, the black student had
his leg in a cast, and his fellow black students saw the incident as a
sign of the racism they felt existed on campus. Thus, the black student's
plight became a cause, and polarization of white and black students
increased. The black students formulated a series of demands that
included a call for the summary expulsion of the white student. Black

students charged that the college president had backed down on a promise to expel the white student, and a call for guns was made by some black students at an open meeting.

The administration and campus life committee, composed of a number of students, quickly saw that a different approach was needed to handle this conflict and sought the services of an impartial, off-campus group—the NCDS. The students and administrators still thought, however, that the central issue was that of determining what disciplinary measures, if any, should be taken against the students involved in the fight. (By this time, some students had called for the expulsion of the black student.) Thus, when the NCDS was asked in, there was talk of simply arbitrating the disciplinary question. The center immediately realized that the fight was not the root of the polarization and that arbitration was not the answer. The center did believe, however, that mediation could help the parties find an answer to their problems.

Willoughby Abner, director of the NCDS, served as mediator. He met with all those who felt they were involved—the two students involved in the fight, the members of the Afro-Latin society, the members of the campus judiciary board, faculty, and administrators. Open hearings and private meetings were held. Through these mediation efforts an agreement that dealt with the fundamental issues—the judicial system, the general problem of racism on the campus, and housing—was worked out between the college administration and the Afro-Latin society, the visible parties to the dispute. The question of disciplinary action against the two students was to be handled through normal campus judicial procedures. The two students had the right to appeal any decisions to an impartial arbitrator appointed by the NCDS, should either student elect to press charges. No charges were filed.

The mediator's first job at this school was to gain the acceptance and trust of the black students. The mediator was able to overcome the suspicions of the black students, partly because he was black and largely because he told the students that they held the power to discharge him and to control his effectiveness. The fight and subsequent events had moved the students to formulate a number of demands, some of which were in fact inconsistent and some of which were considerably more important to black students than to others. By gaining the confidence of the students, asking the right questions, and making objective observations on how the demands might be perceived by others, the mediator was able to get the students to reconsider the issues and to articulate fully and clearly their primary concerns. As a result, the demands of the black students were reordered. For example, the demand that the white student be expelled was originally the first item on the list of demands. In the final set of demands, the first item was that the president of the college apologize to the black students for his actions. The demand that the white student be expelled was placed last.

The mediator helped the administration see that the central issue involved the general feelings of the black students about the judicial procedure, housing, and other university policies. He helped the administration perceive how its actions were interpreted by the black students and how these actions served to escalate the conflict. The mediator also helped the administration repair the damage by taking certain actions and encouraged the parties to find new ways to resolve specific problems, particularly the one of judicial procedures.

Because the power to implement change in the disciplinary system actually rested with the board of trustees and not with the students or the administration, the mediator carefully proposed that the agreement between parties only state a recommendation that the trustees authorize such a procedure. It is crucial to note that the agreement did not promise something that the parties themselves had no power to deliver. Throughout this process the mediator was also teaching the parties something about conflict and its resolution. When a dispute occurred in the spring between black students and the administration over the future operation of a specific program, the students again drew up a set of demands. But this time they were successful in reaching agreement with the administration without having to call in a third party to serve as mediator.

The second example involves a case where a new issue emerged as the subject of the negotiations. The student senate at this school passed legislation calling for a change in the school's policies of regulating visits to students' rooms. The senate legislation was vetoed by the vice-president for student affairs and the university president. The students elected to implement the legislation with a mass "visit-in" and at the same time decided to take the question to the board of trustees. The positions of the students and the administration hardened, and the administration threatened to close the school. The board of trustees, believing this was a question that the campus community should resolve for itself, suggested that various segments of the campus community, including the faculty, meet with representatives of the NCDS.

After meeting with representatives of the center it became apparent—much to the surprise of the campus and trustees—that the fundamental issue was not visitation regulations. (All agreed, however, that at some point and in some manner this problem would have to be faced again.) The real problem involved what role the students should have in the decision-making process of the university. The issue involved university governance and the relationship between the student senate and the rest of the community. The students, faculty, and administration agreed to discuss this issue by developing a joint committee chaired by a representative of the NCDS. Hopefully, an agreement will be reached on a new student senate constitution. Although it is too early to determine the success of this task, one definite lesson can be learned: the problem that everyone thinks is at issue may only trigger reactions to the real problem. Even if the issue of visitation regulations were resolved, undoubtedly the basic problem—the role of the students in formulating and implementing policy—would have surfaced again. The new constitution of the student senate may fail, but mediation was responsible for bringing the fundamental issue to the surface.

The third example of the effective use of a mediator involves a case where a campus community was able to revise its governance system. Early in the year a joint committee was established at this school to negotiate a new governance system for the college. The committee worked for months but was unable to devise a governance system. The school became torn by conflict and was closed due to violence on a number of occasions. The NCDS was called in to help the community handle the problem of developing a new governance system.

The mediator talked with over one hundred individuals and representatives of more than a dozen groups, each sharing different perceptions of one another and of the reasons why things went awry. The critical need was to establish some method for bringing these conflicting groups together to work on the development of a governance system. The original joint committee fell apart because it was given an impossible task. It was established as a negotiating committee; yet it voted on proposals and operated on the principle of majority rule. The concept of agreement by majority rule is antithetical to the concept of agreement through negotiations. To be effective, a negotiating committee must operate on the principle that agreements are reached through consensus.

Because of the nature of the problem and the number of groups involved, the most appropriate course of action for the mediator was to recommend to the campus community, through the college president, a procedure that might be followed to work out a governance plan. This procedure involved the establishment of an ad hoc panel composed of representatives from some sixteen conflicting groups chaired by an impartial member selected by the group. The mediator also recommended guidelines for the operation of the committee, including the requirement that agreement must be reached by consensus rather than majority vote. Any plan agreed to by the committee would then have to be approved by a campus referendum. Should the committee fail to reach agreement, alternatives were also outlined. The mediator's recommendations were acceptable to the campus community and implemented by the college president. The ad hoc committee reached an agreement on a new governance system. The system was subsequently approved by the campus community in a referendum and has been put into effect.

It is important to note that in this situation the mediator did not deal with the substance of the dispute—what the governance system should look like. He did not bring hidden issues to the surface. Instead, he helped the community devise a procedure to deal with the issue that was apparent from the start. High tensions, past failure, and misunderstandings made it necessary for a person experienced in conflict resolution to assist the campus community in devising such a procedure.

The fourth example illustrates the principle that mediation need not be limited in its use to times of crisis. Third-party involvement can help to identify problems before a crisis is allowed to develop. The members of the campus community at this small midwestern college knew that the college had problems, but no one was sure what the problems were or what to do about them. The NCDS was asked to visit; two staff members spent one day on the campus meeting with students, faculty, and administrators to explore areas that posed problems. After separate meetings, representatives of these groups were brought together for a joint meeting during which the NCDS staff members stated some observations. Participants were asked to comment on these observations and to make appropriate suggestions or changes.

As a result of these sessions several things were brought to light. First, some of the areas that initially seemed to pose serious problems were in fact not serious, while problems that were not considered serious had to be given a higher priority. Second, the poor communication between groups and the lack of understanding of the decision-making process was shown to be a serious problem that caused much concern among major segments of the university community. Third, the president had not realized that there were serious disagreements over the effectiveness of the all-campus conference he had sponsored the previous year. The students and faculty questioned the good faith of the administration in implementing some of the proposals that developed out of the conference. In fact, the president was not even sure of the status of the committees and the recommendations that were formed. Following the NCDS visit, a detailed report was made to the campus community, outlining the problems that were revealed. Thus, the campus community could, if it desired, begin to respond to these newly recognized problems before a crisis occurred. Perhaps such problem identifications could take place without the intervention of a third party. In general, however, the NCDS staff member facilitated the process by rendering a sympathetic, objective ear and by presenting no threat of reprisal.

The four examples presented here show the different roles a campus mediator or third-party facilitator may actually play. Mediation can help conflicting parties pinpoint areas of mutual concern. The mediation process can help parties separate the apparent issues from the more fundamental problems underlying the conflict. In the course of this process, the surface issues are dealt with as a matter of course and in a more meaningful way. Mediation can help the parties develop procedures to resolve conflict, or it can help the parties develop new creative ways of identifying the substance of specific conflicts.

Mediation is not the only way a third party might be of assistance in a specific dispute. An arbitrator selected by the parties or appointed by an impartial agency such as the NCDS can play a valuable role in specific procedures such as a campus judicial system. Arbitration is one way to guarantee the accused an impartial hearing in a campus judicial case.

As a point in case, the University of Maryland board of regents has given students the option of appealing the decision of the campus judicial board to an impartial arbitrator appointed by the NCDS. Mediation and, in more limited instances, arbitration are two techniques that the university community might consider in meeting the challenges that the conflicts of the 1970s are certain to pose.

❧ 17 ❧

Paradoxes of Campus Power

Robert M. O'Neil

❧❧❧❧❧❧❧❧❧

In the autumn of 1970, students at Nanterre University in France soaked the dean of the law school in wine because they were unhappy with the operation of the school's restaurant. The dean tried unsuccessfully to convince the students he had nothing whatsoever to do with the restaurant and could not improve its fare. The method of annointment may have been peculiarly Gallic, but the incident was not. It has an American analogue. About two or three years before the incident at Nanterre, students at the University of Colorado seized the cafeteria to protest the quality of the food. They renamed the cafeteria after the state's only convicted cannibal, a snowbound miner who devoured his companion to prevent starvation in the winter of 1883. The differences between the two incidents are revealing. The Nanterre students evidently felt the issue was a matter of governance

172

and accountability but held the wrong person accountable—apparently because the dean was the most accessible symbol of authority. The Colorado students saw self-help as the appropriate remedy. There is no evidence that either protest accomplished its objective. The study and reform of governance in American universities are full of paradoxes. The crosscurrents that exist in policies of university governance have been studied during the past year and a half by the Assembly on University Goals and Governance. In the present paper, some of these paradoxes will be amplified and some tentative recommendations will be offered for redesigning governance of American higher education.

First, there is the paradox of minimal change. Despite enormous pressures for reform, fundamental restructuring of university governance is remarkably rare. Daniel Bell recently observed that during the past decade there have been changes of scale unprecedented in the history of the university—changes which are not simply linear but reflect a change in form, and consequently in institution. Yet as Harold Hodgkinson notes, there have been drastic increases in the populations upon which governments must work, but almost no change in the basic configurations of governance. Second, there is the paradox of disappearing power. Morris Keeton stated in the 1970 yearbook of the American Association for Higher Education (AAHE) that there is a pervasive feeling of disenfranchisement on American campuses today. Detailed studies of the several campus constituencies confirm the impression that all feel they have lost power in recent years—at the very time when unparalleled efforts have been made to expand participation, accountability, and publicity of decision making. Either some groups have gained power without realizing it, or there has somehow been a net reduction in the total amount of power to be shared among competing claimants.

Third, there is a paradox of unselectivity. Despite the unique character of the university and wide differences among institutions of higher learning, little attempt has been made to develop governance models peculiarly suited to academic conditions. There have been few indigenous efforts to devise structures uniquely befitting the needs of particular institutions. Partly because of the sense of urgency to do something about governance (usually in response to student protest), reform has been largely emulative and has often taken a bandwagon approach. Moreover, the unique skills possessed by universities for the study of institutions have been committed generously to external claimants—business firms, hospitals, federal and state governments—

where both the tangible and intangible rewards have seemed attractive. The denial of these rich talents has left universities rather like the proverbial plumber who never gets around to fixing the faucet in his own house.

The fourth paradox in the governance of universities has to do with participation. Because of an assumption that power can be distributed only by increasing the participation of previously excluded constituencies, other methods of power distribution have been largely ignored. Kingman Brewster has suggested that increasing the accountability of decision makers might effectively serve the needs of new claimants without the drawbacks of an undue reliance on participation. Other approaches certainly merit attention—among them collective bargaining (not only by faculty and staff but by students as well) and separation of powers accompanied by formal checks and balances. Not only has there been a fetish about participation as such, but the focus has been unbalanced. Demands for democracy have often been deflected by a single, highly publicized (and minimally effective) change at the top, such as adding one student or faculty trustee. Concern with pressing inequities at lower levels is thus diluted, and the reforming impetus unwisely spent.

Fifth, there is the paradox of formalism. Many recent studies have disproportionately focused on structures, to the neglect of process. The governance of a university is not composed merely of lines and boxes on organization charts; rather, university governance is the way an institution actually operates and makes decisions. The lack of reliable data on the operational aspects has left a critical gap; informal processes and the influence of personality have been largely neglected. Finally, there is the paradox of autonomy. Many students of governance still approach the subject as though the academic community could completely shape its own destiny. This is surely no longer the case. Pressures for replacing internal decision-making processes have come from various sources. A brief review will suggest how far the process of preemption has already progressed.

Ralph K. Huitt suggests that state legislatures would intervene in campus affairs in a minute, if only they knew how to do so. Mounting evidence shows that legislatures do know how to intervene or, at least, are learning faster than the academic community is learning how to protect itself.[1] Virtually every state legislature has now enacted some

[1] See M. O. Hatfield, "Public Pressures on Higher Education." In G. Kerry Smith (Ed.), *The Troubled Campus: Current Issues in Higher Education 1970.* San Francisco: Jossey-Bass, 1970.

repressive measure aimed at controlling campus disorders. Many of these harsh new laws impinge directly upon university governance; an Ohio statute, for example, mandates the dismissal of a student, faculty member, or staff member following conviction for any of a broad range of criminal offenses. The Michigan legislature attached faculty teaching load requirements to the budget, even though the conditions of the statute are not fully honored in practice. The same Michigan legislature intervened unwittingly when it adopted a conflict of interest law several years ago; the state attorney general has ruled that this law precludes any student (and presumably any faculty or staff member) from serving on the governing board of the institution he attends. Other examples of legislative intrusion, deliberate and accidental, are legion.

The courts, too, pose novel and growing threats to campus autonomy. Traditionally, courts have been regarded as the protectors of freedom. In May, 1970, however, state court judges in Ohio ordered Kent State University to close indefinitely, while judges in Florida ordered the University of Miami to reopen. Relevant university constituencies were not consulted in either case. The Ohio judge, moreover, left all decisions about access to the Kent State campus in the hands of the National Guard commander. Several months later, a small claims judge ordered New York University to refund several hundred dollars in tuition and fees to the father of a student whose courses had been reconstituted last May. The judge found the suspension or alteration of classes wholly unwarranted, even though the vital decisions had been made or sanctioned by NYU's new university-wide senate, in which all constituencies were represented. Equally insensitive was the New York trial judge who ordered members of the Queens faculty to furnish prescribed hours of instruction during the summer to make up for classes missed after the events at Kent State and the Cambodian invasion.

A host of suits are still pending, which seek money damages against university officials for exercising goodfaith judgments during the turmoil of last spring. No one interested in university autonomy can overlook the disastrous implications of the sweeping grand jury reports issued against Kent State and Hobart-William Smith. Charges against the latter institution have been dismissed, but a very unpleasant taste and a climate of fear created by the grand jury cannot be readily dispelled. Actions of law enforcement agencies pose two sorts of threats to university autonomy. First, there is the rising incidence of surveillance, such as the FBI interrogation of Kent State students last spring and summer about controversial professors; the monitoring of classes at NYU and Minnesota by army intelligence personnel; and the use of provacateurs by local police at Hobart, Ohio State, the University of Alabama, and the University of South Carolina. Second, there is the central lesson of the tragedies at Kent State and Jackson: when police or National Guard contingents come to the campus, they may completely preempt or displace all internal decision-making processes.

Various other external forces impinge upon campus autonomy and may be briefly noted here. The proliferation of state-wide public systems undoubtedly tends toward centralization and mandates uniformity in areas formerly left to local option. Accreditation may have much the same effect in stifling innovation; with a few notable exceptions like Hampshire and Old Westbury, the governance patterns of the new institutions are emulative and unimaginative. Many pressures may chill the spirit of adventure, but the fear of an adverse accreditation decision may be a prime deterrent to generating innovative governance policies. Austerity, too, is now beginning to take its toll. As funds for supporting higher education become scarce and the competition of nonacademic claimants grows intense, appropriations are bound to carry new fiscal controls that will restrict governance options. Even where the constraints are not explicit, caution may seem the wiser course when financial stringency threatens. Finally, there is the growth of collective bargaining, which has already begun to leave its mark on governance and structure in the City University of New York and will undoubtedly affect every institution that selects a bargaining agent to represent faculty interests.

Much more could be said about the complex of external forces that curtail internal governance options. This brief summary should serve, however, to confirm the folly of studying or restructuring a university's decision-making processes *in vacuo*. The preemption of internal options, moreover, is not an isolated or rare phenomenon. The trends described here continue to grow, and the situation is likely to get worse before it improves. The student of governance must, therefore, be a supreme realist.

We should ask ourselves what approaches to the study and reform of university governance are viable within these constraints. The recent experience of the Assembly on University Goals and Governance has suggested several broad approaches to the problem. First, it is essential to concentrate upon one particular institution. Generalization is hazardous at best. There really is no such thing as an abstract governance model that meets the needs and conditions of any individual university. The current decision-making patterns and distributions of power on each campus significantly shape the options available for the future. At campuses where a faculty is highly organized and wields substantial power, the development of a university-wide senate seems far less likely than at campuses where a loosely organized faculty sees some sharing of power as a possible way of enhancing its own position. The best starting point for university governance reform may be a detailed definition of the communication and decision-making processes. Logan Wilson recently expressed doubt whether anyone has ever made a thoroughgoing empirical study of how decisions are reached on a single American college or university campus. Yet such information seems absolutely essential to a study of governance; without knowledge of present patterns, any discussion of reform is misinformed at best, and misdirected at worst.

The second suggestion made by the Assembly on University Goals and Governance is that a study of the functional aspects of governance may be far preferable to the structural approach commonly employed. That is, the evaluation of existing processes and the assessment of future options should proceed from a definition of the tasks or functions that any system of university governance must perform. This is not the place to enumerate those functions; for the most part they are rather obvious but may vary a good deal from campus to campus. No process of decision making and no allocation of power or responsibility can be judged meaningfully until the specific assignments are placed in perspective.

A third approach to governance reform is to appraise the claims of each of the campus constituencies that participate in the decision-making process. Students, nonacademic staff, alumni, and governing boards are not equally relevent to every internal task, nor are they equally interested in the making of each decision. Thus, a system of governance that accords exactly the same measure of access to each constituent on every question reflects a crude average of participatory claims. A higher degree of selectivity is required, but governance studies often treat the claims of participating constituencies as homogeneous.

A fourth approach to the study and reform of governance procedure is that the options must be reviewed within this selective grid of particular claims and particular tasks. Many alternatives are theoretically available. The relationship of a constituency to a specific university task may be established through participation, either on a direct or a representative basis. As Kingman Brewster has suggested, the constituency that makes the initial decision may be held accountable to those who are vitally concerned but cannot participate directly.

Input is possible at many different stages of the decision-making process, and the access of different constituencies may be assured at different stages without creating a great degree of instability. Authority may be shared effectively, as the Keeton-AAHE governance study now suggests, either through joint participation or through separate jurisdictions. A single comprehensive body may exercise a variety of functions, or separate forums with limited and specialized competence may be created. The range of options is almost unlimited, but only a highly selective approach to the problem permits adequate consideration of that range.

A fifth approach to governance reform suggests that the interdependence of various forces must always be kept clearly in mind. There has been much speculation of late, for example, whether separate faculty and student senates can survive the creation of a single university-wide legislative body. The question cannot be answered in the abstract. The outcome depends chiefly upon the powers given to the new comprehensive body; thus the survival of faculty and student senates may be either assured or precluded by a careful definition of the jurisdiction of the university-wide body. Equally problematical is the impact of collective bargaining. If a group other than the faculty senate is selected as the exclusive bargaining agent for the faculty, the survival of the senate is doubtful. But here again, the probable outcome of inevitable competition for power may depend more on how the contract is written than on any inexorable laws of governance. Faculty participation in the governing board may also be precluded by the advent of collective bargaining, but alternative inputs for faculty views may be devised within a particular bargaining relationship. In these and many other matters, a change in one component of university structure is bound to alter other relationships in ways that simply must be anticipated.

Finally, the external context must constantly be kept in mind. There are, as suggested previously, countless constraints upon internal options for shaping and reshaping governance. The impact of intrusive legislation, litigation, law enforcement surveillance, and the like is only beginning to be felt. Yet the displacement of campus options has not proceeded quite so far as to make the task of governance reform a futile one. To the contrary, the very growth of these external pressures makes the careful study and reform of internal decision making and distribution of power an urgent undertaking.

❧ 18 ❧

New Developments in Governance

John J. Corson

Higher education is embroiled in change—change made manifest by confrontations on the campuses, by vacancies in the offices of president of more than one hundred institutions, by the financial difficulties of a third or more of all colleges and universities, and by the persisting criticism voiced in the daily press, state legislatures, Congress, and in the streets. This campus turmoil is the consequence of social forces the university neither caused nor can influence—the persistence of war, the racial revolution of the sixties, urbanization, and technological advance. These social forces bring about marked alterations in the structure of colleges and universities and in the processes by which they are run.

I am not brave enough—or, at the least, not foolish enough—to predict what the governance of the university will be like in 1980. It is possible, however, to point out with some certainty the central cause of the present sorry state of governance in many institutions. It is also possible to appraise the rash of reforms being proposed in the light of the root cause. In this paper, I should like to identify five modifications in the ways colleges and universities govern themselves or are governed. The logic of these approaches will be assessed, and a rationale as to the future evolutionary course of university governance shall be pieced together.

The central cause of the regretable state of governance in many institutions is an historical misunderstanding of the real nature of colleges or universities. Most American universities inherited a formal organizational structure founded on the concept of hierarchy. That concept presumes that all authority is granted by the founders or the public through a charter granted to a governing board. Theoretically, such a board has the power to exercise all authority. As the theory goes, the board delegates authority to a president who directs and supervises all activities. The president, in turn, delegates authority to deans, department chairmen, and administrative officers.

If this hierarchical structure fit the college or university of the first quarter of this century, it was because the institutions of higher learning in that bygone era had four markedly different characteristics from present-day colleges and universities. First, the trustees and presidents of that period could indeed comprehend the whole body of knowledge their institutions were transmitting. Second, the faculties were made up of men content to sit on the proverbial other end of Mark Hopkins' log rather than men dedicated to or consumed by the rat race of research and publication. Third, the institutions, tucked away in their rural settings, were indeed autonomous rather than subject to a variety of demands made by the larger community; and fourth, the students were a supine lot who would not venture out with their own ideas or fail to conform to the prevailing customs. That was a time when the hierarchical structure, with authority concentrated at the top, did work for most institutions. Now, however, the hierarchical structure that seems a business enterprise simply does not fit the large, complex, multifunctional institution that recruits specialized professors and sophisticated students. The hierarchical structure does not fit because power does not flow from a single source. In a corporation, power flows from the stockholders, or it is passed to the managers of the enterprise; in either event, it flows from a single source and can be delegated. In a college or university, all power—that is, the capacity to make decisions—does not reside in a single source at the top. It resides simul-

taneously and in varying proportions in three or sometimes four groups
that make up the institution: the trustees and administrators; the
faculty; the students; and sometimes the alumni. In short, as an organization, the college or university differs fundamentally from the business enterprise or the governmental agency in the degree to which
power flows either from one source or from multiple sources. With this
basic thought in mind, let us now look at five proposals as to how the
structure of college and university governance should be modified.

The first proposal is that new mechanisms should be established
within the college or university to make possible community-wide
participation in governance. A variety of such mechanisms are actually
being established. Students are being named to sit with faculty members
and/or administrators in committees to formulate decisions on a broad
variety of questions. Faculty members are serving on a variety of administrative and trustee committees. And in a number of institutions
(for example, the universities of Minnesota and New Hampshire,
Pennsylvania State, and Princeton) new councils, senates, or assemblies
have been established to bring together the power holders in the university to discuss issues that require decisions, to confront each other
with their respective views, and to offer advice to the president and
trustees. The reasoning that underlies the formation of such councils,
senates, or assemblies is that the college or university is a political community. In other words, the institution is made up of several factions,
each of which possesses parochial views and the power to disrupt or
endanger university operations. Decisions that will stick can only be
made through a process in which the several factions can voice their
opinions and exercise an influence commensurate with their competence in each particular area of decision making.

Such mechanisms are beneficial in that interaction between
students and faculty and between faculty and administration is taken
out of the president's office. But the perfecting of such mechanisms
requires that further agreements be made as to who shall be represented
on such a council, senate, or assembly; how, and in what proportion,
each faction shall be represented; and what authority the council,
senate, or assembly shall have. In other words, what range of issues
will they be authorized to consider, and what weight will their decisions
have?

The second proposal for modifying university governance is that
the redistribution of authority be made explicit. The power to make or
to exercise authority has been shifting within many institutions. Trust-

ees and presidents, for instance, have been losing the power to exercise authority that theoretically is still theirs, while faculties and students have been gaining power and, hence, gaining effective authority. This redistribution of power creates a need for the redefinition of the authority of each faction (the trustees, the president, the administrative staff, the faculty, the students, and the alumni). This process of redefinition has been initiated in many institutions during recent years and promises to reduce tensions by bringing about an open-minded reappraisal of the role of each faction.

The broad goal is to place authority where the required competence exists. (By competence is meant not only knowledge of the particular issue but also a recognition of the concerns of the whole institution.) Those who are given authority to make decisions should be required to consult continuingly with each faction affected by the decisions. Competence and concern can serve as guides to make feasible the kind of reappraisal that is needed. Redistribution of authority is neither simple nor pleasant when it requires those who have had authority—particularly the trustees and the faculty—to cede it to others. Redistributing authority is made doubly difficult by the idea that educational decisions, financial decisions, and other decisions are of concern to and can be improved by the participation of all or several constituencies.

The third proposal for the modification of governance policies suggests that leadership must be strengthened if the college or university is to remain a viable institution. We may recall the words of two distinguished presidents. Douglas McGregor, after several years as president of Antioch, wrote that he strove to operate as a kind of adviser to the faculty and staff to avoid playing the role of boss. He finally concluded that a leader cannot avoid the exercise of authority any more than he can avoid responsibility for what happens to his organization. Kingman Brewster of Yale complemented this thought in a speech to the Yale Political Union in 1969. Brewster advanced the thesis that the president should be free to make—and should be expected to make— bold, prompt, and decisive decisions on a wide range of issues, always knowing that he will be held accountable by students as well as faculty and trustees. Brewster's comment clarifies that the real nature of the president's office is that of a political leader. The president's task is to give leadership and to maintain the interest, support, and loyalty of the several factions that make up the institution. The president can be an educational leader only if he is effective as a political leader of the whole academic community. However, the strengthening of the office of the president also requires a reaffirmation of his authority and a restructuring of his staff to enable him to carry the responsibilities of leadership.

The reasoning underlying current proposals for the strengthening of leadership rests on pragmatic bases. Institutions of higher education are large and complex; they will not run themselves, and they should not be run to serve the whims of faculty members or students. These institutions are established and supported to benefit the whole society, and all decisions must be tested in the crucible of the public interest. The interests of either faculty or students do not necessarily coincide with public interests. It is not feasible that all factions of the university community should decide everything or even that each faction should be consulted as each issue arises. Ensuring that the institution is run in the public interest and with reasonable economy and efficiency requires strong and effective leadership by those who are thoroughly cognizant of the entire functioning of the institution—its educational philosophy, educational methods, costs of instruction, needed facilities, interdisciplinary relationships, research, and social services of various types. If trustees are to measure up to the demands of such leadership, most existing boards will need to be reconstituted. Board memberships will have to include youthful members, women, blacks, faculty members, and students. Without such broad representation, the boards are ill equipped to translate the society's current concerns to the institution. They cannot make decisions founded on an understanding of the educational process and the capabilities of the institution, nor can they interpret or defend what the college or university is doing.

The fourth proposal for the modification of governance is that every extension of authority must be accompanied by a means to enforce accountability. Whatever form of governance exists must produce results that are acceptable to the several constituencies within the college or university. If the students are given complete authority for student life, the environment they create must facilitate learning in the opinion of the faculty and those who provide financial support. By the same token, if the faculty is delegated authority for the control of admissions, curricula, and certification of educational accomplishment, its members must be held accountable by students as well as by administrators, trustees, and professional groups. The participation of students on departmental advisory committees and student ratings of faculty members are obvious manifestations of the enforcement of such accountability. If the president is granted full authority in matters pertaining to the institution's administration, then he must be held accountable by the trustees and the constituencies he serves, particularly the faculty and the students.

This notion of accountability lies at the root of suggestions that the president's services be evaluated at stated periods. In essence, these proposals suggest that the *quid pro quo* for the reaffirmed executive discretion granted the president is a periodic reappraisal of his performance by the whole community he serves, and that establishment of such a formal arrangement will stimulate regular, widespread, and serious consultation by the president in carrying out his responsibilities.

The final proposal for governance procedures is that the traditional structures of high schools, junior colleges, four-year colleges, professional schools, and graduate schools be modified. The same social forces that lie behind the redistribution of power within the college and university challenge long-standing institutional arrangements in higher education. The present structure of our institutions dates back to the time when only a small, select part of the nation's youth were educated for professions in law, medicine, theology, and education. Institutions now train a greater and less select number of students than in the past. University structures have been extended to perform the research and provide the services that society now demands. The basic structures, however, have changed very little, and many new institutions still imitate both the programs and the structures of long-established, prestigious universities, instead of framing programs and structures applicable to the needs of new and different constituencies.

New developments are altering the landscape of higher education today and suggest restructuring of the present system. Many of these suggestions for new developments were spelled out in a panel headed by Frank Newman of Stanford University.[1] The recommendations called for new types of colleges and special-purpose institutions; off-campus study ventures such as tutoring centers and regional television colleges; flexible systems for earning credits and degrees (including the development of equivalency examinations); increased college enrollment for all age groups; internships and other noncollege opportunities for young people; and restored campus autonomy in a state-

[1] F. Newman and others, *Report on Higher Education*. Washington, D.C.: Department of Health, Education, and Welfare, 1971.

wide system.[2] The welter of change that is visible and the suggestions for restructuring that have been advanced do not provide a neat and comprehensive plan for the reordering of the total structure of higher education. Such a plan is not likely to emerge and is less likely to be achieved.

What is needed at this time is an open-minded, thorough evaluation of these five proposals for the modification of college and university governance. As the Assembly on University Goals and Governance has pointed out, colleges and universities have borrowed their governance from business and public administration for too long.[3] Recent experiences have demonstrated that the governance of colleges and universities cannot be founded on a structure that relies on the authority to command. The foregoing proposals go a considerable way toward devising a system of governance designed to facilitate the engineering of consent. Hopefully, the new structure that evolves will distill the best from each of the five proposals I have described. Only a complete system of governance will be capable of ensuring that freedom of thought and expression for teachers and students alike is maintained, that the knowledge and skills found on university campuses is applied to society's problem, and that bold and effective decision making essential for institutional management becomes the order of the day.

[2] These and other educational reforms are discussed in the essays of Part Two of this volume. [Editor's note.]

[3] *A First Report: The Assembly on University Goals and Governance.* Washington, D.C.: The American Academy of Arts and Sciences, 1971.

PART FIVE:

The Professor as Employee

❧❧❧❧❧❧❧❧❧❧❧❧❧❧❧❧

The essays of Part Five deal with the whole range of academic working conditions, including both their spiritual side (such as the relation between academic freedom and the collective expression of faculty opinion on political issues) and their material side (such as the control of faculty teaching loads). The authors point up the growing chasm between faculty members and the bodies that, in one sense or another, "employ" them: university management, boards of trustees, state legislatures, and the tax-paying public.

❧ 19 ❧

Academic Freedom and Collective Expressions of Opinion

Immanuel Wallerstein

Freedom is a relational, not a formal, characteristic of society. That is to say, there are no formal rules the presence or absence of which denotes the existence of freedom. In every society, there is always the freedom to assent, to speak and act in ways consonant with the views of those in power. The measure of the existence of freedom (which nowhere is absolute) is whether those who fundamentally dissent from the most basic assumptions of the social order are in fact free to act in ways that are most likely to persuade others to change from their views. Thus a very pragmatic litmus tests exists. If a group seeks to engage in certain actions, and if both the group and the powers-that-be believe that such actions may indeed be persuasive to others as yet uncommitted or otherwise movable in their views—to the extent that such acts are forbidden, discouraged or disparaged, freedom is absent.

How is this principle relevant in the university today? Many say we enjoy a large measure of academic freedom in American universities today because certain acts are permitted that were not permitted in times past even though these acts then seemed relevant to the expansion of freedom. Such actions include the right of a professor to hold views at variance with those of the trustees; the freedom to express these views outside the university; and the right to defend the wisdom or expound the merits of unconventional ideas in a classroom debate provided these ideas are formulated in nonpolemical language (that is, are not designated as propaganda) and provided that the professor presents them with a certain moral detachment. I do not doubt that these freedoms are good and that during the early part of our century —or even more recently—the struggle to obtain and defend such freedoms was meaningful and important. But the existence of these freedoms does not demonstrate that we have academic freedom today because they do not touch on the central political struggles of the moment.

The close liaison established between the federal government and our institutions of higher learning during the period from 1940 to 1965 had a distinctly constraining effect upon the development of the university and upon faculty, students, and administrators. This relationship came under severe attack from many students and a growing number of faculty since 1965. As a result, in the last few years many universities have reconsidered their links to the government and many other activities. The consequence is simple: many universities have decided to do things that virtually all administrators and the vast bulk of faculty declined to do in 1965 because such acts were presumably "political". Examples of such previously unthinkable acts are the refusal to permit classified research on the campus or to give class rankings to selective service, or the abolition of ROTC. These are not world-shaking decisions but I for one applaud them. I agree that these acts are "political," but so, I believe, were the converse actions. In any case, such decisions illustrate the fragile life span of the "unthinkable" act.

In times of turmoil, reasonable men seek to determine anew what stance is appropriate with respect to the new dilemmas of the society. I wish to plead the case here for the appropriateness of collective (or corporate) expressions of opinions by the university. Let me review the history. American universities have always overtly supported the government in wartime. During World War I, professors at Columbia University were fired for pacifist views. It is only with the Indochina war that antiwar sentiment has become commonplace. The teach-in, the petition, and the rally were the first steps. The moratorium was the second. The calls for cessation of war by university senates was the third. The Columbia University Senate has, I believe, the honor of being the first to pass such a resolution (on September 26, 1969), to be followed shortly by Harvard. With the invasions of Cambodia and Laos, such collective declarations of opinion have become more common, if still widely resisted because of their inappropriateness.

First let us ask what social function, if any, is fulfilled by a collective expression of opinion by an institution on matters of broad national concern and of deep controversy. The answer is that such collective expressions are a necessary ingredient in the maintenance of a free society. It is not the presence but the absence of collective expressions which is dangerous and to be deplored. A nation is composed of individuals, and in most modern countries individuals do have the right to vote. In many nations individuals also have the right to speak, to write, to assemble, and to campaign. But even if we could say that such individual rights are totally untarnished—and I for one could not say as much for the United States today—the sum of these rights do not add up to a free society. The fact of the matter is that a nation is composed of more than a state machinery, a government, and a mass of individual voters; a nation is also composed of groups (which may or may not be formally organized) and a whole series of major institutions. The latter, in particular, have wealth, personnel, continuity, and prestige at their disposal. Insofar as groups and major institutions are reticent on all matters outside a very narrowly defined purview, they sustain the status quo. Only when the various factions of our nation speak out, will we begin to create the atmosphere of open debate, which we perpetually, but inaccurately, claim to have.

The two institutions, which are by their very nature destined to be in eternal tension with the government, are the church and the university. In theory, both the church and the university appeal to the values and, more significantly, to the norms that lie beyond the social definitions of a given society. I do not say that the church and the university have in fact fulfilled their destined roles. Quite often, even for the most part, they have not, but to that extent they have lost their integrity.

If we look at the church for a moment, we see immediately that it asserts its position on a range of issues from birth control to war. The church acts upon its convictions by sending assistance to revolutionaries in southern Africa, by voting its shares for an ecology ticket in General Motors, or by boycotting banks who refuse to accept moral responsibility for large borrowers. A few churchmen think such involvement is inappropriate, but the majority do not. Most individual church members do not feel that their rights have been infringed upon when collective expressions are not to their liking. Collective expressions have come to be accepted as normal and reasonable—not merely consonant with individual freedom but necessary to national freedom. The same can and should be true of the university.

Basically, there are three arguments against such a position: collective assertions endanger the rights of individual members; collective expressions are time consuming and deviate from the central tasks of the institution; and collective expressions invite social and financial retaliation. Each of these arguments is fallacious. The fallacy in the argument that collective assertions endanger the rights of individuals derives from a simplistic view of social organization. The assumption is that in a complex society individuals only become members of groups that have commonly held viewpoints. This is simply untrue. We are all members of many groups and institutions that occupy differing degrees of importance in our lives. We tolerate a wide range of group or institutional misdeeds or errors before we cut our ties. None of us expects to lead what might be called a perfectly coherent social life. On the contrary, we are socialized to accept both disappointment and ambiguity, and the society could not operate if we were not. No professor resigned from Columbia because he was in disagreement with the faculty senate's view on Vietnam.

Whatever impact a resolution creates externally, it also has some impact on the internal atmosphere of the institution. Nonetheless, the new internal pressures do not necessarily have to be unbearable. Suppression of the minority is not a necessary consequence, particularly—let us honestly note—if the minority within an institution is on the side of the powers-that-be in the nation as a whole. If an individual feels too uncomfortable, the very multiplicity of our universities (as our churches) offers other niches into which he can move. This may be an inconvenience, but we must measure it against the inconvenience to those who wish to counteract the status quo and who could do so most effectively, not as voters, but through their institutions (though there need be no either-or choice here).

The second argument that collective expressions deviate from the tasks of the institution is more than fallacious; it is specious. This argument hinges on the definition of the primary function of the institution. For me, the primary function of a university is neither professional training, general education, nor intellectual research. These are all tasks assigned to the institution. Its primary function is perpetually to question the truths of the time—whether they are the truths of the universe or of the social consensus. The primary function is the Socratic task "to corrupt the youth." To be sure, I would counsel diffidence because the risk of hubris is monumental. But silence is the worst of all solutions, because the most cowardly. As for the additional argument that collective expressions are time consuming, I must say that we are all capable of balancing the demands on us for our limited time. If the university did nothing but pass resolutions, it would become absurdly ineffective. But once again, it is not a question of either-or. I have confidence that we would learn how to give collective expressions of opinion their due amount of time.

The third argument that collective expressions invite social and financial retaliation is backlash. This is fallacious because once again it assumes a very simplified model of social behavior. The assumption is that our society tolerates a range of viewpoints and activities until someone goes too far, at which point the government or some other socially powerful force retaliates. Quite the contrary is true. Our society and all societies constantly exercise social control on their members (individuals, groups, institutions). A range of methods from force to finance to normative constraint is used for social control, but the ideal control is to obtain acceptance within an institution of a constraining norm that will then be enforced by the members of the institution themselves. Thus, we are bound by golden chains at little cost to outsiders. Today, in the American university, this role is played by the norms of professionalism and apoliticism. In point of fact, retaliation is always a function of political strength. If one university gets out of line, it can feel the effects of retaliation immediately. If the collectivity of universities asserted new norms, retaliation would be much more difficult. Can you imagine the government revoking the tax exemption of the National Council of Churches of Christ because the churches called for the recognition of the People's Republic of China? The Council took that very action some ten years ago, when such a call was still considered a very unpatriotic position to take. The fact is that nothing happened because the government was not strong enough to take action against the Council. Thus is freedom preserved by the strength of those dissenting and enhanced by the vigor of their dissent.

The chief danger to academic freedom today comes not from student disruption but from the self-deceptions of the professoriate itself. It is reluctance to take moral risks, which results in mandarinism, discrimination, and collegial pressure. My purpose here is not, however, to condemn my colleagues but rather to urge them to rethink their actions in the light of their ideals. The chief safeguard of academic freedom would be the transformation of the liberal university into the critical university. Asserting the legitimacy of collective expressions of opinion would be the first step on an arduous path to making our quest for freedom relate to the power realities of contemporary American society.

The critical university is now both a desirable and a feasible institution. Only when the major universities of our country define themselves as critical institutions, will we be able to assert that academic freedom genuinely exists in our university system. Opponents of the concept often suggest that the critical university will create seats of orthodoxy, contempt for contradiction, and a stultifying atmosphere of anti-intellectualism. All I can say is that any of these traits would *ex definitio* not be part of what I mean by a critical university. Indeed, my whole point is that, while the liberal university says it is against all of these evils, it in fact fosters them in a hidden and self-deceiving fashion.

A critical university cannot enshrine orthodoxy; it exists to question accepted truths, which means that it is engaged in a perpetual debate with others who are, in social terms, more powerful. The critical university will not, or should not, foster contempt for contradiction, since the voicing of such alternative views are its raison d'être and since the quality of its criticism is a function of the quality of the intellectual defense of the accepted truths. Far from being anti-intellectual, the critical university—and it alone—will demonstrate that intellect and reason are the essential weapons of social analysis and change. The critical university will make reason acceptable to the mass of the population because it will demonstrate the relevance of reason—not merely to the immediate daily tasks of life but to the ideals and hopes of the vast majority. The critical university will make intellectuals self-respecting and hence less alienated from their fellows by integrating them with the real social life of the world. In short, just as the church seeks to be the ethical watchdog of society, so the university should seek to be its intellectual watchdog.

✲ 20 ✲

"Policing" Academic Responsibility

Bertram H. Davis

No one familiar with higher education could have failed to notice that faculty members commonly preach to administrators about freedom, that administrators commonly preach to faculty members about responsibility, and that they both have a great ability to ignore each other. Having laid claim to freedom, faculty members undoubtedly opted for something more exciting and provocative than responsibility. Duty, or as Wordsworth called it, the "Stern Daughter of the Voice of God" has never much piqued the poetic imagination. *Bartlett's Familiar Quotations*, that infallible guide to the human imagination, lists eighty-two entries under "freedom" and only ten under "responsibility." The faculty obviously is in preferred company, but those who carry the banner of responsibility are in good company too. Professional people especially should be ready to regard responsibility highly since they are by definition devoted to the service of man and the public good. In the academic community, responsibility takes on some special dimensions, since academicians are also dedicated to the advancement of their disciplines and of the colleges and universities which allow them to practice their professions.

It is important to take a comprehensive view of academic responsibility, partly because we see and conduct ourselves better as a result and partly because a narrow focus on certain aspects of responsibility is intolerably constricting. Moreover, viewing responsibility too narrowly leads to unfortunate resentments between faculty members and administrators. I am not entirely certain why faculty members and administrators, in their respective emphases upon academic freedom and responsibility, manage to communicate with each other so infrequently. Certainly some faculty members have a regrettable tendency to include under the rubric of academic freedom many things that do not really belong there. Faculty members consequently impair their credibility when they speak out on this subject; academic freedom is a splendid anthem, but we do not always sing it in tune. We do not always take into account that just about every administrator considers himself as devoted to academic freedom as faculty members. We may think that administrators are mistaken in this self-assessment, but it cannot be overlooked when we are trying to communicate.

Some administrators have had a tendency to speak of academic responsibility in terms that suggest a concern to avoid displeasing the board of trustees, the public, or the legislature. One gets the impression at times that the height of irresponsibility is to express publicly a highly unpopular view, but this way of defining irresponsibility inevitably stifles dissent and controversy. In addition, administrators often regard academic freedom and tenure as merely two sides of the same coin; hence, one cannot have academic freedom without having responsibility first. I myself believe it is important to stress the opposite view—that you cannot have responsibility without academic freedom. An individual devoted to the advancement of learning needs the conditions most favorable to learning; the individual cannot adequately discharge his responsibilities without a high degree of freedom. To use another metaphor, let me suggest that academic freedom is the fire that purifies the crude ore of responsibility and gives it maximum potential.

The role of the faculty in policing academic responsibility is a crucial one. In relation to the individual, academic responsibility begins with the appointment process and continues throughout one's career at the institution. In the appointment process, the faculty members are trying to determine which of the available applicants will best discharge the responsibilities expected of him. In subsequent decisions on reappointment, promotion, salary, and tenure, the faculty's responsibility consists in fairly evaluating the effectiveness with which the individual faculty member has discharged his own responsibilities. The 1966 *Statement on Government of Colleges and Universities,* jointly formulated by the American Council on Education, the Association of Governing Boards, and the American Association of University Professors (AAUP), is to a very large extent a statement of academic responsibility, outlining as it does the roles of the board, the president, and the faculty. The *Statement* may be offered as evidence of the leadership role that a professional organization like the AAUP may play in setting the standards of academic responsibility, but its justification lies in the standards that it contains. In matters related to faculty status, the *Statement* places primary responsibility in the hands of the faculty.

I am aware that those who employ the word policing ordinarily have a quite different understanding of it than I do. There are occasions when disciplinary measures must be invoked, and in our time we have heard shrill cries for severe faculty discipline, coupled with the surly observation that faculty members are almost totally undisciplined. I myself think otherwise. Indeed, the academic profession probably polices itself more effectively than any other profession. The medical and legal professions, lacking an institutional base for the implementation of their ethical canons, have been compelled to look for substitutes in the form of state or local boards; but the essential privacy of the doctor-patient or lawyer-client relationship has erected a screen which has been difficult to penetrate. Faculty members can practice their profession only by means of institutional appointments; and like other communities, colleges, and universities faculties have found it necessary to establish rules and regulations for the conduct and performance of their constituents. A faculty member constantly undergoes the scrutiny of his colleagues, and he may at any time be called to account for an alleged infraction of the institution's regulations as well as for a presumed failure to discharge adequately the responsibilities of his position or to observe the general canons of professional conduct. The academic profession is one of the few professions that requires a probationary period for its members. A faculty member may tbe rebuked for an action unacceptable to his colleagues; he may be denied reappointment, promotion, salary increase, or a tenured appointment; and for an egregious act of misconduct he may be dismissed in the middle of an academic year. Even after the granting of tenure, he may be disciplined in similar if not identical ways.

The faculty's role in problems of discipline should be a critical one. Inevitably, a fair appraisal of alleged professional misconduct requires a professional judgment that faculty members are in the best position to make. The role of disciplinarian need not be exercised to the total exclusion of the administration, which may recommend action by a department or faculty committee. In serious cases the administration has traditionally preferred charges for faculty consideration and generally asserts a power of review. The *Statement on Government of Colleges and Universities* concludes that the administration should accept the judgment of the faculty in these matters, except in rare cases and for compelling reasons, which the faculty should have the opportunity to consider.

A well-ordered institution confronts few problems of faculty discipline that it is not equipped to resolve reasonably and fairly. Thus, the role of the professional organization in policing standards of faculty responsibility is likely to be confined to those cases in which the faculty member has been removed from the institution's jurisdiction. The professional organization could not in any event undertake the policing responsibilities of some two or three thousand institutions. The professional organization cannot be expected to attach a penalty to one that the institution has considered sufficient, nor can it impose penalties when the institution has considered none appropriate. This is not to say that the professional organization has no role in such matters: it has in fact a very important role. Having the opportunity to observe policies and practices in a wide variety of institutions, the professional organization has the responsibility of distilling that experience for the benefit of the academic community, most particularly through the promulgation of general standards fitted to the community that the institution serves. Medical and legal organizations have established canons of conduct adapted to the fact that by and large the members of those professions deal directly with the public and may take advantage of private citizens in ways quite foreign to an academic setting. Faced with a very different arrangement in the academic community, the AAUP, through its *Statement on Professional Ethics,* has called attention to the basic responsibility of the faculty member to his subject, his students, his professional colleagues, his institution, and the community in which he lives. The AAUP has supplemented its general standards with a variety of specific recommendations on the wide-ranging responsibilities of the faculty. The numerous policy statements of the AAUP constitute an extensive code of responsible faculty conduct. Some of these policy statements are: the 1940 *Statement of Principles on Academic Freedom and Tenure;* the *Statement on Procedural Standards in Faculty Dismissal Proceedings;* the *Statement on Recruitment and Resignation of Faculty Members; On Preventing Conflict of Interests in Government-Sponsored Research at Universities;* and *The Role of the Faculty in the Accrediting of Colleges and Universities.* Even the *Joint Statement on Rights and Freedoms of Students* was developed initially by an AUUP Committee on Faculty Responsibility for the Academic Freedom of Students.

The policing of academic responsibility covers a broader spectrum than the subject of faculty responsibility alone. The AAUP has joined with other organizations to establish standards of responsible conduct for boards of trustees and administrators, and it has also played a prominent role in the policing of academic responsibility—a role assumed almost as soon as the AAUP was organized. In 1915 AAUP leaders undertook to investigate complaints that faculty members had been dismissed in violation of academic freedom. Almost simultaneously the AAUP took measures to safeguard academic freedom for the future by developing a *Declaration of Principles on Academic Freedom and Tenure.* That unanticipated role has steadily grown, and now the AAUP annually reviews some five hundred to eight hundred complaints and tries to affect corrections when principles of academic freedom, tenure, due process, or notice have been violated. The association conducts formal investigations of one to three dozen cases each year. The purpose of this work is to secure the observance of recognized principles of academic freedom and tenure. The AAUP is by no means alone in its pursuit of this purpose. Indeed, the protection of academic freedom is largely an institutional responsibility, with boards, administrators, faculties, and students all taking part. Large though it is, the fact that the AAUP's workload is not larger still is a result of the efforts of these groups to safeguard academic freedom in college and university communities.

The impact of any action is commonly, though not always, in proportion to the authority of those responsible for the action. At a college or university the impact of an administrative action in violation of academic freedom may be widespread and profound. For very good reasons, administrators are not generally subject to regular campus disciplinary proceedings; they may be accountable to the faculty in many ways, and they are accountable ultimately to the board of trustees. But the record of academic freedom in the United States is stained with numerous incidents which boards of trustees have concurred in, encouraged, and even compelled so that administrative actions violate academic freedom. In the absence of any institutional remedy for this assertion of ultimate authority, the AAUP has had a very vital role to play. The AAUP undertook this role on behalf of the academic community with the conviction that academic freedom is indispensable to the public good, to the welfare of colleges and universities, and to the profession as a whole. In fifty-six years that conviction, far from being shaken, has constantly been strengthened. Had there been other ways in 1915 to assure the protection of academic freedom, the AAUP doubtless would have centered its attention on other professional problems. But in those days the faculty members had recourse only to the courts, which were likely to provide little satisfaction at great expense. Today, partly through the persistence of organizations like the American Civil Liberties Union and the AAUP, the courts are more likely to grant relief. But pursuit of a court case is still an expensive, time-consuming, and uncertain process. Moreover, I do not think we would wish to see the academic community constantly take its direction from the courts. Under the circumstances, the need for professional organizations to assist in policing this delicate and highly significant area of academic responsibility can be expected to continue indefinitely.

In other areas the professional organizations will have to continue using their experience to assist colleges and universities. Because professional organizations consist largely of faculty members, they will inevitably give special attention to asserting the responsibilities of the faculty. I am aware that faculty members have not always sought to meet their responsibilities; they can stand some prodding. But many institutions remain where the administration uses its authority to make a narrow view of the faculty role prevail. In the worst of these situations, the faculty member, hemmed in as he is, will either go elsewhere, draw himself into a private world where neither academic freedom nor academic responsibility has much meaning for him, or try at great risk to correct the conditions he finds oppressive. Increasingly in our time the faculty member is choosing the last of these courses of action. In such instances, academic freedom is generally both the battle cry and the text, even though the basic objective of the faculty member may be the creation of a responsible role for all faculty. Wordsworth's "stern daughter," responsibility, will never get the faculty member much of a following. No doubt, he will be labelled irresponsible by his own chief administrator. It is not to be expected that the words of either the faculty member or the administrator will have much impact upon the other.

21

Prescribing Faculty
Workloads

Richard L. Miller

If legislative actions are accurate barometers of public concern, then there is no doubt that the public wants more for its money from public higher education. Let me illustrate this general point by presenting, in some detail, an analysis of the case in Michigan. I will focus specifically on the establishment of minimum teaching loads for faculty members. The Michigan legislature in recent years has imposed without noticeable public reaction an increasing number of controls on the prerogatives of the boards governing our colleges and universities in the cause of productivity, efficiency and economy. The latest such control establishes minimum faculty teaching load standards for each of the public institutions. As recently as the 1970 general election campaign, there was an opportunity for candidates and the public to register some form of objection to these legislative instrusions. The only issues raised in connection with higher education, however, were campus disorder and costs, reflecting the public's desire for greater productivity and efficiency. In short the people of Michigan care little that the legislature is now deciding how many hours professors must spend in the classroom.

A decade ago the controls now imposed by the legislature would have become political issues in Michigan. The governor and his party would have accused the legislature (controlled by the opposite party) of attempting to rule the universities, making them at best second class institutions of higher education. In that era the public would have been concerned. Today, these legislative controls are virtually ignored. The eroded prestige of higher education and the state's fiscal problems allow the legislature, aggravated by years of frustration over the inviolability of university autonomy, to impose controls without fear of public reprisal.

To understand the impact of Michigan's new rules on faculty teaching loads, it is important to know the structural setting in which these rules have been placed. First, each of Michigan's thirteen public baccalaureate institutions has constitutional status. The Michigan constitution grants to the governing board of each institution general supervision of the institution and the control and direction of all expenditures from the institution's funds. The three largest universities have eight-member governing boards elected at large from the state. The remaining ten colleges and universities have eight-member governing boards appointed by the governor. The junior and community colleges have locally elected boards and are without constitutional autonomy. Michigan also has an elected, eight-member state board of education. The constitution says that the state board is vested with the leadership and general supervision of all public education, including adult education and instructional programs in state institutions, with the exception of institutions granting baccalaureate degrees. The constitution provides in addition, however, that the state board shall serve as the general planning and coordinating body for all public education, including higher education. The parameters of this planning and coordinating authority are undefined by the constitution and to date have not been clarified by the courts.

The legislature's role in higher education is described by the constitution as that of appropriating moneys to maintain the thirteen baccalaureate institutions and other institutions established by law. Operationally, the budget and appropriation process for the baccalaureate institutions excludes the state board. Individually, the colleges and universities prepare annual budget requests that are submitted to the bureau of the budget in the executive office. The executive budget, prepared subsequent to review of the requests, is submitted directly to the legislature. Appropriations by the legislature are made directly to each institution. The state board advises the legislature as to the financial requirements of colleges and universities, but this advice has been uniformly ignored by legislatures. Overall, Michigan's four-year colleges and universities are blessed with the constitutional promise of autonomy, the fulfillment of which fails in the presence of the legislature's power of appropriation.

Into this structural setting the Legislature has now inserted standards of faculty effort, by establishing a minimum faculty teaching load for each of the thirteen public baccalaureate institutions and the twenty-nine junior and community colleges. At our three largest universities—Wayne State University, Michigan State University and the University of Michigan—full-time faculty members are required by the legislature to carry a load of ten classroom contact hours per week. The minimum teaching load for full-time faculty at the other ten baccalaureate institutions is twelve classroom contact hours. For junior and community colleges the minimum load is fifteen hours.

Putting aside for the moment the major issue presented by this new legislative policy—that is, the propriety or perhaps legality of the legislature assuming a direct management role in the operation of the universities—we must consider the immediate problem of interpretation. The legislature has provided no definition of its basic index of faculty load, the classroom contact hour. How shall contact hours be counted in such special types of instruction as supervision or team teaching or arranged instruction? Is the minimum teaching load to apply to each faculty member, or is it intended as a departmental average, school average, or university-wide average? These unanswered questions highlight the importance of a related legislative action that bears directly upon the interpretation of the teaching load policy. In a separate appropriation act in 1970 the legislature ordered the Michigan department of education to "conduct an annual academic staff performance audit of all institutions of higher education." The audit "shall include measures of experience, training, salary and other compensation and productivity in terms of instruction and other duties of all academic staff" and beginning in 1971 must be submitted to the executive office and the legislature by September 30 of each year. By this action the legislature has created the means for annually accounting for faculty efforts at each institution; it is a potentially effective means for enforcing compliance with legislative policy. The legislature did not, however, fill the definitional void created in its teaching load mandate. In effect the responsibility for interpretation was passed on to the bureau, since the data produced in the bureau's audit report will be the only data against which teaching load standards may be compared. Consequently, the bureau's definition of classroom contact hours could well determine the extent to which the standards will be upheld. Therefore, the performance audit has become an integral part of legislative policy and must be viewed as such.

As developed by the bureau, the performance audit attempts to relate faculty education, experience, classroom workload, annual compensation, and distribution of effort at the departmental level at each of the forty-two Michigan institutions. As an example of the type and extent of information required from the institutions responding to the audit, let us look at a hypothetical case of a single department at Eastern Michigan University. The audit would describe this department in the following detail. The headcount of full professors is five, all of whom hold doctoral degrees. Two professors have seven to nine years experience; one has ten to twelve years experience, and two have over twelve years experience. The five full professors are 4.5 full-time equivalents, and all are in the annual compensation range of $10,000 to $14,999. The classroom contact hour load of one of these full professors (.5 full-time equivalent) fall in the load range of 0 to 3.99. This professor has three hours of arranged instruction, teaches three credit hours and generates six student credit hours. The classroom contact hour load of two of the professors (2.0 full-time equivalents) falls in the load range of 8 to 11.99, and these two have one hour of arranged instruction, handle eighteen credit hours and generate 544 student credit hours. And so it goes, as this same set of descriptive information is applied across five compensation ranges and five classroom contact hour ranges at each faculty rank. The institutions must also report the distribution of full-time equivalent academic staff to the functions of instruction, scholarly and creative activity, professional service activity, administrative activity, and committee assignments and other activities. Such distribution is to be done at five compensation ranges for each faculty rank by department. The academic performance audit is exhaustive and exhausting.

Institutional objections to the audit have been registered on several counts—the primary point being that the audit will fail to provide an accurate representation of faculty effort. For better or worse, however, the audit has filled the definitional void left by the legislative mandate. For all practical purposes the legislative policy now is that full-time faculty shall carry a minimum teaching load of twelve class-room contact hours (or ten or fifteen, depending on the classification of the institution), which are defined in the audit as "the number of clock hours per week during the fall term spent in regularly scheduled classes for which credit is offered."

The causes of the new teaching load requirements are directly traceable to the legislature, where the motivation is simply a matter of money. The legislature views its power to establish the annual net state appropriation level for public colleges and universities as an ineffective means for controlling the rising expenditures of higher education. Merely making the appropriations leaves too many loose ends, too much flexibility for the institutions to generate additional revenue locally. This broadens the basis upon which future requests for state appropriations will be made. (Adjusting tuition rates and enrollment policies, for example, are ways by which an institution can broaden this base.) In recent years the legislature has developed several new devices to tie up these loose ends, and the teaching load requirement is just one of these devices. The introduction of the gross appropriation concept was an early invention by which the legislature attempted to set not only the amount it appropriated, but also the amounts of fee revenue and other income that the institutions would realize annually. This device was not totally successful, as the governing boards of institutions continued to exercise their constitutional authority to adjust tuition rates and enrollment policies. The legislature subsequently added to the gross appropriation device new restrictions on enrollments and tuition. First, ceilings were placed on nonresident enrollments, and a nonresident tuition differential was established. Then total enrollment ceilings were imposed on certain of the universities. These additional restrictions were apparently judged by the legislature to be less than totally effective, as more restrictions followed.

The 1969–1970 appropriation act required the institutions to certify to the legislature by April 15, 1970, their resident tuition and fee rates for the following year. This meant that fees were to be fixed prior to the legislative decision on appropriation levels and, hence, would prevent the governing boards from raising tuition rates to support the desired educational programs of their institutions, should the appropriations be too low to do so. To enforce this new certification requirement, the legislature directed that the allocation of appropriations to any university realizing higher revenues from fee increases made subsequent to certification should be reduced by the amount of the excess revenue produced by the fee increase. The noose was tightened in the 1970–1971 appropriation act. As noted previously, the legislature's attempts to place controls on institutional operations through such devices as the minimum teaching load derive from its desire to restrict the flow of dollars from the state to the colleges and universities. Legislative frustration in this task has been aggravated this year by the state's mounting fiscal problems. The slumping national economy has hit Michigan hard, as revenues have fallen far below anticipated levels. The U.A.W. strike at General Motors in the fall of 1970 heavily cut into the state's general fund revenues. The total of revenue costs related to the strike has been set at $50,400,000. Welfare expenditures, which have jumped from 14 per cent of the state's general fund budget in 1965 to 23 per cent in 1971, are increasing by leaps and bounds. Thus, Michigan's legislators are in an irritable state of mind and not too receptive to suggestions that controls on colleges and universities be removed. In 1970–1971, gross appropriations were made on a line-item basis for five functions. Deductions from gross appropriations for nonappropriation institutional revenue were also made on a line-item basis. The tuition certification requirement was repeated, and specific resident tuition rates were listed for all institutions in terms of dollar amount per credit hour. Finally, the legislature plunged deeply into the operation of the university by establishing minimum faculty teaching load requirements.

The response of Michigan's public colleges and universities to these new legislative incursions has generally been one of reasonable opposition. There has been no concerted campaign to take the institutions' argument to the court of public opinion, and no bitter exchange of accusations between institutions and the legislature occurred. The institutions have made it clear to the legislature, however, that these restrictive legislative devices in general, and the minimum teaching load requirements in particular, are direct infringements of governing board prerogatives. Further, the institutions charge that the teaching load levels have been established arbitrarily without benefit of logic or consideration of the full range of faculty effort that goes beyond classroom contact.

As a direct means of voicing their dissatisfaction, the institutions—through a suit initiated by the University of Michigan, Michigan State University, and Wayne State University—have challenged in the Michigan courts the authority of the legislature to attach a whole range of conditional controls to the appropriations. The universities argue in their complaint that the constitution grants to their governing boards exclusive power to make those decisions that the legislature has attempted to pre-empt. Specifically, the suit charges that the legislative mandate on teaching loads "substitutes the judgment of the legislature for the constitutional discretion of the boards to determine the minimum number of classroom contact hours which a faculty member at the universities must teach and unconstitutionally invades the right of the universities to govern their faculties and to compensate their staffs from appropriated funds, regardless of whether or not said funds appear in whole or in part as a so-called line item in the appropriation." The suit has been filed in the circuit court of Ingham County, and oral arguments are expected to be heard by the court this spring.

In view of the clear language of the Michigan constitution, the universities have an impressive argument. The realities of the situation are less promising, however. If the legislature is determined to have its way, a court decision favorable to the universities might not provide an adequate remedy. There are a million and one ways that legislative intent may be implemented through the appropriation process. Even if the universities should win in court and the legislative controls are declared unconstitutioanl, the same legislative intent could be implemented by different means. Higher education might then be forced to carry its case into the political arena to obtain relief from legislative interference. This is an option that colleges and universities have been reluctant to follow in today's political climate.

Since the decision of the court will not be heard immediately, let us ask: What are the implications of the new teaching load requirements for the colleges and universities? First, there is the matter of accountability. All institutions are requested in the academic performance audit to collect and submit detailed information on faculty effort. Also forced compliance with the minimum load requirements is possible through the adjustment of appropriation levels. Significant implications are also found in the impact of the new rules on the unionization of faculty. The teaching load rule is the one legislative intrusion into institutional management that is an immediate and direct threat to faculty security.

Currently, the faculties of two public baccalaureate institutions are organized as units for bargaining purposes. The faculties at the other institutions are in various stages of exploring unionization. The legislative imposition of teaching load standards will certainly quicken the pace of unionization at those campuses where faculties are now weighing the pros and cons of collective bargaining for their profession. Simultaneously, the very legislative actions that are pushing faculties toward unionization are progressively restricting the ability of governing boards to become viable participants in the collective bargaining process. The controls on teaching loads, enrollments, the enrollment mix, educational program decisions, and tuition rates are appropriate examples of how the revenue options and fiscal flexibility of the governing boards are limited. Such limitations are disabling the administrations from becoming effective bargaining participants. If the governing board does not control the resources available to the university, it will be of little use for the organized faculty to join in collective bargaining with the board. The faculty must go where the control is—and where the money is—to bargain. Under the legislative plan of governance that control would reside in the legislature. Given the current set of circumstances in Michigan and the persistence of the legislature in progressively imposing restrictive controls on the governing boards, a bargaining confrontation between faculty and legislature appears inevitable. Such a confrontation would most certainly compound legislative problems and frustrations. But in the absence of a sudden surge of public support for higher education, the confrontation will occur in an environment hostile to faculty goals and will be resolved in the favor of the legislature. Quite possibly, a revision of the mechanisms for governing public higher education in Michigan will be made and will shatter the concept of institutional autonomy now provided in our state constitution.

⚜ 22 ⚜

Tenure and Collective Bargaining

William W. Van Alstyne

In the aftermath of campus unrest and the hard facts of tightened university budgets, tenure has once again become a subject of very general interest. Simultaneously, developments in collective bargaining, boosted by the recent decision of the National Labor Relations Board to extend its jurisdiction to private universities, have already begun to overlap tenure systems on a number of campuses. The coincidence of converging concern over tenure and collective bargaining suggests that it may now be useful to review both forms of professional security.

Tenure, fairly well defined as a concept, does not guarantee lifetime employment. Rather, it provides that no person continuously retained as a full-time faculty member beyond a lengthy probationary period may thereafter be dismissed without adequate cause. The definition of adequate cause is found in the published rules and standards of the university. The standards set by the university are virtually without restriction, with the exception that no rule can violate the academic freedom or the ordinary civil liberties of the individual. Tenure may be conceived as the assurance that one's professional security and academic freedom will not be jeopardized without the full observance of academic due process. This means that, in a particular instance where dismissal has been recommended on grounds of professional irresponsibility or incompetence, a fairly rigorous procedure will be observed. The procedure seeks to ensure, first, that the stated cause is the authentic cause for seeking dismissal, rather than a pretense for considerations that violate academic freedom; second, that the stated cause exists in fact; and, third, that the degree of professional irresponsibility or incompetence warrants outright termination of employment rather than some lesser sanction.

The procedural protections of tenure are analogous to fair hearing requirements now evolving in the federal courts for the protection of various kinds of status in the public sector. Academic due process is also analogous to the statutory procedural protection of civil servants and, indeed, to the weaker conventional grievance procedures in collective bargaining agreements. It has long since ceased to be true that even unskilled workers in a conventional industrial firm may summarily be fired by a unilateral decision of management; typically, the agreement (and labor law) limits the grounds for dismissal, and a grievance procedure is provided to determine the basis and fairness of the proposed termination. Tenure—through its reference to more specific and rigorous forms of academic due process—usually does provide, however, a larger measure of procedural protection than is provided in the *ex post facto* review of the factory worker's grievance.

The concept of tenure may be stated in still another way. The conferral of tenure means that the institution—after a probationary period during which the professional competence, excellence, and responsibility of the appointee has been determined—has rendered a favorable judgment, establishing a presumption of the individual's professional excellence. The presumption, however, can be rebutted. When it can be shown that the individual subsequently misconducts himself, the presumption of fitness may be forfeited. The function of this rebuttable presumption is perfectly clear. The design is not to insulate mediocrity within the sanctuary of the academic institution; rather, it is eminently linked to the public interest in academic freedom and to the protection of personal civil liberty. An individual who can be terminated without adequate cause and irrespective of his length of service must necessarily fear to assert any view or to conduct his private life in any manner that is likely to displease those with summary authority to terminate his career at that institution. (The squeeze on academic freedom becomes acute in a shrinking academic marketplace. Indeed, the concept of tenure, with its provision of academic due process, is most essential in a surplus labor market.) As regards tenure, the individual should reasonably be given the benefit of the doubt, since a lengthy term of probationary service has provided the institution with ample opportunity to determine whether the faculty member is worthy of a rebuttable presumption of professional fitness. Moreover, the institution should have the obligation to show why, if at all, a faculty member should be fired after granting a presumption of fitness.

There are certain circumstances in which tenure will not assure professional security even for a faculty member of unquestioned professional excellence. Two of these may be mentioned to dispel the errant criticism that tenure guarantees lifetime employment. The demonstration of sustained medical disability (established fairly to make certain it is not a masquerade for reasons that violate academic freedom) may result in termination, although disability does not reflect upon the integrity or scholarly competence of the individual. For termination to result, it is enough that the disability substantially impairs the faculty member's regular service to the university, however beyond his control the disability may be. A second instance of bona fide termination may arise if an academic program for which the faculty member is exclusively qualified is cancelled. Declining student enrollments in certain departments have reduced the demand for the services of some faculty members with particular skills. If a tenured faculty member is unable to become professionally competent in some other area of the academic program, he may be terminated simply through the cessation of the program itself. Again, when particular academic programs are terminated because of unavoidable financial stringency, released members of the faculty are in no way charged with misconduct or scholarly incompetence. Nonetheless, the faculty cannot be insulated from the prospect of unemployment when an authentic financial emergency confronts the university. In such cases, certain programs and particular faculty members must be eliminated in a nonarbitrary and reasonable way, and tenure can provide no security.

Briefly to summarize, then, tenure does not protect one from termination because of incompetence or professional irresponsibility, nor does it otherwise guarantee lifetime employment. Tenure means that an institution has found a faculty member worthy of a rebuttable presumption of professional excellence after a lengthy term of probationary service. That presumption of excellence cannot thereafter be divested without academic due process that shows adequate cause for the forfeiture of the presumption.

Let us now turn to a discussion of how tenure can be affected by collective bargaining. The relationship between the concept of tenure and the process of collective bargaining, on a technical level, is quite evident. If the National Labor Relations Act is generally applicable, or if the state statutes that authorize collective bargaining follow the outline of the Wagner Act (as they mainly tend to do), then nothing forbids any institution from maintaining exactly what we have already defined as tenure. According to the acts, tenure would need to be achieved through the negotiation of specific provisions in the collective agreement itself. The Labor Relations Act, for example, authorizes bargaining over wages, hours, and other conditions of employment. Obviously, a provision concerning job security affects a condition of employment. Customarily, in industrial firms the conditions of employment regarding job security do not necessarily involve the kind of thing we have defined as tenure; usually, provisions on job security allow management to fire an employee, but the act is subject to a grievance procedure sometimes culminating in arbitration by third parties from outside the firm and the union. Nothing in the state statutes precludes the modification of this custom in connection with tenure at academic institutions—that is, nothing legally prevents the formation of a faculty union and bargaining in good faith for the setting of precise standards and definitions of tenure, academic freedom, and academic due process. Whether this pattern of negotiation will establish itself in the collective negotiations in higher education remains to be seen. Nothing in the nature of collective bargaining itself, however, precludes the exact duplication of tenure provisions in the collective agreement.

Nonetheless, one or two technical problems exist. Management and labor are both enjoined under the Labor Relations Act to bargain in good faith. That has been interpreted by some to mean that neither party may take an obdurate position, asserting an unwillingness to negotiate on any particular point. According to one view, this means that if management proposes a certain package on a take-it-or-leave-it basis, the publicized proposal itself may be seen as a manifest unwillingness to bargain in good faith. A leading decision on this particular matter—whether obduracy of stance and calculated publicity of that stance on nonnegotiable issues may state an unfair labor practice— appeared a number of years ago in a case involving General Electric and the phenomenon called Boulwarism. The case is seemingly pertinent to our discussion. The concept of academic freedom, at least for the American Association of University Professors (AAUP), is wholly nonnegotiable. Because tenure (and its provision for academic due process) is regarded as indispensable to the protection of academic freedom, it too may be nonnegotiable. Neither academic freedom nor tenure is to be bartered away for better medical plans, lower course loads, free beer on Saturday, or any other benefit. The AAUP feels that the assurance of academic freedom is of constitutional significance. Each individual has a right to academic freedom, and neither the principle nor the right may be waived or subordinated no matter how large a majority would willingly trade them away. As a professional judgment, I believe that the case in which Boulwarism made its appearance is distinguishable in any event. I would not anticipate that it offers any serious problem in accommodating the process of collective bargaining to the concept of tenure.

Aside from the problem of whether the technical processes of collective bargaining will readily lend themselves to traditional academic standards, no clear pattern is emerging as yet. Four areas of possible concern, however, should be mentioned. One of these has to do with the negotiating strength of the particular unit, the circumstances under which the unit is bargaining, and the spirit that animates its desire to reach agreement with the particular college. Specifically, there is a real danger that some very important concepts (academic freedom, tenure, and academic due process) will be traded off when a faculty decides the issues that are to be presented through the exclusive bargaining agent (the union representative). For instance, an extremely weak faculty or a new and indifferent faculty may be more interested in the fringe benefits of a better pension plan, an additional five hundred dollars a year, or an improved medical plan, than in the protection of tenure, academic due process, or academic freedom. This likelihood is enhanced because such concepts are relatively alien to industrial bargaining, since the industrial firm does not serve the same societal interest. The function of the industrial firm is to make profits. The function of the educational firm is the generation and transmission of information and knowledge. The fact is, however, that as national trade unions look for growth by expanding onto campuses (not necessarily in any suspicious or improper fashion but simply to offer themselves to faculty as the suitable, exclusive agent for bargaining), their relative inexperience in the field of higher education tends to make them inattentive to some of the essential constitutional propositions characteristic of higher education.

One may anticipate the appearance of collective agreements that will occasionally turn out to be disastrous in terms of the constitutional rights of academic freedom and academic due process. The individual drawing up a contract based upon a suitable industrial model may not realize that these kinds of precautions should be built into both the negotiations and the culminating agreement. Perhaps the hazards should not be overstressed, but one or two agreements have already appeared that seem utterly heedless of the long struggle for the general acceptance of the concepts of academic freedom and academic due process. Some people now appear willing to abandon these concepts, perhaps because of the shrinking academic market and because of concern for financial rewards and fringe benefits.

A second risk implicit in the use of the industrial firm model of collective bargaining is the prospect of estrangement between the faculty and the university. Currently, the faculty is to a considerable extent a part of management. This is especially true of senior faculty members, who assume authority in matters of curriculum and personnel. Boards of trustees correctly retain but seldom exercise the nominal authority to reject curricular or personnel recommendations issuing from departments. The reserved authority of the board is properly there, but the authority is used only occasionally and even then largely as a veto. The use of a bargaining agent may stretch the distance between the faculty and the college administration. An agent may result in a new degree of alienation and in the emergence of a different point of view: the faculty may no longer identify with the needs of the institution but with their own collectivity as a labor force. Under the industrial firm model, even the line of communication can become severely attenuated, since the union communicates with both the work force and the management. Although our experience is at present too limited to allow a prediction about the possibility, the hazard remains that the administration and the faculty will find their ability to communicate with each other restricted.

A third problem area has to do with the description of the appropriate bargaining unit—specifically, those employees who shall be identified with each other for purposes of representation by an agent who will negotiate a contract in their behalf. In academic life, it has been customary to regard all of the faculty as sharing common concerns. If that custom were to become a legal guideline in regulated collective bargaining, then it is perfectly possible that within a number of institutions the nature of the collective agreement will represent predominantly the wishes of the junior faculty. The prospect should not be endorsed or condemned, but it should surely be recognized. If the union represents the total faculty and the whole faculty votes within the union on a one-man-one-vote basis and if junior faculty outnumber the senior faculty, then the union will seek to negotiate issues that reflect the needs, desires, and insecurities of the junior faculty.

The fourth problem area is the possibility that, as collective bargaining advances in the field of higher education, it will tend to expand, rather than cut back, on tenure. Currently, on most campuses the institution has six years in which to fashion a judgment regarding the professional excellence of the appointee. For each of those six years the appointee may have a new contract, or the institution may refuse to retain the faculty member with only a minimum of academic due process. As collective bargaining becomes prevalent, and as the views of junior faculty members come to weigh heavily in the negotiating process, a condition of instant tenure may be demanded. That is to say, the job security provision could apply even in the first or second year of appointment, so that the termination decision could not be made without a fairly elaborate demonstration of reasonable cause.

Whether this situation would be desirable is another question. Unless, however, the situation is moderate so that academic due process —which the institution is obliged, by reason of its contract, to observe before terminating even the most junior faculty member—becomes accommodative and easily demonstrable, then ultimately we may be heading toward mediocrity of faculty. The institution will be confronted at the hiring stage with making adequate inquiry as to whether the applicant really possesses professional excellence—a difficult judgment to make, when dealing with young men and women who have not yet had an opportunity to show their teaching proficiency or their promise of scholarly productivity.

We have seen then how the subjects of tenure and collective bargaining are related in the academic community. Although experience is presently somewhat limited, one can speculate about the future effects tenure and collective bargaining will have upon one another. Quite possibly, tenure—far from being threatened with extinction by the process of collective bargaining—will be even more widespread than at present.

PART SIX:

Reinterpreting Higher Education

The plight of the university is intimately bound to the course of the cultural revolution our society is now experiencing. If education beyond high school is to meet the future needs of our nation and its individual citizens, the role played by colleges and universities must be redefined. The goals of higher education, its very nature, must be reinterpreted for members of the education profession and for the general public. The authors of the essays in Part Six attempt such a reinterpretation.

23

A Race with Disaster

Ed Riddick

Today we stand in the long shadow of Whitney Young, who once said that his hard life decision was whether to get off the train in Harlem and cuss whitey or go on downtown to try to get jobs for blacks in one of the nation's leading corporations. If he had stopped in Harlem, he might have lived longer. But he decided to go downtown to try to get the jobs. The real issue is not Whitney Young's decision to do one thing or another, but the issue raised by the question itself—an issue of at least four centuries duration for this country. It can be seen in the moral bind in which Whitney Young found himself when he knew he must make one decision or another—whether to go where he could identify with others who shared his grief or whether to attempt to find practical solutions to the problems that caused that grief. I am glad that Whitney Young made the decision he made. I am as oriented toward the practical solutions to problems as anyone; yet I am also aware of the situation in which such decisions leave us.

To understand that situation is to understand the problem now confronting the academic world. It has been said that civilization depends upon education's race with catastrophe. This statement suggests a prophetic role for education, and it assumes that educators hold responsibilities that go beyond mere employment to human involvement and commitment. The academic community, in short, can no longer afford its ivory tower if it expects to win the race with disaster.

The real story of Whitney Young, perhaps, is that he recognized the tragedy of the adjustment he made, because in all of its intricacies and all of its expressions it never gave a large segment of the American community any choices. Neither did it provide any kind of equity (which presumably exists in the country) in the allotment of goods and services. That is the problem all of us must handle today, the problem the academic community must handle.

Let us look at what is happening. A report published by Senator Lee Metcalf reveals that fifty-three American universities hold more than 10.9 million shares of common stock, valued at more than 321 million dollars, in eighty-five electric utilities alone. Some 24.2 million shares of stock, common and preferred, are owned as well in more than 160 energy concerns, and they are valued at more than 905.5 million dollars. This represents a sizeable segment of voting stock in corporations that are tremendously influential in determining the direction of this nation's priorities. Do those who direct the affairs of our universities view this stock as income alone—or as income plus involvement? If they allow this stock, through proxies, to be controlled by the management of the corporations involved, they forfeit choice and stifle voices that ought to take part in making decisions for the nation. We must ask whether ownership of this stock has any meaningful impact on issues that concern the nation as a whole—issues of poverty and race, the question of war, and the question of innovative methods for developing the lives of human beings in our society.

Kenneth Galbraith has observed the effects of what he has described as a national technostructure. He points out that universities and other educational institutions are major facets of this technostructure. The influences of the technostructure are multiplied and heightened by the presence of multicompany corporations and multibank-holding organizations. These groups pervasively seek to control not only aggregates of markets but the very mechanisms of education as well. And this control has a profound effect on all of us—not only blacks, Chicanos, and poor whites, but also middle-management executives and school administrators. We all become aware of our corporate powerlessness. In the academic world, we permit impersonal forces to dominate such a personal process as teaching, and we thereby allow the influences of the technostructure to broaden and deepen. Our silence creates a vacuum where the technostructure can expand. We refuse our moral obligation, and we fail to defend our rights.

Our schools continue business as usual—until one day some of our students decide that matters have gone too far. Then we begin to perceive the situation. We see that we are no longer involved in education for members of our society but that we are taking part in a kind of indoctrination, orienting us toward doubtful goals, precarious objectives, and meaningless postures. We come to ask not what 1984 will be like, but whether we will have a 1984 at all. When our students tell us that our schools and our classrooms are not "where it's at," we know they are right.

If we are serious academic men and women, if we are not merely engaged in defending the ivory tower, we must find out "where it's at." We must, first of all, continually advocate equity in this society—equity as a prerequisite to justice and as an essential and indispensable value. We must question the priorities of our nation and specifically those priorities that are determined on the basis of a need for scarcities in such essentials as food, shelter, and education. Surely it is obvious to all that such scarcities are not necessary, that they are contrived at the expense of those least able to contend with them. As serious academic men and women, it seems to me we must approach the problem at this basic, immediate level.

Perhaps we should begin with the traditional form of conferences of educators. I mean the kind of educational conference where academic people meet only with other academic people. Such meetings provide no opportunity for us to grasp the real problems of society—the social and environmental problems. We ought to plan our educational conferences together with welfare mothers, city planners, and politicians. We ought to wrestle with the whole issue of how education meaningfully interrelates with things that are happening now. If we are truly interested in academic freedom, we must come to appreciate that it is involved with the planning and development of the cities in which we live, with decent medical care for blacks and poor people in these cities, with the distribution of political power to minority groups, and with the sharing of political power on our campuses. We have an obligation as academic people to lobby on our own campuses for the kind of changes that have become exemplary in the remainder of our society. We cannot do these things if the only people we meet and talk to are persons in our own field. I believe that it becomes the role of an academic man to understand the meaning of Aristotle's statement that "Men come together in cities to live the good life." Our campuses should reflect the ingredients of the kind of city that allows for a good life.

We cannot create such a campus with only 6 per cent black students. We cannot do it with the present restrictions in medical and law schools. We cannot do it with the kind of maneuvering that now seems necessary for obtaining grants from the Department of Health, Education, and Welfare. And we will not do it by slipping a couple of blacks or Mexican-Americans in through the back doors of our graduate schools and aiming them toward master's and doctoral degrees. We might begin to build such campuses if we would talk with the people of our cities, including narcotics addicts and mayors. Then we might begin to understand why it is so important for us to make the good life of the campus reflect the good life of the city.

We need to ask ourselves whether, in fact, we have dealt with the question of building a good society, a decent nation that orients priorities meaningfully. Are we spending so much time in competition for funds for defense research that we have no time left for raising appropriations for public education? Are we so busy trying to obtain National Science Foundation grants that we fail to notice that the federal government gave 650 million dollars to white land-grant colleges but less than 75 million dollars to black land-grant colleges? Where are our priorities? We are in a valley of dry bones. When Kenneth Galbraith talks about the academic institution in relation to other structures within our society, he is speaking of an area that has become a part of this valley. It is inhabited by people without guts. We must understand that this is why the students push us up against the wall. They are concerned about what we cannot choose to ignore or overlook.

Much of the problem that plagues New York today is not a mayor who cannot govern it, but a university that owns the real estate of Harlem. Much of the problem in Chicago today involves more than 125 pieces of real estate in Hyde Park and in Woodlawn owned by the University of Chicago. Much of the problem in Philadelphia today— despite its careful and well-publicized selection of black administrators —is the relationship of Temple University to North Philadelphia. Basically, the problems involve the question of whether the university serves the community or whether the community becomes a playground for university research. Unless these matters are understood clearly, it is pointless to try to understand anything else that is going on in the current academic scene. We can begin to deal with the situation only when we decide where we stand as academic men. If we do not firmly declare ourselves to be human beings, we cannot deal with the problems at all. As Norbert Weiner has said, we must make "a human use of human beings." We need creativity, not to fulfill degree requirements, but to fulfill human lives. We must work to fulfill the lives of all members of our community, for we are all victims of racism—including white students and white faculty members.

These large issues bear a direct relationship to other, specific problems on our campuses. They are related to salary schedules for teachers, which ought to reflect the resources of our nation but presently do not. These issues are related to the whole question of the difference in appropriations for white land-grant colleges and black land-grant colleges; they are related to grants for medical colleges. We are all concerned with specific problems of this nature, but the problems do not stand in isolation. The university must see itself as part of a larger community, since the problems of the community are also the problems of the university. The university must not lose sight of this fact. If the university seeks to save itself by withdrawing from the community, it will surely lose itself. And once lost, it might never find its life or its role again.

For the university, the arena for effective action is not the classroom alone—but also includes the streets and the total circumference of the urban complex. The best university in the Midwest has a hospital which alone brings in revenues of 224 million dollars. Yet, within a few blocks of this hospital, forty-seven out of every one thousand babies die before the second week of their lives, and over 36 per cent of the youth between nine and eighteen years of age have intestinal diseases. In this same area, hunger is rampant. Another example is Chicago's uptown area. A new junior college is being built in this area where there is a $22,000 difference in incomes within four blocks. It is called a community college, presumably because it is intended to serve the needs of the community. It is located a very short distance from a grammar school where the turnover rate is 70 per cent each year and where only 42 per cent of the sixth-grade class is reading at its own grade level. The families of a number of these students were forced to move because of housing demolition required for the building of the college. We can only wonder how many students at the grammar school will ever enter the college as freshmen. Large numbers of them will never finish high school; many of them will not complete the eighth grade.

If we are going to make rationalizations about conditions such as these, if we are going to condone the bigotry and inhumanity rampant in the society in which we live as academicians, then we might as well close our colleges and universities and go home. We are not fulfilling the prophetic role required of education, and we have turned ourselves into prostitutes. If, on the other hand, we still believe that educators have responsibilities of human involvement and commitment, we must make some significant choices. These choices are basic: whether we are going to be human; whether we will use the considerable skills and resources available to us to make human decisions; and whether we will participate further in the destructive and morally devastating decisions that have already come to control our society. We of the academic community are as much at fault as anyone for the fact that our government can spend 11 per cent of the gross national product for defense and aerospace research, while devoting only 3.5 per cent to housing and community development. We are at fault for the disparities that exist between black colleges and white colleges. We are at fault for the public housing scandal in the neighborhoods of our cities, inhabited mainly by Puerto Ricans, Mexican-Americans, and blacks. We are at fault for decisions that allow the destruction of housing so that colleges can be built, when those colleges provide no services for the people who remain.

The great black prophet, W. E. B. Du Bois, once warned that "the democracy of which we prate so glibly is being murdered in the house of its friends, and in everyday life more than in broad governmental decisions." The murder is committed each time we say that the university is first of all a research institution. If man is not only to endure but also to prevail, his institutions—especially his academic institutions—must embrace values that merge compassion, planning, and justice. Education must be for all men. Equity is the difference between life and death for many of our schools. It may also be the difference between survival and decay for our nation.

❧ 24 ❧

The Remaking of
American Education

Charles E. Silberman

O urs is an age of crisis—of multiple crises, which are both important and urgent and which are no less real for being frequent. The crisis in the classroom—the public school classroom, the college classroom, and the national classroom created by the mass media and the American political system—is both a reflection of and a contributor to the larger crisis of American society. I would like to concentrate here on the nature of the crisis in the college classroom and the directions in which some solutions may lie.

First, there is an identity crisis that is affecting virtually all Americans in one way or another. College students (at least a significant minority among them) are affected more than the rest of us. This identity crisis involves malaise and anxiety that has become a characteristic of American culture. In part, this anxiety grows out of a change in perception—a belated recognition of and long overdue sensitivity to social ills that should have troubled us all along. Here, the mass media have played a major role in forcing poverty, racism, and bloodshed over the threshold of our awareness; we are the first nation in history to watch a war in the comfort of our bedroom or living room. But the new consensus of anxiety also grows out of a growing concern with the quality of life—a belated discovery that affluence leaves some old problems unsolved and creates a number of new ones. Economic growth reduces poverty but also creates congestion, noise, and pollution. Technological change widens the individual's range of choice and makes economic growth possible, but it also dislocates workers from their jobs and their neighborhoods. Affluence plus new technology forces men to confront the questions of the meaning and purpose of life, even while it destroys the faith that once provided answers.

It is not only affluence that poses problems or causes anxiety. The enormous widening of choice that contemporary society makes possible also appears as a mixed blessing, enhancing our sense of individuality but contributing to the pervasive uneasiness. In the past, men inherited their occupations, their status, and their life style; their wives were selected for them; and their struggle to survive gave them little time to question anything. Today, men are presented with a bewildering range of options. They are forced to choose their occupations, jobs, places to live, marital partners, number of children, religion, political affiliation, friendships, and allocation of income. This widening of the range of choice has had the effect of reducing the authority of tradition, which in turn demands that still more choices be made.

The burden is heavy. The choices are frightening, for they require the individual perhaps for the first time in history to choose and, in a sense, to create his own identity. The young rebels understand this well, even though their rhetoric obscures it. Their actions make it clear that it is the burden of choice that torments or frightens them and that many try to postpone for as long as possible. They understand that the choice of a career involves far more than a choice of how to earn a livelihood. They understand, viscerally if not intellectually, that the question, "What shall I do?" really means "What shall I do with myself?" And that means asking: Who am I? What do I want to be or to become? What values do I want to serve? To whom, and to what, do I want to become responsible? These are existential questions. The students' answers may frequently be irrelevant or naive, but the important fact is that they are confronting—and forcing us to confront—

the fundamental questions of value and purpose. Such students enter college with the expectation that a college education will help them answer these fundamental, existential questions. Part of the crisis in higher education is that so many students are so quickly disillusioned, that so many conclude that the university offers no answers. The result is a frightening rejection of the authority of learning and culture; reacting against the antiseptic mind that the academic world has exalted and its lack of concern for feeling and human relationships, students swing to the other extreme. Hence, the newly fashionable anti-intellectualism of the intellectuals, the insistence that systematic and disciplined intellectual effort is a waste of time, and the accompanying worship of uninhibited sensation that forms the central theme of Charles Reich's *The Greening of America*.

This identity crisis among the students is matched by a parallel identity crisis among the institutions that educate them. What Martin Trow of Berkeley calls the transformation of a system of mass higher education into one of universal higher education is compounding the problem that colleges and universities have been facing since the early postwar period, when the shift from the traditional, elitist system to mass higher education occurred. In a different form, it is the same problem that, early in the century, confronted and largely overwhelmed the high schools. In the phrase of Lawrence Cremin of Teachers College, the question is how to humanize or popularize knowledge without vulgarizing it—how to resynthesize and reorder knowledge so as to make it teachable to the mass of men. We have not done a satisfactory job of humanizing knowledge, partly because academicians have not given this task the priority it deserves. Far more points are given for educating graduate students than for educating raw, untutored freshmen. We must pay heed to Mathew Arnold's reminder in *Culture and Anarchy* that the great men of culture have a passion—*passion* is the word he uses—for diffusing the best ideas of their time.

Higher education needs to rediscover its sense of purpose. It will not be easy to do so, for we are just coming out of a twenty-year absence from serious thought about educational purpose. Wayne C. Booth maintains that there is something irrational in our contemporary neglect of systematic thought about educational goals. The irrationality is all the greater in view of the fact that any curriculum involves judgments about goals and values and the priorities attached to them. But those judgments tend to be unconscious. Joseph J. Schwab observes that the tendency to think about thinking, which is one of the characteristics of the scholar, is notably uncommon and invisible in the one place that matters most to the collegiate community—its curriculum. From the students' viewpoint, the curriculum is not a subject of thought; it merely is.

I can personally attest to Schwab's harsh judgment. In traveling around the country, we made it a practice to ask deans, provosts, and presidents why it mattered that a student attended their institution rather than some other. In what ways were their graduates different from graduates of other institutions? How had attending their college or university affected their students? The usual answers were a blank stare, a long pause, an expression of puzzlement, a confession that this was an interesting question that had not come up before, or an attempt to suggest some answer that would better have been left unsaid. And yet it seems self-evident that this question should automatically be the starting point of any educational program. Plato argued its centrality, some 2,400 years ago, with particular charm in the *Protagoras*. A young friend of Socrates, hearing that the great orator, Protagoras, is in town and is accepting pupils, rushes off to enroll when Socrates stops him and asks him how the studies he is about to undertake will affect him— what kind of human being his education will make him—for education, as Socrates reminds him, is about "the proper way to live."

All is not hopeless. The word *crisis,* after all, has a double meaning. In its most common usage, it means that things are pretty bad. But looking at the etymology of the word, one sees that crisis signifies a turning point—that moment in time when a choice can be made. I have used the term in both senses in the title of my book,[1] and my intuition tells me that we are at a turning point.

What, then, should be done? The starting point, perhaps, is to recognize that no college or university can turn out educated men and women—but that every college can turn out educators, which is to say, men and women who are capable of educating their wives or husbands, their children, their friends and colleagues, and themselves. This, after all, is what liberal education is all about, what it has always been all about. This ability to create educators is also what primary and secondary education is—or should be—all about; education at the college level is no different in essense although it is more complex and learning is more self-conscious. To be educated to the point where one can educate oneself, or others, means not only to think seriously about

[1] *Crisis in the Classroom: The Remaking of American Education.* New York: Random House, 1970.

the means and ends of education but also about the consequences of education—about how education can shape and mold the people being educated. This in turn means that to be an educator is to understand something about making one's education effective in the real world. It means to know something about applying knowledge to one's life and to the society in which one lives it. The aim of education, as Alfred North Whitehead defined it, is the acquisition of the art of the utilization of knowledge. A merely well-informed man is the most useless bore on God's earth.

The most direct and immediate way of finding out what one really knows—the most direct way of finding the purpose and testing the human relevance of what one has learned—is to teach it to someone else. In this sense, teaching is the ultimate liberal art, and some experience with teaching of one sort or another ought to be a part of every student's education. While one cannot be an educator without having received a liberal education, the converse is also true: one cannot be liberally educated without becoming an educator of others and of oneself. One does not really know a subject unless he can teach it—that is, communicate it to others.

In addition to teaching itself, the study of education should also be put where it belongs, at the heart of the liberal arts curriculum, not at its margins. For the study of education is the study of almost every question of importance in philosophy, history, and sociology. Our concept of education, after all, reflects our concept of the good man, the good life, and the good society; and there can be no concept of the good life or the good society apart from a concept of the kind of education needed to sustain it. To do all this would be to return the college or the university to its most authentic tradition: that the education of educators (lawyers, doctors, businessmen, and teachers— all as educators) is the central responsibility of colleges and universities.

Let me emphasize, however, that to argue that all students be liberally educated, or to argue that a liberal education should prepare one to teach, is in no way to suggest that all students should receive a classical education. Those who mourn the decline of classical studies and see in it the triumph of materialism misunderstand the history of the university. When the classics reigned supreme in higher education, it was not because of any inherent superiority—not because they formed the mind or shaped the character more successfully than other studies—but because classics were vocationally useful. Two hundred years ago, for example, no one would have argued that the teaching of

Latin involved anything but Latin; one studied it because it was the communications medium of educated men. It was not until Latin lost this role that its other virtues were suddenly discovered.

It should be clear that there is and can be no one curriculum suitable for all time or for all students at any given time. As Whitehead wrote, the powers of curiosity, foresight, and judgment are not imparted through the study of one particular set of subjects. To insist that there is only one curriculum is to confuse the means of education with the end. There are, in fact, many routes to a liberal education—as many routes, perhaps, as there are students. Certainly it is time we heeded Plato's maxim that the teacher must start where the students are, if he is to take them someplace else.

To suggest that there are many routes to a liberal education is *not* to suggest that colleges do no more than offer a smörgasbord of courses. There is an important, perhaps critical, difference between an individual set of courses that are liberal and liberalizing and an education that is liberal and liberalizing. An education and a curriculum involve more than just a set of courses taken at random. If liberal education is to be more than an occasional happy by-product, there must be some conception of the purposes of education. Thus, the popular substitute for general education or other required courses—in other words, distribution requirements—is no more than a cop-out, an attempt to resolve fundamental questions of educational philosophy through interdepartmental horse trading. Nor is the abolition of all requirements a solution in itself. If students are simply turned loose to do their own thing, the college is not likely to be free to do its thing. Harris Wofford, president of Bryn Mawr College, has said that every college must have a view of what liberal education is, with something to say about how to get it; it is the empty colleges, with nothing to say, that diminish the dialogue.

The dialogue is crucial. To suggest that a college must have something to say is not to imply that there must be only one curriculum; it is to argue that whatever curricula—whatever routes to a liberal education—are offered, each must have coherence and purpose. Students are not likely to know how to choose, how to decide for themselves between the better and the worse, if their teachers convey the notion that the choices do not matter. What made undergraduate education so exciting at Columbia in the 1930s and 1940s was not that either school had, once and for all, defined liberal education, but that it had a conception that shaped the faculty members' and students' lives outside the classroom as well as in. The conception was not one that every faculty member or every student shared; much of the excitement, in fact, stemmed from disagreements over what should be studied. What the faculty did share, however, is critical to liberal education: a concern for the possibilities and character of education, a conviction that the shape and content of the curriculum really matters, that some types of courses are more effective than others, and that the curriculum should be shaped by educational conviction rather than by administrative convenience. Horace Mann, in his 1848 valedictory report to the Massachusetts Board of Education, said that we could not despair in human progress if we believed in education. One experiment that had never been tried, Mann declared, was education in the fullest sense, for it had never been brought to bear with even a hundredth part of its potential upon students and, through them, on the human race. It is about time to try that experiment.

Bridging the Interpretation Gap

Samuel B. Gould

Everyone speaks with feeling these days about the generation gap. Indeed, this term has now become a standard part of our vocabulary along with words like relevance or polarization. The generation gap has always been a yawning abyss to me. The closest I ever came to getting across it was many years ago when my then three-year-old son used to put his little hand on my cheek and laugh at me with a mixture of love and forbearance. This somehow took care of a multitude of misunderstandings, real or imagined. His laughter then and later was a powerful antidote to my inadequacy in the role of the responsible parent and helped me make at least tentative leaps across the years between us. That was magic, however, and the world has no place for magic anymore. Children now belong in day-care centers. Youth are busy with that most unselfish of enterprises, which is called doing your own thing, and adults are still trying to find a way to introduce a little tenderness into a technological world. Everyone has his own particular bag to carry, and he hugs it tightly and defensively and possessively.

But I must not meander over my own canyons of noncommunication or my arroyos of inarticulate failure. I mention them only because gradually I am coming to realize that we have more than a generation gap to deal with; we have a gap generation. All sorts of widely gaping chasms are evident around us. The tension between chronological generations is only one of many such phenomena. There is, for example, the gap between ghetto and suburb, or simply between white and black. There are gaps between employer and employee, between consumer and manufacturer, between conservative and liberal, between technocrat and communist, and between electorate and government administration. Most recently there has even been a systematic movement to widen the gap between the sexes. And, of course, there is the gap between higher education and the surrounding world.

We should remember, therefore, for the sake of perspective, that we are literally surrounded by gap-makers these days. This is not the age of the kind word or the light touch or the hearty laugh. It is not the age for forgiveness of those who trespass against us. In one way or another, just about everyone seems to feel he is being trespassed against and that all sorts of sinister conspiracies are being formed just to do him in. Whatever is, is suspect by the fact of its existence. Perhaps this attitude is another by-product of the scientific world or perhaps it is simply man's plain cussedness.

We should remember also, as we turn our attention to the question of diminished public confidence in higher education, that such suspicions are not so much antagonistic as they are fearful. The public is distressed, not simply because the current troubles of higher education are weakening its effectiveness, but because there is some possibility that many institutions will not survive. To all but a very few this would be a tragedy of the first magnitude; thus, the public is greatly disturbed. I mention this because many of us in education do not realize often enough that some of our severest critics are our friends, not our enemies. They wish us well, and they are saddened as much as angered by our apparent inability to cope and our reluctance to communicate.

To come directly to the point, however, let us ask what higher education can do. First of all, it can be more truthful in its own evaluation of its current weaknesses. Foremost among these weaknesses is higher education's slowness in reacting to change. Many people believe this is an inherent characteristic and that to expect anything different is unrealistic; others are convinced that this slowness is desirable and protects higher education from yielding to every new academic fad or to the pressure from every societal change. The real problem, however, is that too many institutions of learning have no clear conception of their own particular purposes and goals. They all share in a common desire to be of great service, but they have rarely gone through the intellectual exercise of determining just exactly what their roles are in the total spectrum of educational need. The public is inevitably confused either by the lack of a statement of purpose or, when there is one, by the generalities and platitudes such statements reflect. Thus, if higher education is to change its style, structure, or methodologies, it should do so within the boundaries of its own definition of purpose. Higher education can make such changes readily and appropriately so long as this definition exists and is clear to everyone.

Another weakness about which all of us need to be more truthful relates to finances. There is no question about the magnitude of the financial problems facing all institutions of higher education, public as well as private. Needs will always outstrip resources, and the distance between the two grows greater every year. This has been a fact of life even in the best of times. But we have forgotten two elements that unfortunately make the public less concerned in the financial plight of higher education today than it has been in the past. First, education has now become only one of many social problems deservedly clamoring for support; and, second, it has never made a clear case of accountability and efficiency for the funds it does receive.

There was a time when we were sure that education was the answer to all our social ills, and, in a very broad sense, it still is. But when a nation is beset with a mounting list of truly horrendous problems, education can only take its place among them. Higher education is a means toward the solution of other problems, but it has not thus far identified its role in such solutions with specific and dramatic actions. It has not even determined to its own satisfaction exactly what such a role should be. These dilatory tactics have not inspired public confidence.

In the matter of stewardship, higher education has a poor track record of efficiency. Granted that institutions of learning have inherent or traditional peculiarities that make them different from business, industry, or government, legitimate questions can all too frequently be raised about how institutions use the funds they do have. Their endowment investment procedures, their antiquated and sometimes whimsical budget practices, and their unwillingness to search for innovative ways to ward off financial crises are viewed by the public with suspicion and almost total lack of understanding. If higher education is looking for increased support from many sources, it will have to exhibit a readiness to abandon its old attitudes. And let it be remembered that its reputation for irrelevance in the conduct of its financial affairs bears direct relationship to its reputation in academic program development. The two are inextricably joined together. In the matter of courses of study, for example, higher education seems to have mastered only two of the four arithmetical techniques: it is superb in addition and multiplication, but it normally ignores subtraction or division.

If higher education wishes to regain public confidence, it will have to reorganize itself to be closer to the community it serves. This is a community with a number of components, all essential to the acceptance and ultimate support of what academic institutions hope to do. The community includes students, faculty, and alumni; business, industry, and civic leaders; cultural and social agencies; and any groups or any individuals concerned about the present and future patterns of American life. As a first step, higher education can revise its governance structure so that students, faculty, and alumni have an appropriate role. This does not mean taking the governance of institutions away from those who have responsibility; rather, it means a system of broad participation in the process of decision making and a guarantee that decisions are made after careful interpretation to these constituencies. In addition, institutions can go far beyond their present practices in opening their cultural and academic doors to adults of all ages so that the latter may share in the wealth of intellectual and artistic resources. This is not only a move toward lifetime learning (in itself a vital concept of education), but it is also a way to make the growing or waning strength of colleges and universities an active concern to all adults.

Still further, as basic problems of higher education (such as purpose, physical growth or finances) are being studied, community leaders should be sought out to join in the studies and in some instances to assist in the resultant actions. Such studies can sometimes lead to a division of labor between colleges or universities and the various agencies of the community that are themselves engaged in educative or training programs. Business and industry can also share in this task. A joining of forces can frequently result in efficient and effective means of education, which avoids a replication of programs and facilities.

Higher education can also urge students to participate in community life by volunteer work in cooperation with various agencies. There is great mutual benefit in this: the students acquire a realistic picture of what it means to deal with social problems, rather then to theorize about them, and the community acquires an assessment of what students are like in their abilities, their enthusiasms, their goals. Underlying all this interaction between the internal and external community is a great interpretive process—regularized, constant, truthful. Frictions will occur inevitably, but in times of impending crisis individuals on one side of a disagreement are likely to recognize the good will and intentions of those on the other side.

A serious commitment on the part of higher education to gain public confidence is bound to make the matter of self-interpretation paramount in importance. The peculiarities of academic institutions and their goals and achievements call for careful explanation to a curious and often confused citizenry. Out of the many areas that constantly call for careful explanation, we can name five that are broad in scope and perhaps of key significance. These are, in fact, principles of interpretation.

The first principle is that higher education should take the public into its confidence. Instead of rumor and half-truth stimulated by idle talk and hearsay, there should be systematic attempts to give information quickly and accurately, together with a frankness that can eventually eradicate most suspicion. When the layman feels he is being told in full what is actually being done or planned, along with the reasons for such planning or action, he may disagree; but he is more likely to understand our motives and respect them. Conversely, when he is led to believe that the institution's work is beyond his comprehension or is none of his business, he is ready to be critical and antagonistic even before he finally learns the substance of the matter.

The second principle of interpretation is that higher education should talk to the public in terms the latter can understand. We all realize how important it is for us in the academic world to be scholarly and even esoteric in whatever we say. It gives an air of profundity to the most shopworn platitudes and a certain panache to the speaker or writer who wants to set up unintelligibility as one of the criteria of scholarship. But one does not communicate to the public when writing for professional journals or presenting papers before colleagues—t at is, not if one expects to achieve anything of interpretive value. Clarity is essential.

The notion that higher education should emphasize its positive achievements is the third principle of interpretation. In the great welter of accusations and counteraccusations, the many accomplishments of academic institutions have been ignored. Every college or university of consequence has a story to tell about its research, exceptional teaching, community action, or intelligent action in response to societal needs. This story remains untold, unfortunately; and the presently emerging picture of the progress of higher education is inaccurate and distorted. This is a situation that can and must be remedied.

The fourth principle of interpretation is that higher education should make sure that the public understands and appreciates the values of scholarship. In a pragmatic, technological, and materialistic society, the enduring qualities of the world of thought are of inestimable importance. Academic institutions should not encourage such qualities with a sense of shame or apology. Rather they should explain repeatedly and painstakingly how vital these qualities are to the future of America. Only then can some sort of balance be struck between practical necessities and the inculcation of habits of rational discourse and exploration.

The fifth principle of interpretation is that higher education should disclaim responsibility for what it has not brought about or what it should not be expected to control. Many of today's most shattering problems did not originate in colleges or universities, nor does higher education have the power to deal with them. These problems emerge from difficulties generated by the total society, and the campus is only a microcosmic reflection of these problems. Higher education should make this point bluntly and fearlessly, not as a way of evading responsibility, but as one way of clearly fixing responsibility and calling upon the public to shoulder its share of the task of providing remedies. Conversely, colleges and universities should give unmistakable evidence of their ability to keep their own houses in order, when dealing with matters plainly within their purview. Institutions of higher learning should be able to act with speed and calm assurance when campus crises arise.

Many lessons have been learned during these past few years, and new perspectives have emerged. It is apparent by now, for example, that the violent efforts to destroy colleges and universities have been limited to the activities of a very small group who are discredited and rejected among their own peers. Such a group will always be a threat and will have to be contained. But one of the important ways to contain them is for higher education to seize the initiative in changing its outmoded patterns. It must lead the way toward adapting to the times, instead of being content merely to find techniques for protecting itself; and it must do this within a framework of realistic expectations, whether academic, or social, or financial. Promises of change cannot be made lightly, lest they return to haunt the maker and eventually crush him.

One perspective remains constant, however: maintaining the integrity of the intellectual process, encouraging the growth of the individual, and holding fast to the humane values of life must be placed foremost in the order of academic priorities. There will always be those among the public who are unalterably opposed to such a perspective. They can never be the friends of higher education regardless of how much we try to explain and interpret. But then, everyone worth his salt has enemies; so has higher education. What we do not realize often enough is that higher education has a great host of friends who wish it well and who can be partners in the educational renaissance that is imminent. We need this kind of partnership and should work to make it a reality.

❧ 26 ❧

Is Higher Education a Commodity?

Louis T. Benezet

We have embarked upon an adventure to bring higher learning to the many. We are finding that it is costly to do this, and the public is balking at paying the price. Still, other elements of society are asking that the price be paid. Higher education is less costly, they say, then continual war overseas or revolution at home. It is unfortunate, however, that in the public mind (aside from the long-haired radicals who must be quieted down now and again), the central problem facing higher education is conceived in purely fiscal terms. This is unfortunate on two counts: first, the criteria by which any solution is judged becomes financial rather than educational; and, second, education is conceived as a commodity. This thinking is pervasive, for it characterizes not only the general public but the state and federal officials and legislators, and even the President of the United States. And this emphasis on the financial aspects of higher education has been encouraged by the publications of the Carnegie Commission on Higher Education.

It is depressing that the President's message on higher education in 1970, and again in 1971, has rested its case upon financial aid to the student. Little is offered for the colleges except a prospect of research studies from a National Educational Foundation. As a *New York Times* editorial observed, that is like offering a drowning man research on improved swimming techniques. It is safe to presume that Richard Nixon (while at Whittier College), Robert Finch (while at Occidental), and Elliot Richardson (while at Harvard) heard many times that education was costing their colleges more than it was costing them. We may presume also that this message was in their alumni letters in years following. We are told, however, that the federal administration was caught by surprise when the higher education community reacted negatively to the September, 1970, message.

The series of lucid reports that have come from the Carnegie Commission under Clark Kerr's direction have helped the professional in higher education understand why we are in such trouble. But the Commission has not sufficiently helped the public understand the crisis. With its national prominence, it could help direct the country's attention to the basic error that pervades public thinking about college education. This is the same error that was implicit in the President's message of September, 1970—namely, the notion that college education is a commodity, which a person by various means purchases for his own benefit.

Higher education is not a commodity. The chief beneficiary of higher education is not the person who gains its credits and degrees. Higher education is a series of experiences which, if successful, create changes. These changes enable a human being to be of greater value to society. The beneficiary is society itself. The social benefits derived from higher education can make the difference between an enlightened society of men and women and a mass of humanoids who will fall back into varying stages of retrogression.

When economic times are bad, or should we say recessed, the commodity view of higher education increases. A clear fallacy in the commodity theory of college is reflected today by the unemployment of over 50,000 of our highly educated Ph.D. holders. Yet the economic subtleties involved are not well understood. When students demonstrate, the commodity view of public education becomes a club wielded with zeal by old grads, hard hats, legislators, and here and there a state governor. The thought that young people should behave so badly after all that charity and taxes have done for their education brings many people, including some who have gone to college, to the point of anger. Few administrators would be rash enough to suggest that some students might be demonstrating for a long-range benefit to society.

The concept of higher education as social benefit above individual benefit had its day following the Soviet Sputnik in October, 1957. All at once the public realized that the university does have something to do with national well-being. A period ensued that was characterized by public demands for rocketry in kindergarten But the social benefit attached to college education was mainly identified with the production of celestial hardware. Then in July, 1969, the Americans got to the moon, and the twelve-year saga of educational excellence was declared successfully concluded.

The current Carnegie proposals for a three-year baccalaureate, for credit for outside experience, and for other types of extramural education are being widely studied. Such proposals will have a large impact upon educational processes in the next few years. With the critical financial state that colleges are in, we would probably be driven to explore such options even if they did not have a solid educational rationale behind them. Thus, ironically, the new emphasis on nonresidential and career-centered methods of earning a college degree could make college look even more like a commodity to the public than it does now. Members of the public may become convinced that four years spent roaming from dormitory to classroom to library to student union to gymnasium does indeed represent a waste of expensive time. The rationale will be that you can get it all by smart living and reading a book now and then. If we plunge into short courses, three-year degrees, credit for outside experience, and all the rest, the question inevitably arises as to the future of residential four-year baccalaureate education. The trouble is, we have never discovered how to determine when a person can be said to be college-educated. We don't know the inside ingredients or the mental processes that go into it. Nor do we know how to distinguish a college-educated person in the best liberated sense from a person who has gone through the same four years only to emerge as a narrow, self-serving soul incapable ever again of absorbing a new thought. Perhaps the case for the residential college cannot be made. We might be facing the era of its passing; economic indices alone have all but written the epitaph for its headstone. If so, let us make the obsequies brief, lower the coffin quickly, and turn to other forms of dispensing the higher learning.

It is not the particular forms of higher learning we should be fighting to preserve. What needs most to be emphasized is that higher learning is not a commodity. Higher learning is a process of human growth and change. It can happen through self-teaching or through contact with broadening experience; or it can happen best when students and professors are brought together in a certain environment so that time, steady influence, and freedom from distraction can work to produce the changes in people that our future society must have if it is to survive.

I spoke briefly of the era of the sixties when we were pursuing excellence by shooting at the moon. Something else happened during that decade. It was a turbulent, anxious time as it still is today. Yet in that decade there grew on many campuses, perhaps for the first time, the base of a widespread belief in the humanity of all men—rich and poor, black and white, man and woman, American and Asian, educated and uneducated. Students have pressed this credo upon their elders. They accuse the elders of refusing to practice humanity in national policy or even in the educational processes on the campus itself. Younger professors, some of whom started the decade as undergraduates, have joined the new priesthood of believers. Young doctors and young lawyers are turning from more lucrative aspects of their trade to do service in needy places. Such idealism is hard for some to keep at a time when we have been incapable of removing ourselves from a brutal and futile war overseas. Still it has come out of this past decade.

If we can maintain the humane spirit and at the same time retain substance and process in higher learning, then our campuses may still lead the way to an era finer than any we have seen. There is on American campuses a current desire to connect education with a wider view of humanity. Some of its implications are disturbing; some of its protagonists appear intolerant and at times irrational. Anti-intellectualism on campus is always a paradox. Demonology and animalism as reactions to academe are so grotesque as to be hard to believe. Yet good things are happening also, which work to make higher education a growth process rather than a commodity. The current press toward environmental studies is a student reaction that is promising. It is worth our effort to seek effective and efficient ways of bringing higher education to the many. Meanwhile, we must keep working to persuade the public that a full investment in higher learning for the many will be the best investment we ever made. If the investment does not return to ourselves, then it will return to our great-grandchildren. Let us hope that we may be fortunate enough to have them.

27

Destiny—Not So Manifest

Clark Kerr

Higher education in the United States is entering a great climacteric—a period of uncertainty, of conflict, of confusion, of potential change. Its present health is in doubt; its future fortunes are obscure; its fundamental constitution is being challenged. It is entering more than just another new decade among many decades past and prospective. It enters this new period with little to guide it in its past experiences. Only once before in its three and one-third centuries since the founding of Harvard has it faced such a period of great transition, such a hinge of history, such a turning point in its axes of development.

For most of this one-third of a millenium higher education has had a manifest destiny—its course of progress marked by clarity and confidence. Its first era of manifest destiny was from 1636 to about 1820, or about two centuries. Higher education then served the great forces unleased by the Renaissance and the Reformation. European

culture, built on classical Greek and Roman foundations, was brought
to and extended within the new society, and the doctrines of the
Protestant sects animated all of the colleges and most of the teaching.
The old culture and the new religious morality were the great themes
of the academic world. The colleges drew their students largely from
the upper middle classes and directed them toward the historic professions of teaching, law, medicine, and the ministry. There was a clear
idea of the attributes of the educated man and of the curriculum that
would prepare him best. The colleges at Oxford and Cambridge were
the models.

By 1820, this established concept of the good academic life
began to be challenged more and more. By 1870 its fate was sealed. It
was doomed to eclipse by a new vision. It would survive only as a
dwindling element of American higher education. By 1970, the small
(twenty instructors or less) [1] residential college with a single curriculum
for all its students was as rare as it was standard in 1820. The period
from 1820 to 1870 may be instructive at the present moment, for it
also was a time marked by academic turmoil. Students were restless.
They were protesting against *in loco parentis* and the fixed curriculum.
One-half of the graduating class of 1823 was expelled from Harvard.
Young faculty members had new ideas. Ticknor, fresh from studies in
Germany, began teaching and agitating at Harvard in 1819. He
favored the system of electives and the higher intellectual standards
then spreading through the German universities. Some presidents later
joined the fray, like Wayland at Brown and Tappan at Michigan.
State colleges and universities, free from control by any single religious
denomination, had already been founded, beginning with Georgia and
North Carolina, and were spreading in their appeal. Oberlin opened
as the first coeducational college in 1833. The Land Grant idea, of
service to all the people, was first propounded in 1850. The nation,
also, was increasingly torn by social hostilities that led to the Civil War.

The central debate was over electives,[2] between the proponents
of the classical curriculum and those who favored new subjects, like
modern foreign languages and science. But there were many other
issues: the degree of public control of colleges (as debated in the

---

[1] Harvard, the largest college, had twenty-three instructors (including
tutors) in 1839.
[2] John S. Brubacher and Willis Rudy, *Higher Education in Transition:
A History of American Colleges and Universities, 1636–1968*. New York:
Harper & Row, 1968, p. 98.

Dartmouth College case); "godliness" versus "godlessness"; teaching versus research; liberal versus practical education; the cosmopolitanism of the Old World versus the provincialism of the New World; elite versus mass education; the old academic and moral standards versus the increasing rebellion of the students against them; and others. The old regime remained largely intact for most of the half century after 1820, but the new order prevailed in the end. The crucial victories came with the passage of the Land-Grant Act by the national Congress and the appointments of Eliot as president at Harvard and Gilman as president at Johns Hopkins. At least by 1890, the new university was there for all to see, although in historical perspective, it can be seen that it was already taking shape twenty years earlier.

The new century for higher education that began with the end of the Civil War and ended recently reflected the forces that also animated the nation. The manifest destiny of America then was to develop much of a continent for the life of free men. Industrialization, populism, and nationalism were the new themes. And higher education followed them too. Skilled persons were trained and technology developed for more efficient agriculture and industry; college places were created for not 2 per cent but 50 per cent of the age group; and the national purpose was served through research particularly during and after World War II. The goal of the nation and of the college was "success." [3] The colleges and universities of America came to lead the world in the transition from elite to mass higher education, in service to the productive forces in society, and in the pursuit of scientific discoveries. It was an heroic century.

Throughout these three periods, at least two things remained constant. One was the consistency between the nature of the college and that of the surrounding society; the campus and the society were both changing but always in essentially compatible ways. The other was the constant public belief in and support of higher education. Each new town wanted its own local college; more and more families looked upon college attendance as the key to a better life for their children.

Now we are entering a new time of troubles. For not much longer will higher education be one of the rapid growth points in our society. For one hundred years, the number of students in higher education has doubled about every fifteen years. In the 1980s, there will

[3] Laurence R. Veysey refers to the university after 1890 as a "success-oriented enterprise." See *The Emergence of the American University*. Chicago and London: University of Chicago Press, 1955, p. 439.

be no growth at all; and after that decade, the growth will be more nearly in accord with that of the total population and, thus, at a much slower rate. This is a traumatic shift. We are also no longer so sure about service. We ask more questions about what kind of service and to whom—research for the military? advice to the city? health service for the poor? It is no longer sufficient to offer almost any service to the powerful. And science has become suspect in some quarters; it may not lead to the golden age but rather to feared brave new worlds. Beyond that, society and the campus are in conflict as never before. The campus is now the chief locus of dissent, not the farm or the factory. Much of the public dislikes this dissent. It senses an inherent conflict between the meritocracy of the campus and the democracy of the common man. The public also fears the impact that new ideas originating on the campus will have on the life of man and the impact that new life styles originating on the campus will have on the life styles of their children, alienating them from their parents. As a consequence, public support has suddenly become more doubtful.

Other things are also happening. As in the period between 1820 and 1870, students are restless, and the faculty consensus developed over the past century is again being shattered by basic disagreements. Once again, American society is marked by social divisiveness. How long may this new period of uncertainty last? Will it once again be for half a century? No one can really know. Certainly, however, the next two decades at least, and each for different reasons, are likely to be difficult ones. In the 1970s, higher education will add by one-half to its student population under conditions of a prospective shortage of resources; and then, in the 1980s, for the first time in over a century, it will add no students at all. The 1990s, however, for demographic reasons, will once again be a decade of expansion. I should like to comment briefly on what I consider some of the great uncertainties of this coming period and then to end with a few notations on what seem to me to be clear new directions in higher education.

First, the uncertainties. Higher education in the United States has always developed in close relation to American society as a whole. This is true (although occasionally to a lesser extent) of systems of higher education throughout history and throughout the world. Henry VIII in England, Napoleon in France, the Meiji restoration in Japan, Lenin in Russia, Mao in China—all profoundly affected higher education. Industrialization and the rise of science have affected higher education everywhere they have taken place. Consequently, to predict the future of higher education in this country, one must first predict the general future of the United States. And that is by no means entirely clear. In particular, the more divisiveness there is in society, the more there will be on the campus also. Higher education is a subsystem of the larger society, and it is a more integrated subsystem as a higher percentage of young people go to college and as knowledge becomes more central to the conduct of society. Higher education will rise and decline and change as the nation may rise or decline or change. The modern campus exists in dependency on its environment.

More broadly, on the world scene, we cannot yet be sure of the impact of the cultural revolution. It is possible that we are witnessing the early stages of a substantial change in styles of thought as happened, for example, with the shift in viewpoint from aristocratic to democratic doctrines at the time of the American and French revolutions. We may now be moving from an emphasis on self-denial inherent in the Protestant ethic (but also in all successful take-off periods of industrial development) to one of greater self-gratification; from saving for the future to immediate consumption; from hard work to sensate pleasure. The classical college may be viewed as related to Consciousness I; the multiversity to Consciousness II; and the free university, or no university at all, to Consciousness III.[4] But it is not certain that Consciousness III will triumph or even can triumph in a society grown accustomed to the discipline of modern technology and dependent upon its products. The cultural revolution might take a Maoist form of emphasis on the supremacy of political thought, including at least theoretical rejection of the role of the expert. Whether in its sensate or ideological form, the cultural revolution could have a great impact. Certainly we see today some consequences of the view of college as a place for enjoyment as well as for preparation for the future, as a place for ideology as well as for self-advancement. Until we know what form the cultural revolution may take and how effective it may be, we cannot be certain of the new directions for higher education. Full knowledge of the dynamics of this social process may be a long way off.

The new technology in higher education is only beginning to take hold. Eric Ashby[5] once spoke of the four revolutions in educational technology: the transfer of education out of the family to the specialized

---

[4] Charles A. Reich, *The Greening of America*. New York: Random House, 1970.

[5] Eric Ashby, "Machines, Understanding, and Learning: Reflections on Technology in Education," *The Graduate Journal*, Spring 1967.

teacher, then the invention of the written word, then the invention of the printed word, and now the electronic revolution with the radio, television, the computer, and the video-cassette. Each method of instruction continued as each new method became available in the past, and this, undoubtedly, will be true now also. But this new revolution will come faster around the world than the early ones. It may turn out to be as important.

The proper functions of higher education are under renewed debate. How much service and to whom? How much research and for what purposes? How much general and how much specialized education? How much defense of the status quo? How much dissent and how much revolutionary effort? Paul Goodman has new supporters for his apprenticeship approach; Hutchins for the great discourse; Flexner for pure research; and the revolutionaries for the campus as a base of operations. Some of the debate is like that which raged around the Yale Report of 1828; but the alternatives now are more numerous and the differences in position even more fundamental.

Governance is in dispute. Higher education in the United States has been governed by its several estates—the student, the faculty, the staff, and the trustee estates—each with its own jurisdiction. Now nearly everybody wants to take an interest in nearly everything, and there is less consensus about the whole endeavor. The estate system of governance depended on consensus about functions, on mutual tolerance among the estates, and even on apathy. The consensus, the tolerance, the apathy that made this system work no longer exist to the same extent. Two quite contrary forces are at work. One is to create a more vertical system of authority leading from the governor or the legislature or the trustees. The other is to provide a more horizontal system of authority with one person one vote or, beyond that, participatory democracy by the activists.

Financing is in doubt. How much by the students; how much by the state; how much by the federal government? How much for this higher education priority as against other social priorities? Never in a period of relative prosperity have the colleges been in so much of a depression and so uncertain of future resources. These are some of the uncertainties, and there are no foreign models to guide us toward solutions as did once the British model and then later the German model. We may hear, however, a good deal about Maoist theories and those of the early Marx—more about the theories than about the actual resultant practices.

Finally, a few comments about new directions. These, of necessity, will be more short run in character and more specific than the uncertainties. We will continue with the unfinished business of the past century—the extension of opportunity to young persons regardless of family income, race, and geographical location. We will extend service more evenly to all parts of society and not so much to the powerful in particular; and we will provide lifetime chances at access to higher education. We will develop clearer rules governing the conduct of all members of the academic community, more formal policies about enforcement, and more independent processes for adjudication of disagreements. In the absence of consensus and goodwill, the campus will become a more formal political entity and less of an informal community.

Cost effectiveness of operations will be more carefully examined. More visible presidential leadership is likely to emerge during this period of transition as it did during the last one. The federal government has become much more of a force in the 1960s (as it did in the 1860s), and this development, this time, is likely to be more permanent. The labor market is already turning against the college trained. This is likely to continue. The premium paid for college training will go down as the supply of trained persons goes up. This process has already gone quite far in Sweden. The college trained will take jobs of lower status than they have historically (and they may change the nature of these jobs as they do) or go unemployed, and the range of wages and salaries will narrow to the disadvantage of the college trained. This is happening around the world. The coming revolt may be of the meritocracy against the egalitarianism of the common man, instead of the common man against the meritocracy.

The intellectuals will be in tension with the surrounding society. This has often been true throughout history. Now there are many more intellectuals. They are, by nature, divided among themselves and, in part, against society. Technetronic society requires more intellectuals but some of these intellectuals also tend to rebel against some aspects of it. The campus will be involved in this tension.

Higher education in the United States, in the perspective of history, has been quite fortunate. In 330 years of existence, it has had only about fifty years of substantial uncertainty—between 1820 and 1870. Now, however, it faces the prospect of a second such period of unknown duration and, as yet, of uncertain outcome. Climacteric I was survived, and higher education came out of it stronger and better than ever. Climacteric II is now upon us. One thing is certain and that is that the answers are not all predetermined, that the final outcome will depend on the quality of our decisions as we move along and, particularly, on the early decisions as we begin to chart the directions of this new era.

Index

DATE DUE

6. 7.'84	

BRODART, INC.   Cat. No. 23-221